On Understanding
Intervention in Psychology
and Education

On Understanding Intervention in Psychology and Education

HOWARD S. ADELMAN
and LINDA TAYLOR

Westport, Connecticut
London

Library of Congress Cataloging-in-Publication Data

Adelman, Howard S.
  On understanding intervention in psychology and education / Howard
S. Adelman and Linda Taylor.
      p. cm.
  Includes bibliographical references and index.
  ISBN 0–275–94888–9 (alk. paper)
  1. Counseling. 2. Children—Counseling of. 3. Educational
counseling. I. Taylor, Linda (Linda L.) II. Title.
  BF637.C6A   1994
  158′.3—dc20   94–2986

British Library Cataloguing in Publication Data is available.

Library of Congress Catalog Card Number: 94–2986
ISBN: 0–275–94888–9

First published in 1994

Praeger Publishers, 88 Post Road West, Westport, CT 06881
An imprint of Greenwood Publishing Group, Inc.

Printed in the United States of America

The paper used in this book complies with the
Permanent Paper Standard issued by the National
Information Standards Organization (Z39.48–1984).

10 9 8 7 6 5 4 3 2 1

Contents

Tables and Figures

Preface

Intentional intervention remains a relatively uncharted phenomenon. Yet everyone does it. Family and friends intercede in each other's lives. Psychologists, teachers, social workers, case managers, work supervisors, organization managers, and many others intervene for a living.

Interveners differ not only in their roles and functions but also in how systematically they approach their work and in their efforts to find better ways. Some are extremely reflective and wonderfully articulate about what they do and why they do it, and they are consistently improving current practices. Others want improvements but are so enmeshed in daily demands that they hardly have time to think. Differences are seen in views about labelling, about attending to causality, and about approaches to planning, implementation, and evaluation. Asked their orientation, an increasing number of practitioners say they are eclectic. Observations of their work bear this out. The data also suggest that the endeavors covered by this term range from somewhat naive to highly sophisticated.

Over the past twenty-five years, we have pursued an eclectic brand of intervention research and practice in clinical and school settings. In doing so, we have drawn on an emerging literature and learned from challenging interchanges with colleagues, clients, and students. At times, our focus has been on improving current practices; at times, we have struggled to transform such practices. Always we have tried to learn and build on fundamentals. Always the problems involved in understanding the essence of intervention have confronted and humbled us.

In this brief monograph, our purpose is to sketch out what we have come to see as fundamental problems that must be addressed in pursuing effective eclecticism and understanding intervention as a generic phenomenon. We approach these problems from the perspective of psychology and education, but with a view to analyzing them as generic intervention concerns. We identify and describe essential pieces of intentional intervention, explore how they relate to each other, and try to produce an outline picture of the whole. Our approach involves analysis and commentary; we offer conceptualizations, examples, and opinions.

Have we misidentified or misdescribed certain pieces and relationships? Certainly. *What are the pieces and relationships we missed?* We're still trying to understand these. *Will some of our analyses seem unfairly critical of present practices and unrealistic in their implications for change?* Chances are that overworked professionals will think so and will see us as unsympathetic and quixotic. Therefore, let us say at the outset, we do mean to risk exploring ideas that ultimately may prove impractical. In doing so, however, we don't mean to cast aspersions on anyone who strives to live up to current standards for practice. We know that the demands placed on many practitioners go well beyond what common sense says anyone should be asked to endure.

Intervention is an intriguing and at times a troublesome phenomenon. This monograph is meant for those who already are intrigued and those we hope will become intrigued. Implicit throughout is an agenda for theory building and research. There is a great deal of work to be done and too few who are doing it; please join us.

As always, our work owes so much to so many—colleagues, clients, students, family, and friends. Their contributions are reflected throughout this volume. No listing of names could enumerate all from whom we have learned. We take this opportunity simply to acknowledge our enormous debt.

On Understanding Intervention in Psychology and Education

Introduction: Fundamental Problems in Understanding Intervention

There is nothing as practical as a good theory.

Lewin

In a recent analysis of programs addressing psychosocial problems, Schorr succinctly defines intervention as "any systematic attempt to alter the course of development from either its established or predicted path"[1]—a useful definition, but not a comprehensive one. Intervention is something everyone does, but few people take the time to fully understand it. To appreciate the full nature and scope of intervention, one must adopt a broad definition and attempt to answer such questions as

Why intervene? (What should be our goals? What is our responsibility with respect to facilitating human functioning? Should we intervene whenever there is a problem? When is consent required?) and

What is the best way to intervene? (What makes some ways better than others? How do we know which ways are best?)

Questions about ends and means can be asked in a straightforward way, but the answers are complex and difficult to articulate.

Whether articulated or not, each professional's partial insights guide decisions about goals sought and processes used; they become the bases and biases shaping intervention. Conflicting bases and biases are seen in how professionals address concerns associated with intervening in psychology and education. With a view to improving intervention research and practice, we group these concerns under four inextricably interrelated and fundamental topics or problems for exploration. As graphically presented in Figure I.1, these are (1) the classification problem (i.e., differentiating phenomena—conceptually and methodologically—into relevant subgroups for purposes of planning, implementing, and evaluating intervention), (2) the underlying rationale problem (i.e., assumptions shaping intervention aims and means), (3) the planning and implementation problem (i.e., processes for optimizing intervention), and (4) the evaluation problem (i.e., describing, judging, and advancing intervention knowledge and practice).

Each basic problem has major implications for intervention research, theory, and practice, and the four are so interrelated that work done on any one potentially contributes to increased understanding of the others. Several implications are appreciable simply by noting the sequential relationship among the four problems. For instance, logically, if valid differentiations are not made among persons or environments, valid assumptions about appropriate intervention processes and outcomes are difficult to make. When those assumptions are invalid, effective planning, implementation, and evaluation are jeopardized. The remainder of this chapter provides an overview of the four fundamental intervention problems; then, we move on to explore each in greater detail in the rest of the book.

THE CLASSIFICATION PROBLEM

Scientists know that distinguishing among phenomena is both a practical necessity and an ethical imperative in advancing knowledge. Conceptual and methodological schemes for differentiating people, places, problems, programs, actions, outcomes, and so forth are key to efforts to improve interventions. The problem is how to do this in ways that maximize benefits for science and practice while minimizing negative consequences to individuals and society.

No one doubts that the act of assigning certain labels, especially to individuals, can produce negative consequences, such as harmful stereotyping, stigmatization, undermining self-esteem, generating negative expectations, misidentification, and misprescriptions. The hope is that the benefits accrued will be greater than the costs.

Figure I.1
Four Fundamental Problems for Intervention Theory

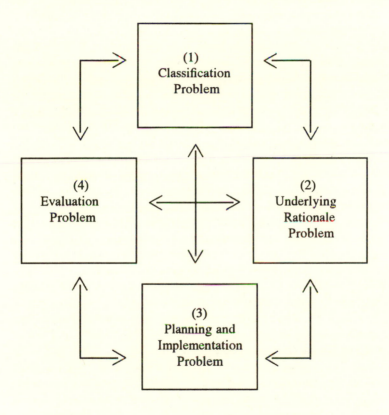

Source: H.S. Adelman and L. Taylor (1988). Clinical child
psychology: Fundamental intervention questions and
problems. *Clinical Psychology Review, 8*, 637-665.
Reprinted with kind permission from Pergamon Press
Ltd., Headington Hills Hall, Oxford OX30BW, UK.

Unfortunately, in most instances research must still find that the good outweighs the harm. This is true even for the dominant labelling systems for emotional, behavioral, and learning problems. In the absence of clear evidence about costs and benefits, it is not surprising that changes in terminology stem as much from socio-political-economic considerations and rational analyses as from scientific activity.

The history of science is marked by frequent changes in classification terminology. Categories and subgroups are added, deleted, and modified. In psychology and education, considerable attention is paid to classification of individuals with problems (i.e., diagnostic classification). Elaborate diagnostic schemes are widely used, and criticism and revision of prevailing schemes are ongoing. Criticism ranges from philosophical and conceptual to methodological and legal. For example, in writing the summary for the Project on Classification of Exceptional Children, Hobbs concluded: "Available classification systems are gross and inadequate. They obscure both the uniqueness of individual children and the similarities of children assigned to various categories. Gross classification leads to gross and inadequate solutions to problems at every level of concern. Federal, state, and local governments are organized on the basis of outmoded classification concepts. . . . The familiar categories of exceptionality have limited value in planning education or treatment programs for most exceptional children."[2] Similarly, in reviewing classification of psychopathology, Ross and Pelham concluded, "The current state of nomenclature and diagnostic criteria in the field of adult psychopathology is barely more than one of organized confusion, but compared to the chaos that reigns in the realm of child psychopathology it is one of rigorous exactitude."[3] Such comments characterize the state of the art currently and for the immediate future and are taken by some as support for the position that the entire process of diagnostic classification is so flawed as to warrant noncategorical identification of problems.[4]

From another perspective, present diagnostic practices are criticized for colluding with the presumptive tendency toward viewing all emotional, behavioral, and learning problems as caused by pathology within the individual. Such a tendency downplays the possibility that the problems of many individuals assigned labels were initially caused (and perhaps are maintained) by environmental factors. One result of systematically downplaying the environment's role is that intervention is kept narrowly focused on individuals. That is, interventions to alter environmental systems that cause problems for individuals are de facto deemphasized, and strategies to increase individual coping and adaptation are overemphasized. Increased attention to classifying environmental phenomena represents a step toward countering these trends.

Given the scope of concerns, dissatisfaction with current labels and procedures is quite understandable and appropriate. Calls for improvement in classification and identification systems certainly are warranted; calls for eliminating all classification and identification are premature. At this time, addressing the classification problem means finding better ways to classify phenomena, rather than finding ways to do away with classification.

We hasten to add that to argue for classification is not to argue for tying the provision of all forms of special help to formal diagnoses. The point simply is that classification is fundamental to scientific research, as well as to efforts for improving intervention efficacy in fields such as psychology and education. The nature of intervention planning, implementation, and evaluation is inextricably intertwined with how the classification problem is handled.

In Part I, we discuss the question of what phenomena should be labelled to guide intervention theory, research, and practice, the focus of current categorization efforts, and guidelines for minimizing negative effects of classification.

THE UNDERLYING RATIONALE PROBLEM

Intentional interventions are rationally based. Thus, those concerned with studying and advancing intervention must be concerned with the rationale underlying such activity, even though it may not be explicitly stated.

An underlying rationale for intervention is a framework outlining and shaping the nature of intervention aims and procedures. It consists of views derived from philosophical (including ethical), theoretical, empirical, and legal sources. Rationales are expected to include general orientations or "models" of the causes of behavior (including problems), tasks to be accomplished, and intervention processes and outcomes.

Ample statements are available about the role played by underlying rationales. As a general proposition, Markley and Harman state, "Images of humankind which are dominant in a culture are of fundamental importance, because they underlie the ways in which the society shapes its institutions, educates its young, and goes about whatever it perceives its business to be." In discussing instruction, Bruner stressed that instructional interventions reflect "a theory of how growth and development are assisted by diverse means." Rossi and Freeman indicate that interventions are based on hypotheses drawn from causal and predictive studies, from theories, and from clinical impressions. And Howard and Orlinsky propose that underlying psychotherapeutic intervention is "some conception of *human nature* or personality (the 'material' to be worked with), *human fulfillment* (the ideal to be sought), *human vulnerability* (psychopathology), of *therapeutics*, and of the therapeutic *profession*. Taken together, they comprise . . . the Therapeutic Belief-Value Complex."[5]

Although rationales guide intervener thoughts and actions, there is little evidence that they are systematically formulated and explicitly stated by most professionals. Even when not explicitly stated, however, underlying rationales have major ramifications for outcomes because they both guide and limit the nature of subsequent activity. As Brickman and his colleagues suggest, "Each set of assumptions has characteristic consequences for . . . competence, status, and well-being . . . [and] the wrong choice . . . will undermine effective helping and coping."[6]

Of course, not all intervention rationales are equal. Some reflect a higher level of scholarly sophistication; some cover a broader range of relevant considerations; some have greater philosophical, theoretical, and empirical consistency. And an intervention rationale's sophistication, breadth, and consistency are not the only important considerations. Systematic biases that arise from dominating models also are of concern. For instance, prevailing views of intervention for emotional, behavioral, and learning problems tend to (1) attribute cause to factors within the individual, and (2) focus intervention on changing the individual. As suggested above, this shapes classification activity and plays down the causal role of environmental factors, such as social policies, characteristics of community, home, work, and school settings. It also underemphasizes environmental factors as a primary focus in correcting the problem.

More generally, dominant models for intervention reflect society's conserving tendencies, and therefore stress system maintenance and the socialization of groups and individuals as the most pressing goals for interveners. This is unfortunate because of the significant number of cases where such goals are counterproductive to progress, and their pursuit significantly limits the quality of life for many in the society.

Sophistication, breadth, consistency, bias—all must be considered and can be judged appropriately only if an underlying rationale is explicitly stated. Generally speaking, all efforts to understand, improve, and diffuse successful intervention activity are hampered by the absence of explicitly stated underlying rationales. As Rossi, Freeman, and Wright have cautioned, "If the parties involved in program development and implementation fail (or refuse) to apply themselves to unraveling and specifying the assumptions and principles underlying the program, there is no basis for understanding what they are doing, why they are doing it, or for judging whether or not they are doing what they intend to do."[7]

In our discussion of the underlying rationale problem in Part II, we examine concerns and ideas relevant to formulating underlying rationales. We begin by looking at how intervention is defined, then we discuss what is involved in deciding on ends and means, and finally we explore several matters of relevance to the contractual bases for intervention.

THE PLANNING AND IMPLEMENTATION PROBLEM

Intervention rationales are abstract and usually in a state of continuous evolution. Thus, it is inevitable that difficulty and controversy surround efforts to translate a rationale into a specific plan of action and then to carry the plan out.

To underscore the connection between an underlying rationale and planning, Banathy emphasizes that intervention, or from his perspective *system design*, is guided by the designers' vision and images, including an underlying philosophy and core values and ideas. For example, he distinguishes between a design based on a rationale that intends to maintain or improve the status quo, and one based on a vision of transforming "what is" into "what should be." In this regard, he recognizes that goals and strategies are easy to perceive. However, he stresses that it is the design of a system that creates the model shaping and guiding strategies and goals. In his words, the design or model of a system "endows people in the system with a common purpose, assists them in understanding their specific contributions in the attainment of the purpose, and guides them in operating their system as a collective venture. Furthermore, the design or model of the system, once made public, informs the environment that embeds the system, and other systems in the environment, about what the system does, how it works, and how it is related to the environment and other systems."[8]

In clarifying the nature and value of planning, advocates also acknowledge problems related to excessive planning. For example, Hartley states: "To some persons, planning conjures up the image of a totalitarian society embracing centrally planned economic objectives and activities. In this case, self-expression and human freedom may approach a kind of universal triviality. The requisite assumption . . . is that some planning is desirable; exactly how much is less clear. . . . [Planning] is a way of attempting to somewhat control the future instead of merely reacting to it and being controlled by it."[9]

Decisions about what phenomena will be the focus of intervention and how such phenomena are labelled guide the translation process from rationale to planning and implementation. As translations are made, concerns arise about the appropriate relationship of means to ends, the desirability of specific ends, the processes by which ends and means are decided upon, the degree to which planning should be participatory, and so forth. For example, as immediate objectives and means to accomplish them are specified, intervener agreements with respect to the abstract rationale often turn into disagreements. Furthermore, because few interventions are devoid of iatrogenic effects (i.e., negative consequences), planning and implementation also encompass concerns about unintended and undesired outcomes.

In addition to controversial theoretical and philosophical concerns, planning and implementation also enmesh interveners in major methodological and practical problems. Methodologically, difficulties arise from the limited validity of current intervention (including assessment) approaches. Practically, difficulties are imposed by forces that resist change and by competing priorities and limited resources; such factors include restrictive policies and deficiencies in personnel availability, motivation, and competence. That is, planning and implementation not only are guided by classification decisions and underlying rationales, but also are shaped by some of the same personal, professional, socioeconomic, and political factors. For instance, agencies and individual professionals often must operate within current national, state, and local policies when addressing emotional, behavioral, and learning problems. When the formulation of policy guidelines is dominated by a particular philosophy, theory, or pragmatic need, the ways in which ends and means are translated into practice can become standardized. This can result in widespread institutionalization of a particular set of theories, beliefs, and values. The inherent dangers are obvious.

Analyses of processes, mechanisms, and products related to translating an underlying rationale into action are essential to appreciating the factors that shape everyday psychological and educational practices. In making such analyses, we find it useful to think in terms of *phases* of intervention planning and implementation. Intentional intervention is viewed as having a normative planning phase, a phase for planning specific practices, an administrative planning phase, and an evaluation planning phase. During these planning phases, each abstract intervention *aim* is translated into sets of somewhat less abstract *goals*, and then each goal is translated into specific (and sometimes concrete) *objectives*. Similarly, abstract processes are turned into specific procedures and activities. Such *planning* concepts and related concerns are covered in Part III.

Of course, not all that is planned is carried out; not everything done is planned. *Implementation* requires understanding what is intended and what isn't and how to accomplish the former and avoid the latter. The discussion in Part III also emphasizes that such understanding is built on an appreciation of the role of assessment and specific concepts and concerns related to facilitating implementation.

THE EVALUATION PROBLEM

Everyone evaluates interventions with which they come in contact. (Evaluation involves determining the worth or value of something.) Whenever anyone decides that an intervention is or isn't a good one, an evaluation is made. Interveners judge whether their own and others' programs are going well. Clients are quick to formulate likes or dislikes with respect to interveners and programs.

Often such evaluations only reflect an individual's or a group's informal observations. At other times, the judgments reflect careful data gathering and analyses and the use of an appropriate set of standards. Sometimes the judgments reflect differences in opinion about what a program should do; sometimes the judgments are about the degree to which the program is effective.

Interventions may be evaluated simply in terms of whether they accomplish intended outcomes. Indeed, accountability needs and demands tend to narrow discussion of the evaluation problem to a focus on maximizing the quality of data on intended outcomes. People, however, also evaluate in terms of whether they agree with what a program is trying to do. What an intervention intends to do is reflected in its rationale. Thus, evaluations of whether an intervention is any good usually reflect judgments about the appropriateness of its rationale—with specific reference to the major ways the rationale results in the intervention differing from others.

For example, all interventions for individuals with emotional, behavioral, and learning problems are designed with the hope that those served eventually will be able to cope effectively with day-to-day demands. All such interventions intend to do something positive and to minimize negative side effects. Some interventions, however, focus on a narrow range of socialization skills; others stress a broad range of goals related to helping an individual cope and grow. When one doesn't agree with an intervention's rationale, one will not likely approve of the intervention—even when evaluation data indicate it is effective.

Intervention evaluation involves decisions about focus, methods, standards to be used, and the best way to proceed in gathering and interpreting data. In making such decisions, controversy may arise over whose perspective is to prevail in making decisions. Concerns also arise because what can be evaluated currently is far less than what an intervention may intend to accomplish and because evaluation processes can produce significant negative effects.

Besides addressing concerns related to evaluating intervention, the evaluation problem underscores the role of evaluative research in advancing basic knowledge about intervention. That is, when intervention evaluation is analyzed within the context of the other three fundamental intervention problems, it becomes clear that evaluation is shaped profoundly by current understanding of these problems and contributes immensely to improved understanding. Work on the evaluation problem not only is essential to ensuring that intervention practices meet society's needs and expectations, it is fundamental to enhancing basic knowledge about intervention as a phenomenon.

In Part IV, we discuss the essence of evaluation, the process as it relates to the other three basic intervention problems, and how the process must be expanded if it is to improve intervention and advance intervention knowledge.

CONCLUDING COMMENT

On a broad theoretical level, in-depth understanding of the fundamental intervention problems introduced in this chapter has significant potential for improving practice and advancing knowledge. As more and more professionals address these problems and approach intervention in generic terms, they not only will improve understanding of their own interventions but will contribute to fundamental knowledge regarding intervention as a pervasive phenomenon in society.[10] What follows is a progress report on our efforts along these lines.

NOTES

1. L.B. Schorr with D. Schorr (1988). *Within our reach: Breaking the cycle of disadvantage.* New York: Doubleday, p. 31.

2. N. Hobbs (1975). *The future of children: Categories, labels, and their consequences.* San Francisco: Jossey-Bass, pp. 233, 236.

3. A.O. Ross & W.E. Pelham (1981). Child psychopathology. *Annual Review of Psychology, 32*, 243–278 (p. 244).

4. National Association of School Psychologists, (1986). *Rights without labels*. Washington, DC: Author. (Reprinted in *School Psychology Review, 18*, 1989.)

5. O.W. Markley & W.M. Harman (1982). *Changing images of man*. London: Pergamon Press. J.S. Bruner (1966). *Toward a theory of instruction*. New York: Norton. P.H. Rossi & H.E. Freeman (1982). *Evaluation: A systematic approach* (2nd ed.). Beverly Hills, CA: Sage. K.I. Howard & D.E. Orlinsky (1972). Psychotherapeutic processes. *Annual Review of Psychology, 23*, 615–668 (p. 617).

6. P. Brickman, V.C. Rabinowitz, J. Karuza, Jr., D. Coates, E. Cohn, & L. Kidder (1982). Models of helping and coping. *American Psychologist, 37*, 368–384 (p. 368).

7. P.H. Rossi, H.E. Freeman & S.R. Wright (1979). *Evaluation: A systematic approach*. Beverly Hills, CA: Sage.

8. B.H. Banathy (1991). *Systems design of education: A journey to create the future*. Englewood Cliffs, NJ: Educational Technology Publications, pp. 27–28.

9. H.J. Hartley (1968). *Educational planning-programming-budgeting*. Englewood Cliffs, NJ: Prentice-Hall, pp. 2–3.

10. Over twenty years ago, Urban and Ford noted with respect to intervention: "We share with a growing body of scholars the conviction that the heterogeneity of theory and method that has taken place over the last century obscures some underlying interrelationships, and that the task at this juncture is one of sorting out the interrelationships which are presumed to exist. We believe that interrelationships do exist and that they will be identified and verified if they are sought. The most likely outcome of such a search would appear to be more adequate and comprehensive theoretic formulations." H.B. Urban & D.H. Ford (1971). Some historical and conceptual perspectives on psychotherapy and behavior change. In A.E. Bergin & S.L. Garfield (Eds.), *Handbook of psychotherapy and behavior change*. New York: Wiley & Sons, p. 6.

Systematic efforts to address intervention concepts and ideas in fundamental terms are seen in the work of a smattering of writers. Besides those cited above, over the years our thinking about intervention has benefitted from reading the following: S.S. Brehm & T.W. Smith (1986). Social psychology applications to psychotherapy and behavior change. In S.L. Garfield & A.E. Bergin (Eds.), *Handbook of psychotherapy and behavior change* (3rd ed.). New York: Wiley & Sons. D.H. Ford & H.B. Urban (1963). *Systems of psychotherapy: A comparative study*. New York: Wiley. J.D. Frank (1973). *Persuasion and healing* (2nd ed.). Baltimore: Johns

Hopkins University Press. S.L. Garfield (1980). *Psychotherapy: An eclectic approach*. New York: Wiley. M.R. Goldfried (1980). Toward a delineation of therapeutic change principles. *American Psychologist, 35*, 991–999. M.R. Goldfried (1982). *Converging themes in the practice of psychotherapy*. New York: Springer. B. Joyce & M. Weil (1986). *Models of teaching* (3rd ed.). Englewood Cliffs, NJ: Prentice-Hall. H.L. Hodgkinson (1989). *The same client: The demographics of education and service delivery systems*. Washington, DC: Institute for Educational Leadership, Inc./Center for Demographic Policy. F.H. Kanfer & A.P. Goldstein (Eds.) (1991). *Helping people change: A textbook of methods* (4th ed.). New York: Pergamon. J.G. Kelly, L.R. Snowden & R.F. Muñoz (1977). Social and community intervention. *Annual Review of Psychology, 28*, 122–143. J. Miller (1978). *Living systems*. New York: McGraw-Hill. J.O. Prochaska & J.C. Norcross (1994). *Systems of psychotherapy. A transtheoretical analysis* (3nd ed.). Pacific Grove, CA: Brooks/Cole. W.C. Rhodes & M.C. Tracy (1972). *A study of child variance: Intervention* (Vol. 2). Ann Arbor: University of Michigan Press. H.H. Strupp & S.M. Hadley (1977). A tripartite model of mental health and therapeutic outcomes with special reference to negative effects in psychotherapy. *American Psychologist, 32*, 187–196. N.D. Sundberg, J.R. Taplin, & L.E. Tyler (1983). *Introduction to clinical psychology: Perspectives, issues, and contributions to human service*. Englewood Cliffs, NJ: Prentice-Hall.

PART I

THE CLASSIFICATION PROBLEM

"What's the use of their having names," the Gnat said, "if they won't answer to them?"

"No use to them," said Alice, "but it is useful to people who name them, I suppose. If not, why do things have names at all?"
                    Lewis Carroll, *Through the Looking-Glass*

What's in a name? Assignment of a label plays a major role in decisions to intervene and may profoundly shape a person's future. In psychology and education, for example, particular attention has been paid to classifying problems in human functioning with a view to their amelioration. And in attaching names to problems, there generally is some implication about what caused the problem and what to do about it.

People tend to associate strong images with specific labels and act upon these images. Sometimes the images are useful generalizations; sometimes they are harmful stereotypes. Because of the potential harm caused by diagnostic classification, the practice of labelling individuals is widely criticized. Attacks range from critiques of specific categories to arguments against all diagnostic labelling. Even among the lay population, one hears:

"The label stigmatizes the person. People tend to expect the worst of a person who has a diagnostic label; they often avoid and act differently toward them. This may make a problem worse." "If you tell people they have problems, they often make your words come true." "When the label is wrong, serious errors in treatment can be made."

Those who study diagnostic classification are especially concerned about the role labelling plays in segregating individuals with physical, cognitive, social, and emotional differences—including a disproportionate number from minority groups. In this regard, many writers discuss how society's interests shape decisions about which psychological and educational phenomena are given primary attention. Political processes establish guidelines used in defining problems, differentiating one phenomenon from another, and planning, implementing, and evaluating intervention.

With respect to diagnostic classification of children, cautions about potential abuses highlight society's role and interests.

Categories and labels are powerful instruments for social regulation and control, and they are often employed for obscure, covert, or hurtful purposes: to degrade people, to deny them access to opportunity, to exclude "undesirables" whose presence in some way offends, disturbs familiar custom, or demands extraordinary effort. . . . Society defines what is exceptional or deviant, and appropriate treatments are designed quite as much to protect society as they are to help the child. . . . "To take care of them" can and should be read with two meanings: to give children help and to exclude them from the community.[1]

Not all critics of diagnostic practices are against labelling in some form. Many desire to replace present categories with a system that identifies the need for intervention and uses processes and terminology that minimize negative consequences.

Few would deny that labelling can have negative effects. Awareness of this possibility is a good reason for care in how labels are used. Moreover, evidence that negative effects outweigh benefits is a good reason to do away with a particular label. But such concerns are not sufficient reasons to stop classifying phenomena. They simply underscore that diagnostic labelling, like all classification in science, is an essential but flawed enterprise.

As Neisser states, "We cannot perceive unless we anticipate, but we must not see only what we anticipate."[2] Even writers who challenge the basic tenets of logical positivism and those who stress the holistic nature of phenomena find it necessary to conceive parts of the whole in order to advance understanding.[3] Despite the risks involved in breaking phenomena apart, classification remains an indispensable tool. As Aristotle, the father of all classificationists, stated, "To think is to order." Ultimately, classification schemes are meant to facilitate understanding of phenomena (permitting parsimony without simplicity and aiding recognition of fundamental structures and relationships) and can both improve and provide new directions for theory, research, and practice.

Given the need and the concerns about classification, the search continues for the most useful labels and for ways to minimize negative effects that arise when labels are used. From this perspective, one criterion of a "good" label is that the designation helps more than it hurts. This, of course, raises the question, Who is the label supposed to help? Researchers? Practitioners? Clients? Society? Each may have a vested interest; each may have a different need for labelling, may use different labels, and may use different criteria in weighing benefits and costs. Thus, how "good" a particular label is usually depends on whose interests and needs are used in making the judgment.[4]

In sum, classification is both a practical necessity and an ethical imperative for significant advancement of knowledge about facilitating human functioning and ameliorating problems. Conceptual and methodological differentiations among phenomena are essential to improving intervention planning, implementation, and evaluation. At the same time, the potential negative consequences of labelling raise an ethical imperative to minimize such effects and ensure that benefits outweigh costs.

In working on classification as a fundamental intervention problem, then, primary concerns are: What phenomena should be classified? How can the phenomena be classified so that benefits for advancing and applying knowledge are maximized and negative consequences to individuals and society are minimized? A central task in all this is ongoing refinement (including modification and replacement) of classification schemes through developmental stages based on systematic evaluation.

Toward outlining key facets of the classification problem, Part I provides a brief exploration of five topics: (1) the question of what phenomena should be labelled to guide intervention theory, research, and practice; (2) broadening the classification of problems; (3) classifying positive functioning; (4) the difficulty of categorizing environmental variables; and (5) minimizing negative effects of classification.

NOTES

1. N. Hobbs (1975). *The future of children: Categories, labels, and their consequences*. San Francisco: Jossey-Bass, pp. 8–11, 20–21.

2. U. Neisser (1976). *Cognition and reality: Principles and implications of cognitive psychology*. San Francisco: W.H. Freeman, p. 43.

3. The long-standing controversies over holism and reductionism permeate the study of intervention. As will become evident, we approach intervention from the perspective of transactional models of behavior. A transactional view implies the type of holistic perspective that often is seen as at odds with the analytic approach called for by the logical positivist tradition. Clearly, scholars break the whole apart (e.g., sort into taxonomies) at considerable risk of distorting the phenomenon under study. However, pragmatically and realistically, there seems no alternative way to maintain all options for advancing knowledge. Examples of contemporary discussions of holism and the debate over logical positivism include D.P. Briggs & F.D. Peat (1984). *Looking glass universe: The emerging science of wholeness*. New York: Simon & Schuster. P. Checkland (1981). *Systems thinking, systems practice*. Chichester: Wiley & Sons. C.H. Cherryholmes (1992). Notes on pragmatism and scientific realism. *Educational Researcher, 21*, 13–17. E. Eisner (1991). *The enlightened eye: Qualitative inquiry and the enhancement of educational practice*. New York: Macmillan. E. Guba (Ed.) (1990). *The paradigm dialogue*. Newbury Park, CA: Sage. E.R. House (1991). Realism in research. *Educational Researcher, 20*, 2–9, 25. F. Schrag (1992). In defense of positivist research paradigms. *Educational Researcher, 21*, 5–8.

4. Parties with interests in matters related to intervention are grouped as those who are directly or indirectly involved. The former include (a) *subscribers* (e.g., private individuals and representatives of organized bodies who are seeking intervention for themselves, others, or both), (b) *systems focused upon* (e.g., individuals and those in settings who seek change or are referred by others), and (c) *interveners* (e.g., those who, in addition to whatever self interests are involved, may base their activity on the stated desires or interpreted needs of subscribers, the objects of change, or both). Indirectly involved interested parties include anyone else whose influence has the potential to produce a major impact on the intervention, such as (a) *first level environmental influences* (e.g., family, friends, employers, teachers, co-workers, local representatives of funding sources) and (b) *second and third level environmental influences* (i.e., those who lobby for, underwrite, study, evaluate, and teach about intervention, such as governmental agents related to health, education, welfare, and law enforcement; professional and lay organizations; theorists, researchers, and instructors).

Although focused on the topic of psychotherapy evaluation, a seminal discussion of different interested parties and examples of varying criteria is found in H.H. Strupp & S.M. Hadley (1977). A tripartite model of mental health and therapeutic outcomes with special reference to negative effects in psychotherapy. *American Psychologist, 32*, 187–196.

With direct relevance to classification of individuals' problems, see the following: American Psychiatric Association (1980/1987). *Diagnostic and statistical manual of mental disorders* (3rd ed./rev.). Washington, DC: American Psychiatric Association.   T.A. Widiger & T.J. Trull (1991). Diagnosis and clinical assessment. *Annual Review of Psychology, 42*, 109–133.   R.l. Cromwell, R.K. Blashfield, & J.S. Strauss (1975). Criteria for classification systems. In N. Hobbs (Ed.), *Issues in the classification of children* (Vol. 1, pp. 4–25). San Francisco: Jossey-Bass.   P. McReynolds (1989). Diagnosis and clinical assessment: Current status and major issues. *Annual Review of Psychology, 40*, 83–103.   M.C. Reynolds (1984). Classification of students with handicaps. In E.W. Gordon (Ed.), *Review of research in education* (Vol. 11, pp. 63–92). Washington, DC: American Educational Research Association.   M. Rutter & M. Gould (1985). Classification. In M. Rutter & L. Hersov (Eds.), *Child and adolescent psychiatry: Modern approaches* (2nd ed.). Oxford: Blackwell.   M. Rutter & A.H. Tuma (1988). Diagnosis and classification: Some outstanding issues. In M. Rutter & A.H. Tuma (Eds.), *Assessment and diagnosis in child psychopathology*. New York: Guilford.   E. Zigler & L. Phillips (1961). Psychiatric diagnosis: A critique. *Journal of Abnormal and Social Psychology, 63*, 607–618.

1

What Phenomena Should Be Classified?

Normality and exceptionality (or deviance) are not absolutes; both are culturally defined by particular societies at particular times for particular purposes.

Benedict[1]

Exploration of the classification problem requires that psychologists and educators begin with the most fundamental labelling question, What phenomena should be classified? The answer to this question guides development of all classification schemes, including diagnostic classifications, and thus is a primary factor shaping the focus of intervention theory, research, and practice. In this respect, a particular concern is the degree to which classification is limited to persons or pathology.

Comprehensive formal classification schemes in psychology and education are designed primarily to differentiate *individuals who are viewed as having or making problems* and doing so with respect to *negative features*. For example, there are schemes for diagnosing psychopathology, behavior problems, and those with special education needs; there are also emerging schemes for categorizing more delimited phenomena such as types of criminal acts and subgroups among the homeless.[2]

In general, available classification schemes convey the impression that individuals' emotional, behavioral, or learning problems are instigated by internal *pathology* (i.e., are attributable primarily to *nature*—using the term broadly). In some cases, this impression is tempered by a view that the pathology is a vulnerability that manifests as a problem only under stress. At the same time, however, bias toward person pathology in classifying problems may be bolstered by the tendency (outlined in attribution theory) for observers to perceive the problems of others as rooted in stable personal dispositions. This tendency may be further promoted by societal and professional interests (e.g., economic and political) that favor a view of such problems in terms of personal rather than social causation.[3]

An overemphasis on classifying problems in terms of personal pathology skews theory, research, and practice. One example is seen in the fact that comprehensive classification schemes do not exist for environmentally caused problems (i.e., those attributable primarily to improper *nurture*) or for psychosocial problems (i.e., those instigated by both *nature and nurture*).[4] Critics suggest that this results in proportionately less attention for interventions designed to (1) address psychosocial problems and (2) enhance human functioning among those not manifesting problems. There is considerable irony in all this because it is likely that on a theoretical level many who use prevailing diagnostic schemes think in terms of the interplay of person and environment in viewing the etiology of most problems in human functioning—with differences in view concentrating on the amount of variance hypothetically attributed to each.

To counter nature versus nurture biases in thinking about problems, it is beneficial to approach all classification and intervention guided by a broad model that incorporates both views in thinking about human behavior (including problems). In psychology and education, such a model is the currently prevailing transactional view.

A BROAD VIEW OF HUMAN FUNCTIONING

Before the 1920s, psychology was dominated by models of human behavior that viewed the determinants of behavior as primarily a function of person variables, especially inborn characteristics. With the rise of behaviorism, a strong competing model stressed that behavior was primarily a function of the environment, for example, the stimuli and reinforcers one encounters.

The contemporary model for understanding human functioning is a transactional view that emphasizes the reciprocal interplay of person and environment.[5] However, there is a continuing tendency to attribute human problems primarily to either person or environment variables. This is both unfortunate and unnecessary. It is unfortunate because, as already suggested, it limits efforts to advance knowledge and colludes with prevailing tendencies to focus intervention on individuals, rather than fostering consideration of interventions directed at environmental system causes. It is unnecessary because a transactional view encompasses functioning determined by person, environment, or both and encompasses a comprehensive perspective of cause and correction.

To illustrate the nature of transactional thinking, let's use the example of youngsters at school. In teaching a lesson, the teacher finds that some students learn easily and some do not; some misbehave, some do not. Even a good student may appear distracted on a given day. Why the differences?

A common-sense answer suggests that each student brings something different to the situation and therefore experiences it differently. And that's a pretty good answer—as far as it goes. What gets lost in this simple explanation is the essence of the differences and the reciprocal impact student and situation have on each other—resulting in continuing change in both.

For our purposes here, any student can be viewed as bringing to each situation *capacities and attitudes* accumulated over time, as well as *current states of being and behaving*. These "person" variables transact with each other and also with the environment.

At the same time, the situation in which students are expected to function not only consists of *instructional processes and content*, but also the *physical and social context* in which instruction takes place. Each part of the environment also transacts with the others.

Obviously, the transactions can vary considerably and can lead to a variety of outcomes with respect to changes in the students. At any given time, those noting student outcomes may judge them as positive, negative, or some combination of both. For example, in Figure 1.1 the types of potential changes in accumulated capacities and attitudes can be described as

- desired functioning—with possible changes and expansion of capacities and attitudes in "approved" ways

- deviant functioning—with possible changes and expansion of capacities and attitudes but not in "approved" ways
- disrupted functioning—interference with ability to function, including distorted attitudes and possibly a decrease in capacities
- delayed and arrested functioning—with little change in capacities and perhaps in attitudes

Such outcomes, of course, are accompanied by concomitant shifts in current states of being and behaving. Any specific outcome (e.g., deviant functioning) may *primarily* reflect the contribution of person variables, environmental variables, or both. Similarly, subsequent changes in functioning (e.g., amelioration of problems) may require interventions that focus primarily on person, environment, or both.[6]

IMPLICATIONS FOR CLASSIFYING INTERVENTION PHENOMENA

Now, let's return to the original question. What phenomena should be labelled to guide intervention theory, research, and practice? In psychology and education, interveners are interested in both fostering positive growth and dealing with problems; in each case, they must decide whether to focus intervention on environments, persons, or both. However, as noted above, in both fields professionals focus primarily on developing schemes for labelling the problems of individuals (and framing problems in individual rather than societal terms). As a result, few resources are devoted to creating formal schemes for classifying problems caused by environmental factors (classification of environmental phenomena remains in its infancy) or for comprehensive categorization of positive human functioning. This state of affairs probably is a contributor to the relatively weak knowledge base for enhancing positive functioning and developing interventions focused on environmental determinants.

From the above perspective, a critical need exists for taxonomic categories that differentiate positive and negative functioning with respect to internal causes, environmental determinants, or the transaction of both. The absence of such categories limits understanding of human behavior and thus unduly restricts intervention

Figure 1.1
Learning and Behavior as a Function of Person-and-Environment Transactions*

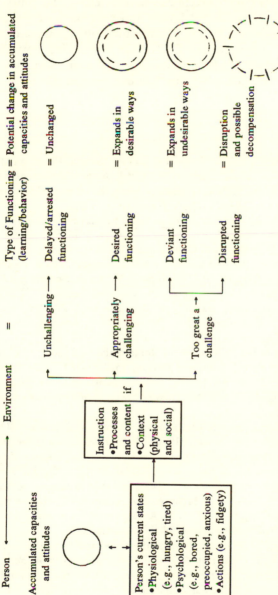

| Person | = | Environment | = | Type of Functioning (learning/behavior) | = | Potential change in accumulated capacities and attitudes |

Unchallenging → Delayed/arrested functioning = Unchanged

Appropriately challenging → Desired functioning = Expands in desirable ways

Too great a challenge → Deviant functioning = Expands in undesirable ways

→ Disrupted functioning = Disruption and possible decompensation

Accumulated capacities and attitudes

Instruction
•Processes and content
•Context (physical and social)

if

Person's current states
•Physiological (e.g., hungry, tired)
•Psychological (e.g., bored, preoccupied, anxious)
•Actions (e.g., fidgety)

*See Table 2.1 for examples of person-and-environment factors—and their transactions—that lead to problems.

Source: H.S. Adelman and L. Taylor (1993). *Learning problems and learning disabilities: Moving forward.* Pacific Grove, CA: Brooks/Cole. Reprinted with permission.

theory, research, and practice.

One further point: Practitioners, researchers, and policy makers usually require different labels and processes. Furthermore, practitioners in one field (e.g., education) often denigrate labelling schemes developed in other fields (such as medicine or psychology). Therefore, multiple classification schemes seem inevitable, and to minimize confusion, cross translations are essential.

NOTES

1. R. Benedict (1934). *Patterns of culture*. Boston: Houghton Mifflin.

2. In addition to the American Psychiatric Association's scheme found in the *Diagnostic and statistical manual of mental disorders* (DSM) (periodically revised—see DSM-IV), others are pursuing empirical and theoretical approaches to the classification of individual problems. Examples include: World Health Organization's International Classification of Diseases (ICD-10). T.M. Achenbach & C. Edelbrock (1983). *Manual for the Child Behavior Checklist and Revised Child Behavior Profile*. Burlington: University of Vermont. R.J. Thompson, W. Kronenberger, & J.F. Curry (1989). Behavior classification system for children with developmental, psychiatric, and chronic medical problems. *Journal of Pediatric Psychology, 14*, 559–575. K.A. Farr & D.C. Gibbons (1990). *International Journal of Offender Therapy and Comparative Criminology, 34*, 223–237. J.E. Berecochea & J.B. Gibbs (1991). Inmate classification: A correctional program that works? *Evaluation Review, 15*, 333–363. G.A. Morse, R.J. Calsyn, & G.K. Burger (1992). Development and cross-validation or a system for classifying homeless persons. *Journal of Community Psychology, 20*, 228–242.

3. For an issue-oriented psychological discussion of attributional bias, see the following: G.W. Bradley (1978). Self-serving biases in the attribution process: A reexamination of the fact or fiction question. *Journal of Personality and Social Psychology, 36*, 56–71. E.L. Deci & R.M. Ryan (1985). *Intrinsic motivation and self-determination in human behavior*. New York: Plenum Press. D.T. Miller & C.A. Porter (1988). Errors and biases in the attribution process. In L.Y. Abramson (Ed.), *Social cognition and clinical psychology: A synthesis*. New York: Guilford.

For a range of perspectives on professional and societal biases, see the following: H.S. Becker (1963). *Outsiders: Studies in the sociology of deviance*. Glencoe, IL: Free Press. A. Chase (1977). *The legacy of Malthus: The social costs of the new scientific racism*. New York: Knopf. K. Heller,

W. Holtzman, & S. Messick (1982). *Placing children in special education: A strategy for equity*. Report of the National Academy of Sciences' Panel on Selection and Placement of Students in Programs for the Mentally Retarded. Washington, DC: National Academy Press. N. Hobbs (1975). *The future of children: Categories, labels, and their consequences*. San Francisco: Jossey-Bass. S.R. Lopez (1989). Patient variable biases in clinical judgment: Conceptual overview and methodological considerations. *Psychological Bulletin, 106*, 184–203. T.E. Schact (1985). DSM-III and the politics of truth. *American Psychologist, 40*, 513–521. J.C. Wakefield (1992). The concept of mental disorder: On the boundary between biological fact and social values. *American Psychologist, 47*, 372–388.

4. Although the term *psychosocial problems* connotes problems that arise because of the way specific person and environmental factors transact, for convenience in the present discussion the label also is used to encompass problems instigated primarily by environmental variables.

5. For a brief overview, see A. Bandura (1978). The self system in reciprocal determination. *American Psychologist, 33*, 344–358.

6. For a more in-depth discussion, see H.S. Adelman & L. Taylor (1993). *Learning problems and learning disabilities: Moving forward*. Pacific Grove, CA: Brooks/Cole.

2

Toward Broadening the
Classification of Problems

By embracing and acting on a society's or an organization's
definitions of problems and of deviants, interveners work to
maintain the status quo.

Bermant & Warwick[1]

Continuing debates over how to define and differentiate problems
are one indicator of the importance of and difficulty in dealing with
diagnostic classification. We have touched upon some of the
concerns. In this chapter, we specifically address the matter of
classifying problems in ways that differentiate those caused by
internal factors, environmental variables, or a combination of both.
Before doing so, however, it will help to review the basic nature of
diagnostic classification.

SOME FUNDAMENTALS

Conceptually, the task of defining and differentiating psychological
and educational problems is tantamount to the general task of
classification or taxonomic sorting. Wojciechowski nicely places the
task in philosophical and empirical perspective: "To take the
problem of classification seriously is, and has always been, a sign of
intellectual maturity and a prerequisite for effective investigation of
reality. [The problem is] as old as philosophy and as open and
unsettled as a philosophical system." He argues that the problem
remains unsettled because two opposing factors are at play and
counterbalance each other: "the imperative desire of the intellect

to understand the overwhelming richness of the phenomena . . . and the varied and varying, seemingly endless multiplicity of data." Given this, our choice is to attempt to formulate a global and exhaustive classification ("reach for the apparently supreme intellectual ideal of the total conceptual horizon") or to be less grandiose and opt for what is more attainable and less controversial—partial classification. Wojciechowski goes on to stress that, in fact, the two choices are complementary (but this is not to say that total classifications result from combining partial classifications).[2]

Providing a psychological perspective, Datta and Farradane postulate that the desire to find order is a basic human "drive." They argue that, as a cognitive activity, classification involves more than ordering entities, activities, or other elements of external reality; it is an "organization of our mental concepts or constructs of external entities and elements." Moreover, they see classification as not just concerned with grouping concepts by selected characteristics, but focused on the relationships between concepts or groups of concepts.[3]

Theoretically generated classification begins with a definition of the domain that is to be described, decisions about level of generality, and creation of categories into which phenomena will be ordered. Categories are formed along vertical (i.e., hierarchical) and horizontal dimensions. The process of constructing categories may be inductive, deductive, or both. How many categories are created depends essentially on one's ability to abstract from one's experience (including statistical analyses). The categories may range in level of abstraction from highly descriptive to extremely abstract.

Principles used in constructing such classes usually are closely related to the purposes for which the classification scheme is developed. In this regard, researchers may adopt different principles than practitioners, and both may prefer to classify phenomena differently from policy makers and administrators.

The task of classification, of course, involves more than development of a conceptual scheme; it requires reliable procedures for differentiating (e.g., operationally identifying) phenomena of interest. Differentiations may be of a qualitative (i.e., different kinds) or quantitative nature (i.e., differences in degree). The end result is meant to be differentiations that reduce heterogeneity (e.g., partition out variance) in desired ways. A constant problem, however, is the graduated rather than discrete nature of so many phenomena that are of interest.[4]

The Problem of Heterogeneity

A great deal of criticism aimed at psychiatric and special education classification activity stems from the fact that current identification procedures result in heterogeneous groupings. For example, with respect to individuals, those assigned the same diagnostic label may differ with reference to symptoms, causes, current performance, and prognosis. At the simplest level, this criticism raises the point that a group assigned a particular label encompasses important subgroups. At a more complex level, this criticism suggests that the diagnostic label does not capture the essence of an important class of phenomena.

To clarify this crucial matter: Homogeneity is not a quality inherent in a phenomenon, but a construction of the observer and classifier. Take, for example, the delineation in biological classification of a genus and the species it encompasses. If a particular diagnostic label (e.g., depression, learning disabilities) is like a genus, it cannot be criticized for not designating the significant subgroups (species) within it. However, if the label is more akin to a species than a genus, the group of which it is a subgroup should be clarified. In either case, the problem is not heterogeneity per se. From this perspective, Zigler and Phillips conclude, "it would perhaps be more fruitful to dispense entirely with the homogeneity-heterogeneity distinction ... allowing us to direct our attention to the underlying problem of the relative merits of different classificatory principles."[5]

Current State of the Art

Heterogeneity aside, present efforts to classify psychological and educational problems use taxonomies and typologies defined in terms of current dysfunctioning, causal factors, intervention implications, or some combination of all these. (For our purposes here, we will ignore the debate that distinguishes taxonomies from typologies.)

Taxonomy building generally is based on observation or multivariate statistical techniques. The specific variables and criteria used in defining a category usually are chosen because they have immediate relevance for research, intervention, administrative, or policy matters. For many labels, however, the difficulty in validly identifying cause precludes doing more than grouping by symptoms and handicapping condition. Psychiatric and special education classifications, for example, use a polythetic approach whereby those persons who share a number of attributes usually are assigned the same label. It should be noted, however, that designated symptoms have constituted a relatively limited range of the potentially important correlates, and the classification schemes have not adequately dealt with the dimensions of severity and pervasiveness or with causality.[6] As greater attention is given to classifying other phenomena (such as psychosocial problems), these factors should reemerge as essential concerns for differential categorization.

Severity and Pervasiveness

The dimensions of severity (mild to profound) and pervasiveness (narrow to broad) have fundamental significance for planning, implementing, and evaluating intervention. As graphically presented in Figure 2.1, treating the combination of pervasiveness and severity as discrete categories rather than continuous variables yields nine classification groups. When *paradigmatic* causes of dysfunction are added as a third dimension, the schema jumps to twenty-seven groups. If duration is added, another large leap in categories results.

The relatively straightforward nine-group classification of severity and pervasiveness underscores a simple but critical fact: planning, implementation, and evaluation *minimally* must make differentiations with regard to such basic dimensions. For example, in making prognoses and evaluating intervention efficacy, one must account for severity given comparably pervasive problems. That is, realistic intervention requires recognition that comprehensive improvements are more easily accomplished with those whose problem severity is

Figure 2.1
Four Key Dimensions of Concern in Classifying Psychosocial and Educational Problems

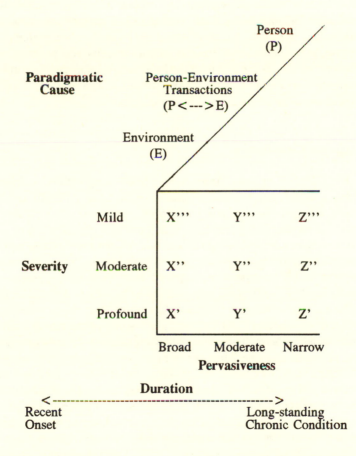

mild (X''') as contrasted to profound (X')—given equal pervasiveness.

Issues do arise, however, because of lack of agreement about how to define severity and pervasiveness. For example, in assessing individuals, severity might be defined in terms of intensity and frequency of specified deviant and devious behavior and/or nonoccurrence of adaptive skills and behavior. Pervasiveness might be defined with respect to the range of developmental areas and/or situations affected. Satisfactorily operationalizing these dimensions remains a major task confronting classification researchers. The problem, of course, is that specific criteria for judging severity and pervasiveness depend on prevailing contextual norms and standards, such as expectations related to age, sex, subculture, and social status. Deviance, after all, is defined by social groups.

Causal Classification

Classification by cause demonstrates other complexities. It may be done with reference to paradigmatic cause or in terms of specific instigators (primary/secondary contributing factors). The number of possible specific instigating factors is immense; indeed, a list of such factors related to psychological and educational problems would fill the rest of this monograph. For our purposes here, the broad reciprocal deterministic paradigm of cause is used to generate an outline of general factors hypothesized as causing emotional, behavioral, and learning problems (see Table 2.1).

A critical look at Table 2.1 suggests some of the empirical and conceptual problems associated with using cause to classify problems. For example, many variables may be primary or secondary instigating factors. And, of course, secondary causal factors interact with primary instigators. In general, the degree to which secondary factors exacerbate problems is determined by type of primary instigator and the degree of dysfunction produced by it. This is exemplified when a genetic anomaly or physiological "insult" causes a major central nervous system (CNS) disorder and the effect on behavior is so severe and pervasive that resultant dysfunctioning cannot be significantly worsened. In contrast, when CNS disorders are minor, a great many secondary variables can aggravate existing dysfunctions and create other problems.

As the above analysis suggests, sometimes causal factors and their effects are logical indicators for intervention decisions and are potential predictors of outcome. That is, outcomes should differ for groups who differ in the degree to which the pathological impact of causal factors can be compensated for or reversed.

From the above perspective, classification by causal factors and their immediate effects and current manifestations could be of great significance in intervention planning, implementation, and evaluation. The problem, of course, is that available methods for assessing causes (e.g., testing causal hypotheses) have major limitations.

CLASSIFYING EMOTIONAL, BEHAVIORAL, AND LEARNING PROBLEMS: A WORKING EXAMPLE

Efforts to improve classification of problems in psychology, psychiatry, and education involve an interplay of conceptual and empirical activity. Progress has accelerated with advances in methodology, especially improved measurement, sequential decision making, and use of multiple approaches. However, the continuing consensus among reviewers in this area is that considerable work remains to be done, especially with respect to developing and validating categories or dimensions that are distinguishable from other syndromes (to facilitate reliable diagnosis) and that also are associated with different causes, outcomes, or interventions.[7]

A clear indication of the need to address a wider range of variables in labelling emotional, behavioral, and learning problems is seen in efforts to develop multifaceted classification schemes. The multiaxial classification system developed by the American Psychiatric Association in its *Diagnostic and Statistical Manual of Mental Disorders* (see DSM-IV) represents the prevailing approach in the United States.[8] To account for the possibility that problems do not completely stem from within the individual, the system includes a dimension acknowledging "psychosocial stressors." However, this dimension deals only with the environment as a contributing factor, so such stressors are not viewed as primary causes. Moreover, this dimension is not included in making the official diagnosis; rather it is limited to ad hoc clinical and research uses.

Table 2.1

Factors Instigating Emotional, Behavioral, and Learning Problems

Environment (E) **(Type I problems)**

1. Insufficient stimuli
   (e.g., prolonged periods in impoverished environments; deprivation of learning opportunities at home or school such as lack of play and practice situations and poor instruction; inadequate diet)

2. Excessive stimuli
   (e.g., overly demanding home, school, or work experiences, such as overwhelming pressure to achieve and contradictory expectations; overcrowding)

3. Intrusive and hostile stimuli
   (e.g., medical practices, especially at birth, leading to physiological impairment; contaminated environments; conflict in home, school, workplace; faulty child- rearing practices, such as long-standing abuse and rejection; dysfunctional family; migratory family; language used is a second language; social prejudices related to race, sex, age, physical characteristics, and behavior)

Person (P) **(Type III problems)**

1. Physiological insult
   (e.g., cerebral trauma, such as accident or stroke, endocrine dysfunctions and chemical imbalances; illness affecting brain or sensory functioning)

2. Genetic anomaly
   (e.g., genes which limit, slow down, or lead to any atypical development)

3. Cognitive activity and affective states self-experienced as deviant
   (e.g., lack of basic knowledge, skills, or cognitive strategies; inability to cope effectively with emotions; low self-esteem)

(cont.)

Table 2.1 (cont.)

4. Physical characteristics shaping contact with environment and/or experienced by self as deviant
   (e.g., visual, auditory, or motoric deficits; excessive or reduced sensitivity to stimuli; easily fatigued; factors such as race, sex, age, or unusual appearance that produce stereotypical responses)

5. Deviant actions of the individual
   (e.g., performance problems, such as excessive errors in performing; high or low levels of activity)

Interactions/Transactions Between E and P* (Type II problems)

1. Severe to moderate personal vulnerabilities and environmental defects and differences
   (e.g., person with extremely slow development in a highly demanding environment—all of which simultaneously and equally instigate the problem)

2. Minor personal vulnerabilities not accommodated by the situation
   (e.g., person with minimal CNS disorders resulting in auditory perceptual disability trying to do auditory-loaded tasks; very active person forced into situations at home, school, or work that do not tolerate this level of activity)

3. Minor environmental defects and differences not accommodated by the individual
   (e.g., person is in the minority racially or culturally and is not participating in many social activities because he or she thinks others may be unreceptive)

*May involve only one (P) and one (E) variable or may involve multiple combinations.

Source: H.S. Adelman and L. Taylor (1993). *Learning problems and learning disabilities: Moving forward*. Pacific Grove, CA: Brooks/Cole. Reprinted with permission.

The following conceptual example is offered to illustrate the type of broad scheme that might be a useful *starting* place in classifying emotional, behavioral, and learning problems with a view to differentiating psychopathology from psychosocial problems. From the perspective of a transactional view of the determinants of behavior, it is useful conceptually to differentiate along a continuum in ways that separate problems initially caused by internal factors, environmental variables, or a combination of both. As can be seen in Figure 2.2, problems caused by the environment can be placed at one end of such a continuum and referred to as Type I problems. At the other end are problems caused primarily by pathology within the person and designated as Type III problems. In the middle are problems stemming from a relatively equal contribution of environmental and person sources, labelled Type II problems.

To be more specific: In this scheme, diagnostic labels connoting *extremely* dysfunctional problems caused by pathological conditions within a person are most appropriate for individuals whose problems fit the cluster designated as Type III problems. Obviously, some problems caused by pathological conditions within a person are not manifested in severe, pervasive ways, and there are persons without such pathology whose problems do become severe and pervasive. The intent is not to ignore these individuals; as a first categorization step, however, it is essential that they not be confused with those seen as having Type III problems.

At the other end of the continuum are individuals with problems arising from outside the person (i.e., Type I problems). For example, many persons grow up in impoverished and hostile environmental circumstances; based on the best evidence available, such environmental conditions should be considered first in hypothesizing the *primary instigating* causes of the behavioral, emotional, and learning problems these individuals manifest. (Once such conditions are ruled out as the basis for observed problems, hypotheses about within-person causality become more viable.)

To provide a reference point in the middle of the continuum, a Type II category is used. This group consists of persons who do not function well in situations where their individual differences and vulnerabilities are poorly accommodated or are responded to hostilely. The problems of an individual in this group are a relatively equal product of person characteristics and failure of the environment to

Figure 2.2
A Continuum of Problems Reflecting a Transactional View of the Locus of Primary Instigating Factors

Primary Locus of Cause

Problems caused by factors in the environment (E)		Problems caused equally by environment and person		Problems caused by factors in the person (P)
E	(E<-->p)	E<-->P	(e<-->P)	P
Type I problems		Type II problems		Type III problems

- caused primarily by environments and systems that are deficient and/or hostile
- problems are mild to moderately severe and narrow to moderately pervasive

- caused primarily by a significant *mismatch* between individual differences and vulnerabilities and the nature of that person's environment (not by a person's pathology)
- problems are mild to moderately severe and pervasive

- caused primarily by person factors of a pathological nature
- problems are moderate to profoundly severe and moderate to broadly pervasive

In this conceptual scheme, the emphasis in each case is on problems that are beyond the early stage of onset.

accommodate that individual.

There are, of course, variations along the continuum that do not precisely fit a category. That is, at each point between the extreme ends, environment-person transactions are the cause, but the degree to which each contributes to the problem varies. Toward the environment end of the continuum, environmental factors play a bigger role (represented as $E < — > p$). Toward the other end, person variables account for more of the problem (thus $e < — > P$).

Clearly, a simple continuum cannot do justice to the complexities associated with classifying and differentiating individuals' problems. Furthermore, some problems are not easily assessed or do not fall readily into a group due to data limitations and comorbidity (two of the frustrating realities confronting classifiers). As an example, however, the above conceptual scheme serves to suggest the value of initially using a broad, paradigmatic conception of causality. Specifically, the approach minimizes the presumptive tendency toward viewing problems as caused by deficiencies or pathology within the individual. In doing so, it helps avoid tendencies toward "blaming the victim."[9] It also helps broaden the focus of intervention by highlighting that a prerequisite and sometimes sufficient approach to ameliorating some problems involves improving the environment's accommodation of individual differences.

After the general groupings are identified, it becomes relevant to consider the value of differentiating subgroups or subtypes within each domain and major type of problem. For example, subtypes for the Type III category might first differentiate behavioral, emotional, or learning problems arising from serious internal pathology (e.g., structural and functional malfunctioning within the person that causes disorders and disabilities and disrupts development). In doing so, the need for a category to cover problems that pervade all three domains also is evident. Then subtypes might be differentiated within each of these categories. For illustrative purposes: Figure 2.3 presents some ideas for subgrouping Type I and III problems; Figure 2.4 presents ideas for further subtyping misbehavior within the Type I category. In formulating subtypes, basic dimensions such as problem severity, pervasiveness, and chronicity continue to play a key role, as do considerations about development, gender, culture, and social class.

Obviously, the point in offering the preceding examples is not to argue for their adoption but to emphasize that discussion of classifica-

Figure 2.3
A Categorization of Type I, II, and III Problems

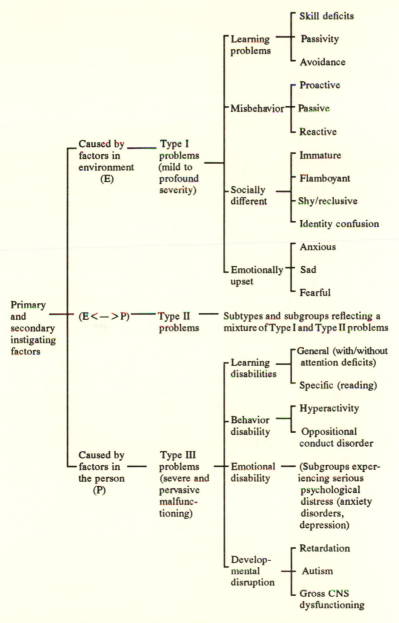

Source: H.S. Adelman and L. Taylor (1993). *Learning problems and learning disabilities.* Pacific Grove. Brooks/Cole. Reprinted with permission.

Figure 2.4
Subtyping Intentional Misbehavior (a Type I problem)

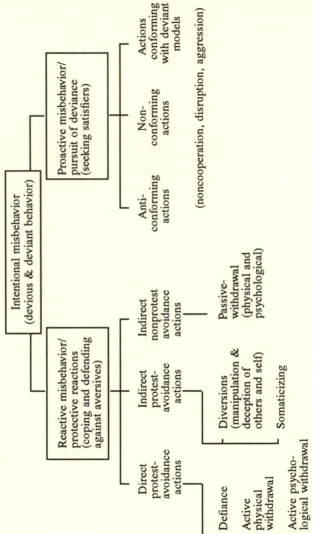

tion raises theoretical, practical, legal, and ethical matters of profound concern to researchers, practitioners, and policy makers. For example, as the examples underscore, efforts to improve classification are essential to improving differential diagnoses related to psychopathology and psychosocial problems. The clearer the image of phenomena that are of interest, the sharper the focus of discussion related to cause and correction, and the greater the chances are for advancing knowledge.

NOTES

1. G. Bermant & D.P. Warwick (1978). The ethics of social intervention: Power, freedom, and accountability. In G. Bermant, H.C. Kelman, & D.P. Warwick (Eds.), *The ethics of social intervention*. Washington, DC: Hemisphere (p. 392).

2. J. Wojciechowski (1974). The philosophical relevance of the problem of the classification of knowledge. In J. Wojciechowski (Ed.), *Conceptual basis of the classification of knowledge: Proceedings of the Ottawa Conference*. Pullach/Munchen: Werlag Dokumentation (p. 13).

3. S. Datta & J.E.L. Farradane (1974). A psychological basis for general classification. In J. Wojciechowski (Ed.), *Conceptual basis of the classification of knowledge: Proceedings of the Ottawa Conference*. Pullach/Munchen: Werlag Dokumentation (pp. 320–321). Datta and Farradane go on to stress that scientific classifications have been "almost purely generic in type, constructed by 'synthesis' from the particular to the general" (p. 322). The synthetic method is seen as needing to satisfy five requirements: (1) creation of only one place in a scheme for each concept, (2) assurance of complete freedom of interpolation and extrapolation as knowledge advances, (3) representation of compound or complex subjects by synthesis of simpler concepts, (4) explicit expression of relationships between concepts in compound or complex subjects, and (5) separation of the different lines of relationship. Building on the work of J.P. Guilford, they suggest that in classifying concepts and their interrelationships there are four basic types: entities, activities, "abstracts," and properties.

Currently, theory and research by cognitive and social psychologists are providing basic insights into why and how people categorize and the impact of such categorization. For example, in the 1970s Rosch outlined a psychological theory of categorization. *Categorization theory* focuses on the way individuals organize their world by forming and using natural and social concepts related to objects; this contrasts with *script theory*, which focuses on schema for specifying the sequencing of events. See E. Rosch (1978). Principles of categorization. In E. Rosch & B. Lloyd (Eds.), *Cognition and categorization*. Hillsdale, NJ: Erlbaum (pp. 27–47). Also see C.B. Mervis & E. Rosch (1981). Categorization of natural objects. *Annual Review of Psychology, 32*, 89–115; S.T. Fiske (1993). Social cognition and social perception. *Annual Review of Psychology, 44*, 155–194.

4. For an overview of the pros and cons of dimensional (quantitative) versus categorical (qualitative) classification of pathology, see T.A. Widiger & T.J. Trull (1991). Diagnosis and clinical assessment. *Annual Review of Psychology, 42*, 109–133.

5. E. Zigler & L. Phillips (1961). Psychiatric diagnosis: A critique. *Journal of Abnormal and Social Psychology, 63*, 607–618. (The example of biological classification comes from this source.)

6. For some time, controversy has raged over what constitutes a symptom and how specific symptoms relate to etiology and intervention. Controversy is likely to continue as long as (1) the current limited range of correlates (i.e., symptoms) remains the primary focus of research and (2) researchers are unable to establish cause-effect relationships with respect to a wide range of problem determinants and intervention processes and outcome.

7. See review by H.C. Quay, D.K. Routh, & S.K. Shapiro (1987). Psychopathology of childhood: From description to validation. *Annual Review of Psychology, 38*, 491–532.

8. American Psychiatric Association (1980/1987/1994). *Diagnostic and statistical manual of mental disorders* (4th ed./revised). Washington, DC: American Psychiatric Association. (Outside the United States, the World Health Organization's International Classification of Diseases—ICD-10—is widely used.)

Criticisms of the schemes used by practitioners for classifying pathology are legion. In general, it is recognized that such systems are not scientific products but are designed to meet a number of pragmatic needs (e.g., clinical, legal, public health). With respect to coverage, concerns are raised over what is included and what is not. For example, citing the Group for the Advancement of Psychiatry Committee on the Family, Widiger and Trull note: "A major limitation of the DSM-III-R is its confinement to organismic/mental disorders and its failure to recognize social, relational pathology." See Widiger & Trull (1991). *Annual Review of Psychology* (p. 113).

9. W. Ryan (1971). *Blaming the victim*. New York: Random House.

3

Nondiagnostic Classification of Persons

Measurement is essential to science, but before we can measure, we must know what it is we want to measure. Qualitative or taxonomic discovery must precede quantitative measurement.

Eysenck[1]

The complexities of classifying problems in human functioning are multiplied exponentially when one tries to classify human behavior in general. Thus, it is not surprising that multifaceted, comprehensive schemes have not emerged.

In psychology, those concerned with personality, social, and developmental theory and research use various ways to describe persons, their development, and their ways of functioning. The most systematic categories produced so far are classifications of personality traits. Early work developed lists of traits that presumably characterized functioning across domains and situations (e.g., creative-uncreative; extrovert-introvert; reflective-impulsive; aggressive-unaggressive). After it became evident that thousands of such traits can be specified, taxonomists took another tack. The emphasis turned to differentiating traits with respect to whether they permeate a person's behavior or appear only in some situations, and groups of traits were designated as core personality dimensions. As a result, considerable agreement has been reached that there are five basic personality dimensions. But no consensus exists about labels for these dimensions. As a recent review indicates, however, the following trait names capture their flavor:

(1) extraversion/introversion (or surgency), (2) friendliness/hostility (or agreeableness), (3) conscientiousness (or will), (4) neuroticism/emotional stability (or emotional stability), and (5) intellect (or openness).[2]

A related trend categorizes *types of behavior* along basic dimensions. A person's actions might be labelled as friendly or hostile, outgoing or shy, aggressive or submissive, altruistic or selfish, and so forth. Such concepts, however, require considerable refinement. For example, with respect to aggression, care must be taken not only to avoid interpreting a hurtful act as indicating an aggressive trait, but also to avoid misinterpreting the act itself. Individuals may have a pattern of hurting others but may not do so intentionally or with aggressive feeling; and they may commit the acts only in one situation or at one time and not another. Thus, hurtful behavior requires further differentiation, such as whether it is sanctioned, intentional, proactive or reactive, antisocial or prosocial. Similarly, acts cannot readily be labelled as altruistic or not. Helping behavior may not be motivated primarily by a person's unselfish desire to help another; a person may feel altruistic under some circumstances and not others.

As a reciprocal determinist perspective has become the prevailing view of behavior, greater attention is paid to how the same person functions differently at different times, in different places, and in different domains. Of particular interest is functioning in the major developmental domains (sensory, perceptual, motoric, cognitive, linguistic, social, emotional). In each developmental domain and subdomain, classification schemes must address contrasting determinants (person, environment, or both) and differences in functional intensity, cross situational stability, and consistency over time, as well as accounting for developmental stages, gender, culture, and social class.

As with human problems, a multiaxial framework is needed to integrate the multiple aspects of positive human functioning. Compas provides a useful example in discussing positive mental health. He proposes an approach outlining five axes. The two core axes involve, first, skills and motives for protecting the self from stress, and second, skills and motives for involving the self in meaningful activities. The third axis addresses the divergent perspectives and sources of information: adolescents, parents, teachers, and mental health professionals. The fourth axis accounts for developmental changes, and the fifth incorporates sociocultural differences.[3]

Obviously, a lifetime of work remains with respect to establishing nondiagnostic classification schemes for human functioning. Equally obvious is the fact that relatively few professionals are pursuing this area. More than with problems, most practitioners probably feel they don't need to classify nonproblem behavior in order to intervene. We would encourage some rethinking of this position. Among the immediate benefits that should accrue from such work is improved understanding of contrasting determinants that produce similar behavior. In turn, this can lead to a better understanding and more effective and efficient intervention strategies to foster positive functioning.

NOTES

1. H. Eysenck (1952). *The scientific study of personality*. London: Routledge & Kegan Paul (p. 34).

2. J.M. Digman (1990). Personality structure: Emergence of the five-factor model. *Annual Review of Psychology, 41*, 417–440.

3. B.E. Compas (1993). Promoting positive mental health during adolescence. In S.G. Millstein, A.C. Petersen, & E.O. Nightingale (Eds.), *Promoting the health of adolescents: New directions for the twenty-first century*. New York: Oxford University Press. In keeping with his framework, Compas defines positive mental health during adolescence as "a process characterized by development toward optimal current and future functioning in the capacity and motivation to cope with stress and to involve the self in personally meaningful instrumental activities and/or interpersonal relationships. Optimal functioning is relative and depends on the goals and values of the interested parties, appropriate developmental norms, and one's sociocultural group" (pp. 165–167).

4

The Difficulty of Categorizing Environmental Variables

Environments [like people] can be ... portrayed with a great deal of accuracy and detail. Some people are supportive; likewise some environments are supportive. Some [people] feel the need to control others; similarly, some environments are extremely controlling. Order and structure are important to many people; correspondingly, many environments emphasize regularity, system, and order.

Insel & Moos[1]

As difficult as it is to classify persons, an individual is at least contained within reasonably well-delineated boundaries. The same is not true of the environment. Everything that is not person is environment (or the product of person-environment transactions).

Work on multifaceted, comprehensive environmental classification is in its infancy, and this profoundly limits the way the environment is discussed in the intervention literature. This is ironic given that the essence of what an intervener does mostly involves arranging subsets of environmental variables.

EFFORTS TO CLASSIFY ENVIRONMENTS

The literature describing environmental influences on human

functioning has a distinguished history. As early as the 1920s, Jacob Kantor was differentiating between the physical and psychological environment. In the 1930s, Kurt Lewin, Edward Tolman, and Henry Murray all stressed that behavior was a function of both person and environment and set out to characterize the environment. Complex pictures of the environment emerged in terms of a psychological topography, physical variables, and objective and perceived "presses."[2]

Ongoing efforts to address the problem of classifying environments are found in a variety of literatures. Of particular relevance to intervention are approaches to environmental classification found in the work of (1) researchers studying ecological and environmental influences on human functioning, (2) systems theorists and organizational researchers, and (3) those concerned with social and community interventions. The following examples will suffice to illustrate the nature of such work and underscore its relevance for intervention theory, research, and practice.

Ecological and Environmental Psychology

In building what he called eco-behavioral science, Roger Barker described the environment generally as a behavior setting. As embellished by Wicker, this term refers to small-scale social systems (people and physical objects) with naturally occurring, specifiable temporal and spatial features configured to carry out routinized activities. Examples of behavior settings include a grocery store, a regular classroom, a basketball game, a therapy session, and so forth.[3]

Having identified a behavior setting, the question arises about what phenomena to classify within the setting. Moos and his colleagues suggest five ways to conceptualize such environmental factors: (1) physical factors in the natural and built environment (e.g., architecture and design of space), (2) group characteristics (e.g., the personal characteristics of the group), (3) organizational structural variables (e.g., size, distribution of power, turnover rate), (4) reinforcement consequences, and (5) organizational or social climate (e.g., perceptions and beliefs of those in the setting). Subgroupings within each can be made. For instance, with specific regard to organizational or social climate, three basic dimensions are delineated: (1) relationships (e.g., the extent to which individuals are involved in the environment and help support each other), (2) personal growth (e.g., the availability of opportunities for self-enhancement and development of self-esteem), and (3) system maintenance and system change (e.g., degree of structure, clarity of expectations, openness to change).[4] An example of how such dimensions are operationalized can be seen in the *Classroom Environment Scale*.[5]

Complementing eco-behavioral science, early work on environmental stimulation and perception categorized "collative" variables, such as novelty, complexity, surprisingness, and incongruity. With the growth of the field of environmental psychology, there has been a major research focus on environmental cognition, attitudes, and stressors. Particular attention is paid to territoriality, personal space, crowding, privacy, and social networks. In moving toward a synthesis, Saegert and Winkel provide an analysis indicating that three models shape how the environment is defined (and thus categorized) in environmental psychology.[6] One model views the environment in terms of physical qualities, interpersonal interactions, and information—all of which are seen as stressors necessitating adaptation. A second model approaches the environment as consisting of sociophysical constraints and opportunities allowing for goal-directed action. Using this approach, the environment is defined in terms of temporal and spatial structures of land uses, services, and facilities from which the best options can be selected. The third model emphasizes socially and culturally defined settings and systems; from this perspective, sociocultural factors are viewed as influencing how the environment is perceived and categorized. The limitations of each model underscore the need for synthesis.

Systems Theory and Organizational Research

Checkland, a systems theorist, argues that the "absolute minimum number of systems classes needed to describe the whole of reality is four: natural, designed physical, designed abstract, and human activity systems."[7] Environments fit into each class. Viewed as a system, environments are differentiated in terms of levels, for example, in descending order, a country, region, state, city, neighborhood, and school or workplace. Each system level consists of sets of interacting (related) units with boundaries that shape the nature and scope of relationships.

James Miller's theorizing represents the most detailed effort to distinguish system characteristics. He treats all systems as living (including organizations and nations) and views all systems and subsystems as interrelated. He describes three broad environmental subsystems: those that deal with matter or energy, those that deal with information, and those that deal with both. He then proceeds to differentiate nineteen subsystems with respect to their functions.[8] In applying Miller's theoretical work to intervention activity, Sundberg, Taplin, and Tyler differentiate subsystems in the person and environment using identical characteristics. That is, for both person and environment, they categorize key subsystem features in terms of mechanisms related to (1) decision making (about purposes, priorities, problem solving); (2) boundaries; (3) perceptual and feedback functions; (4) input, central processes, and output; (5) memory (e.g., institutional); (6) formal and informal structures; and (7) linkages to other subsystems and systems. Interveners assess each feature to determine the need for addressing structural and functional problems, enhancing system efficacy, or both. And given the interrelationship of subsystems and systems, all features are continuously monitored—especially when an intervention is implemented.[9]

The influence of systems theory is seen in organizational research, as is the tradition of human factors psychology. Not surprisingly, much of this literature focuses on workplaces. Porras and Silvers, for example, categorize the workplace first into two major sets of organizational variables: organizational vision and the work setting. In turn, organizational vision is divided into (1) the guiding beliefs and principles of the organization, (2) its enduring purpose (stemming from those beliefs), and (3) its catalyzing mission (the specifying of organizational purpose to direct and move the organization toward desired ends). Work settings are divided into four clusters of variables shaped by the organization's vision: one, organizing arrangements (e.g., goals; strategies; formal structure; administrative policies, procedures, and systems; formal reward systems; ownership), two, social factors (e.g., culture, such as values, norms, language, rituals; interaction processes; social patterns and networks; individual attributes; management style), three, technology (e.g., equipment; technical expertise; technical systems), and four, physical setting (e.g., space configuration; physical ambience; interior design; architectural design).[10]

Also focusing on the workplace, Katz and Kahn categorize five functional subsystems: (1) production (the subsystem that carries on the organization's fundamental work), (2) support (the subsystem providing the operational material), (3) maintenance (the subsystem that coordinates and motivates action), (4) adaptation (the subsystem that anticipates changes and appropriately alters subsystem processes), and (5) management (the subsystem that coordinates the whole). Clearly, workplace categorizations have relevance for identifying environmental variables of concern to interventionists.[11]

Community Research

Environmental categories of interest to interveners also are generated by the study of social and community interventions. Drawing from environmental psychology, workers in this area are concerned with environmental quality and stressors and with such specific constructs as privacy, territoriality, and crowding—all of which may be objectively or subjectively defined. In categorizing communities, they stress types and levels. Their intent is to facilitate understanding of the relationship between environmental variables and psychosocial problems.

Hunter and Riger, for example, view the community as a *place* and classify each in terms of (1) resident demographics or social characteristics (e.g., social class, ethnicity), (2) land use and quality of housing (e.g., low-density single-family homes, high-density apartments), and (3) institutional and organizational composition (e.g., presence or absence of schools, recreation facilities, churches, civic groups).[12]

Communities also are categorized in terms of *relationships and resources*. For instance, neighborhoods are grouped by the degree to which they provide psychosocial and human service supports. Emphasizing *social organization*, Warren and Warren focus on three dimensions: interaction, identity, and connections. Using these, they differentiate six types of neighborhoods—each with different implications for interveners: (1) integral (high on all three dimensions), (2) parochial (high interaction and identity, low connections), (3) diffuse (low interaction and connections, high identity), (4) stepping-stone (high interaction and connections, low identity), (5) transitory (low interaction and identity, high connections), and (6) anomic (low on all three dimensions).[13]

PERSON-ENVIRONMENT MATCH

After presenting a framework for classifying the physical environment, Wachs offers the following caution:

> It is possible to classify objective dimensions of the . . . environment, . . . but it will be difficult to understand the functional significance for development of stimuli in different dimensions without an understanding of how [the actor's] characteristics interface with both physical and social stimuli. . . .
>
> At some point it will be necessary to bring both individual and environment together to achieve a complete understanding of the role the environment plays in the developmental process--which does not mean that it is not necessary to have an adequate classification system for the environment. What is essential, first, is to develop independently both environmental classification systems and individual difference taxonomies.[14]

Emerging from the complementary literatures on organism-environment interaction and on the reciprocal transaction between the person and the environment is an expanded understanding of the environment and the person, and their relationship to each other.[15] The work shows special promise for generating new environmental classifications that can advance intervention theory, research, and practice.

The work of Holland provides an example of how environmental - classification is affected by looking at the influence of the relationship (e.g., the match) between person and environment. Holland starts with a six-category classification of personality: (1) the realistic type, (2) the investigative type, (3) the artistic type, (4) the social type, (5) the enterprising type, and (6) the conventional type.

He makes the assumptions that for each personality type there is a parallel model environment and that people tend to move toward environments congruent with their personality type. Thus, he categorizes environments as Realistic, Investigative, Artistic, Social, Enterprising, and Conventional. Of relevance to intervention, Holland assumes that when the person successfully moves toward a congruent match, the result will be reinforcing and satisfying and associated with personal and vocational stability and productivity. A mismatch (i.e., a state of incongruence) is seen as unsatisfying and a stimulus for change.[16]

Putting discussion of the merits of Holland's formulation aside, one can appreciate the potential value to intervention theory, research, and practice of classifications of persons and environments that are conceived with respect to their relationship to each other. A transactional view of the person and the environment encourages holistic classifications of individuals and the patterns of environmental stimulation they encounter. It also encourages categorization of transactional patterns that characterize effective and ineffective intervention processes.

Another effort to deal with interactional and transactional classification schemes is seen in relation to the conceptual-level matching model (CLMM) classification scheme, which focuses on interactions between a person variable (i.e., conceptual level) and differing types of environments described in terms of structure. One application of this work is seen in studies of criminal offender treatment/rehabilitation programs.[17]

Work on individual-organization fit also illustrates the potential of schemes that bring individual and environment together. For example, Chatman has used a categorization of identical value dimensions to describe organizations and new employees as a basis for refining understanding of which newcomers stay and which leave.[18]

SOME BASICS IN ENVIRONMENTAL CLASSIFICATION

Based on analysis of available conceptualizations, some basic dimensions and steps for environmental classification emerge. Each dimension is conceived at different levels of abstraction and can be classified through the filter of an objective observer or as experienced (perceived) by the person whose functioning is the focus of interest.

A reasonable first step in classifying environments involves identifying specific types of behavior settings, such as home, neighborhood, classroom, school, workspace, and recreation area, and clustering them with reference to the broader context in which they are embedded (e.g., culture, political system, economic status). For some intervention purposes, behavior settings also might be categorized with respect to their stage of development.

To help clarify the structure and functions of each setting, environments can be hierarchically organized (e.g., macro-micro) with subdivisions at each level. Furthermore, the stimuli affecting behavior in the setting can be grouped broadly as biochemical, physical, and social and also differentiated as proximal or distal and as static or dynamic.

Table 4.1 presents our attempt to categorize groups of environmental variables as a guide for analyzing intervention and planning ways to influence client functioning during intervention. In doing so, we recognize that such variables are likely to be perceived differently by the various parties involved in an intervention. These differences can profoundly influence the course of intervention and should be identified.

NOTES

1. P.M. Insel & R.H. Moos (1974). Psychological environments: Expanding the scope of human ecology. *American Psychologist, 29*, 179–188, p. 179.

2. As an example, see K. Lewin (1935). *A dynamic theory of personality: Selected papers*. New York: McGraw-Hill.

3. A.W. Wicker (1992). Making sense of environments. In W.B. Walsh, K.C. Craik, & R.H. Price (Eds.), *Person-environment psychology: Models and perspectives*. Hillsdale, NJ: Erlbaum.

4. R.W. Swindle, Jr., & R.H. Moos (1992). Life domains in stressors, coping, and adjustment. In W.B. Walsh, K.C. Craik, & R.H. Price (Eds.), *Person-environment psychology: Models and perspectives*. Hillsdale, NJ: Erlbaum. Also see R.H. Moos & T.G. David (1981). Evaluating and changing classroom settings. In J.L. Epstein (Ed.), *The quality of school life*.

Table 4.1

Environmental Variables of Particular
Concern to Interveners

I. *Setting and context characteristics*

A. **Organizational format** (e.g., personal patterns, client groupings)

B. **Locale, nature, and scope** (e.g., geographic context, architectural features, availability and use of materials and furnishings, population "density")

C. **Climate** (e.g., perceptions of physical, social, intellectual, political, and moral atmosphere)

II. *Characteristics of the participants*

A. **Format role identification** (e.g., intervener, client, student, parent, societal agent, association with specific organizations)

B. **Demographics** (e.g., urban/rural, ethnicity, socioeconomic status, gender and age distribution, association with specific groups)

C. **Individual differences in current motivation and development** (e.g., competence, commitment, perceptions of self and others)

D. **Criteria and standards used in judging person characteristics** (e.g., absolute or relative standards about good-bad, normal-abnormal, success-failure; psychological, socioeconomic-political criteria)

III. *Task-process-outcome characteristics*

A. **General features**
   1. Quantitative (e.g., amount to be accomplished; sequencing, duration, pacing, and rate; number of persons required or involved)
   2. Qualitative (e.g., underlying rationale; intrinsic and extrinsic value; cooperative or competitive; actual and perceived difficulty)

B. **Specific types, areas, and levels of tasks and outcomes** (e.g., focus on contemporary tasks; focus on prerequisites needed to perform contemporary tasks; remediation; treatment; enrichment)

C. **Specific processes**
   1. Procedural methods and models (e.g., helping or socialization; mechanistic-behavioral, industrial, humanistic; role of participants; nature of structure)
   2. Tools (actions/experiences/materials) (e.g., communication, practice, learning; printed materials; computer and audiovisual presentations; game-like activities)
   3. Techniques (e.g., variations in the characteristics of a tool or the way it is applied, such as varying intensity, duration, patterning, cueing; systematic or unsystematic feedback, rewards, punishments)

Lexington, MA: Lexington Books.

5. R.H. Moos & E. Trickett (1974). *Classroom Environment Scale manual.* Palo Alto, CA: Consulting Psychologists Press.

6. S. Saegert & G.H. Winkel (1990). Environmental psychology. *Annual Review of Psychology, 41*, 441–477.

7. P. Checkland (1981). *Systems thinking, systems practice.* Chichester: Wiley. Checkland concludes: "The case of what in everyday language are called 'social systems' shows that real-world entities may well not fit easily into one class. . . . Nevertheless, the gradual development of tested conceptual models of the four classes of system, with the logical, structural, and regulatory entailments worked out, should make simpler the interpretation and holistic analysis of complex activity" (p. 122). Also note the congruity between the four systems' classes and the four basic types formulated by J.P. Guilford and by Datta & Farradane. See S. Datta & J.E.L. Farradane (1974). A psychological basis for general classification. In J. Wojciechowski (Ed.), *Conceptual basis of the classification of knowledge: Proceedings of the Ottawa Conference.* Pullach/Munchen: Werlag Dokumentation.

It should be pointed out that Checkland builds on the seminal work on general system theory done in the 1950s by Bertalanffy and Boulding and the work of Jordan in the 1960s. For more on this early work, see the following: L. von Bertalanffy (1968). *General systems theory.* New York: Braziller. K.E. Boulding (1956). General systems theory—The skeleton of science. *Management Science, 2.* N. Jordan (1968). *Themes in speculative psychology.* London: Tavistock. E. Laszlo (Ed.) (1972). *The relevance of general systems theory: Papers presented to Ludwig von Bertalanffy on his seventieth birthday.* New York: Braziller.

8. J. Miller (1978). *Living systems.* New York: McGraw-Hill.

9. N.D. Sundberg, J.R. Taplin, & L.E. Tyler (1983). *Introduction to clinical psychology: Perspectives, issues, and contributions to human service.* Englewood Cliffs, NJ: Prentice-Hall.

10. J.I. Porras & R.C. Silvers (1991). Organizational development and transformation. *Annual Review of Psychology, 42*, 51–78.

11. D. Katz & R.L. Kahn (1966). *The social psychology of organizations.* New York: Wiley. Also see P. Rich (1992). The organizational taxonomy: Definition and design. *Academy of Management Review, 17*, 758–781, and J.S. Schippman, E.P. Prien, & G.L. Hughes (1991). The content of management work: Formation of task and job skill composite classifications. *Journal of Business and Psychology, 5*, 325–354.

12. A. Hunter & S. Riger (1986). The meaning of community in community mental health. *Journal of Community Psychology, 14*, 55–71.

13. R.B. Warren & D.I. Warren (1977). *The neighborhood organizer's*

handbook. Notre Dame, IN: University of Notre Dame Press.

14. T.D. Wachs (1989). The nature of the physical microenvironment: An expanded classification system. *Merrill-Palmer Quarterly, 35*, 399–419 (p. 417).

15. For a recent overview of the work in this area, see the following: T.D. Wachs & R. Plomin (Eds.) (1991). *Conceptualization and measurement of organism-environment interaction*. Washington, DC: American Psychological Association. W.B. Walsh, K.C. Craik, & R.H. Price (Eds.) (1992). *Person-environment psychology: Models and perspectives*. Hillsdale, NJ: Erlbaum.

16. W.B. Walsh & J.L. Holland (1992). A theory of personality types and work environments. In W.B. Walsh, K.C. Craik, & R.H. Price (Eds.), *Person-environment psychology: Models and perspectives*. Hillsdale, NJ: Erlbaum.

17. M. Reitsma-Street & A.W. Leschied (1988). The conceptual-level matching model in corrections. *Criminal Justice and Behavior, 15*, 92–108.

18. J.A. Chatman (1991). Matching people and organizations: Selection and socialization in public accounting firms. *Administration Science Quarterly, 36*, 459–484.

5

Minimizing Negative Effects

> We should turn self-fulfilling prophecies into suicidal prophecies.
> As implied by Merton[1]

As the preceding discussion underscores, the negatives related to classification activity go beyond the impact of labelling. Decisions about what phenomena to categorize have potential negative consequences both for what is labelled and for what isn't. Moreover, in fields such as psychology and special education, the deficiencies of current labelling practices limit progress and often generate public censure, both of which affect a field's reputation and support. Thus, the classification problem encompasses concerns about how to minimize negative consequences.

Fundamentally, consequences can be minimized by improving existing classification schemes and methodology, and by anticipating and addressing negative effects arising from labelling practices. The following brief comments will suffice to clarify the points.

IMPROVING CLASSIFICATION SCHEMES AND METHODOLOGY

Many of the difficulties involved in devising classification schemes are not amenable to easy solution. They are rooted in complex problems of an epistemological, philosophical, theoretical, and methodological nature. Despite this, some emerging directions have promise for improving classification schemes of relevance to intervention. One is the continued refinement of the multiaxial approach to diagnosing pathology, paired with efforts to place pathology in perspective using a reciprocal determinist view of behavior. In turn, this should lead to improved schemes for multidimensional classifications of psychosocial, environmental/organizational, and transactional problems. Another promising direction focuses on ways to move beyond the emphasis on deviance, weaknesses, and limitations to classify nonproblem functioning and strengths.

Methodologically, the path to improvement remains one of enhancing reliability and demonstrating the differential validity of each category in a scheme. This involves not only development of precise criteria and readily applied operations but also effective training procedures for those who do the labelling (including error reduction strategies).[2]

In terms of general guidelines, we can adapt those suggested by Jablensky. He states that a good classification is designed for a clearly stated purpose and that it (1) divides the universe of observations into heuristically useful units leading to action (e.g., research, intervention), (2) generates new observations and questions, (3) is reliable, (4) satisfies the cognitive needs of users (i.e., is in "accord with their 'world maps'," avoids jargon, and is easy to learn and internalize), (5) is adaptable and meaningful in a large number of cultural settings, and (6) can be related to previous and other current classification systems.[3]

GUIDELINES FOR MINIMIZING NEGATIVE CONSEQUENCES

Minimizing potential negative effects of labelling requires delineating procedures and criteria for assessing the benefits and negative consequences of current approaches and weighing costs versus benefits. In practice, of course, no agreement exists about processes for determining cost versus benefits. There is consensus, however, that intervention ethics requires that steps be taken to minimize negative effects. The following guidelines illustrate the minimal requirements that should be expected of those involved in labelling others.

Persons responsible for assigning labels must acquire a fundamental awareness of potential immediate and long-term negative impact on individuals, groups, and society. Based on this awareness, proactive steps must be taken to:

1. provide those potentially affected with information about possible negative consequences (e.g., indicate risks during the consent process);

2. maximize the valid application of assessment practices and decision processes used in arriving at a label (e.g., actively seek both confirmatory and disconfirmatory data in arriving at a differential diagnosis);

3. prevent inappropriate communication and use of labels (e.g., protect privacy through confidentiality procedures, clarify limitations of a label with respect to its valid applications);

4. take specific actions to counter reactive effects (e.g., prepare those potentially affected to use protective strategies, encourage others not to react in harmful ways).

As steps are taken to minimize negative consequences, a shift should occur in the cost-benefit equation related to a particular label and classification scheme. How to gather and weight the data used in such an equation, however, remains a problem.

NOTES

1. Although identifying and labelling problems can lead to what Merton described as self-fulfilling prophecies, interveners can take steps to turn this potential negative consequence into the opposite phenomenon—what Merton called the suicidal prophecy. That is, interveners can reach out to encourage others to understand and react to the labelled client in ways designed to correct rather than exacerbate the problem. R.K. Merton (1948). The self-fulfilling prophecy. *Antioch Review, 8*, 193–210.

2. Error detection studies are essential to the development of error reduction strategies. For example, see H.S. Adelman, B.A. Lauber, P. Nelson, & D.C. Smith (1989). Minimizing and detecting false positive diagnoses of learning disabilities. *Journal of Learning Disabilities, 22*, 234–244 and D.A. McKenzie (1991). A proposed prototype for identifying and correcting sources of measurement error in classification systems. *Medical Care, 29*, 521–530.

3. A. Jablensky (1988). Methodological issues in psychiatric classification. *British Journal of Psychiatry, 152* (suppl. 1), 15–20 (p. 20).

A Few Concluding Comments about the Classification Problem

Discussion of the classification problem as it applies to intervention raises theoretical, practical, legal, and ethical matters of profound concern to researchers, practitioners, and policy makers. Classification tends to determine the nature and scope of what is studied and what interveners do. Even more fundamentally, disciplines and applied fields profoundly shape their very essence as they adopt classification schemes. For example, in psychology, psychiatry, and education, the schemes adopted have far-reaching effects. They determine the ways individuals are described, studied, and served; they shape prevailing practices related to intervention, professional training, and certification; and they influence decisions about funding. It is not surprising, therefore, that debates about classification schemes, specific diagnostic procedures, and the very act of labelling are so heated.

As occurs with all abstract constructs, operationalizing categories is difficult and fraught with complex problems and issues. Consequently, any particular scheme is an easy target for criticism and controversy. Such critiques cut two ways. They can hurt a field's image by laying out its deficiencies. At the same time, the criticism can be a stimulus for improving the unsatisfactory status quo.

A particular danger with respect to contemporary approaches to classification of problems in psychology and special education is that the widespread criticism may be misinterpreted. That is, the general public may see the criticism as evidence that current efforts are invalid or that it is not worth investing in finding better ways to classify. The hope of responsible critics is that their primary influence will be to counter the tendency of many to ignore the classification problem in psychology and education.

At a time when so many disciplines have the potential to make outstanding advances related to psychological and educational interventions, there is no more fundamental problem than that of refining existing classification systems and developing new ones. As the discussion in Part I indicates, efforts to improve classification of persons, environments, and their transactions are essential to advancing knowledge related to all intervention.[1] And, as will become evident in the next sections, the clearer the image of phenomena that are of interest, the sharper the focus of discussion related to other fundamental intervention problems.

NOTE

1. Growing interest in the principles and practices of classification in various disciplines led to founding of the Classification Society in 1964. Several branches emerged, going their separate ways but relating to each other through the International Federation of Classification Societies. Most of the societies have a strong bent toward mathematical methodology (although the British Classification Society notes that this is true for a smaller proportion of its membership). One major classification periodical is the *Journal of Classification*, published by the Classification Society of North America.

PART II

THE UNDERLYING RATIONALE PROBLEM

I never would have seen it if I hadn't believed it.

Foster, Ysseldyke, & Reese[1]

Professionals associated with psychological and educational interventions have produced an immense body of work that reflects fine accomplishments and a clear recognition that there is much more to do. Perhaps the weakest facet of the literature is the dearth of specific discussion dealing with underlying rationales for intervention. As noted in the introduction, interveners differ in the degree to which their activity is guided by a coherent philosophy, well-developed theory, and sound empirical findings and experiences. Moreover, underlying rationales often are not explicitly stated or are stated in ways that ignore or mask fundamental philosophical, theoretical, empirical, and legal concepts and concerns.

Optimally, rationales encompass models of the determinants of behavior and views about the purpose and focus of intervention; they also include ideas about how best to plan, implement, and evaluate intervention. These ideas are shaped by explicitly or implicitly held positions on such matters as preferred orientation to intervention, ethical considerations, and a wide range of process topics. Prominent among the process topics are the role of assessment and the client's role in decision making, as well as positions about structure, activities, techniques, working relationships, personalizing intervention, addressing transitions, and dealing with negative consequences.

We do not mean to suggest that every intervener should, could, or needs to write out a complete statement of rationale. Obviously, good work can be done and is done in the absence of such statements and, indeed, without total realization on the part of interveners as to why they function as they do. We do, however, believe that the desired avenue to wide-scale improvements in intervention theory and practice must be paved with articulation and analyses of underlying rationales. It is through increased discussion of intervention rationales that researchers and practitioners can achieve expanded awareness of fundamental ideas and beliefs shaping intervention, which in turn will enhance sensitivity about basic concerns and biasing factors.

As a step in this direction, the discussion in Part II sketches a range of fundamental concerns and ideas relevant to formulating underlying rationales. These are explored within the context of six basic topics: (1) defining intervention, (2) deciding about purposes, (3) general analyses of processes, (4) the psychology of clients, (5) ethical considerations, and (6) improving intervention through transforming rationales. Other topics relevant to an underlying rationale are discussed in Parts III and IV. Throughout, an attempt is made to address psychological and educational intervention in a generic way.

NOTE

1. G. Foster, J. Ysseldyke, & J. Reese (1975). I never would have seen it if I hadn't believed it. *Exceptional Children, 41,* 469–473 (p. 469).

6

Defining Intervention

"To take care of them" can and should be read with two meanings.
                                                                    Hobbs[1]

A tendency for professionals to stress benefits in defining intervention is not surprising. Intervention according to Suran and Rizzo
"is a general term that refers to the application of professional skills
to maintain or improve a child's potential for ongoing healthy
development."[2] Methods used to intervene are described by Kanfer
and Goldstein as "designed to help people change for the better."[3]

With reference to children's problems, Rhodes and Tracy provide
a more neutral definition. They describe intervention as "any
directed action upon the deviance predicament between child and
community."[4] Even more neutral is Schorr's definition of intervention as "any systematic attempt to alter the course of development
from either its established or predicted path."[5]

On a less positive note, critics accentuate the fact that intervention is an interference into the affairs of another.[6]

Extracting from various definitions, intentional intervention is
viewed as encompassing planned actions designed to produce
intended outcomes related to existing (usually problematic)
conditions. To leave it at that, however, ignores several basic
matters and risks misinterpretations.

A definition of intervention should be broad enough to account
for the full nature and scope of intervention means and ends.
Minimally, it should account for

* *all processes and transactions—including the fact that unplanned processes
  occur*

- *all outcomes—including those that are not beneficial*
  (Interventions maintain, develop, improve, or transform. Besides positive outcomes, every intervention has the potential to produce negative side effects or costs. And, whether positive or negative, unintended outcomes are inevitable.)
- *conditions that are problematic and those that are nonproblematic*
  (Intervention may focus on unhealthy/negative functioning or healthy/positive functioning.)
- *a variety of systems—persons, environments, or both.*

(To avoid an overemphasis on persons, environments, or transactions, the term *system* is used frequently in what follows. As used in systems theory, person, group, organizations, and societies are all conceived as systems. In addition, we use the term *client* to denote any system that is the object of an intentional intervention; the term *intervener* is used for anyone who intervenes, such as a professional, parent, or friend.)

As a broad working definition, then, we propose the following: *Intentional intervention aims at producing intended outcomes through planned processes. The intended outcomes encompass maintenance, change (development, improvement), or transformation with respect to problematic or nonproblematic conditions of systems (person, environment, or both). Besides planned processes, unplanned transactions occur. The combined processes may or may not produce intended outcomes, and may produce unintended outcomes; also some outcomes may be negative* (see Figure 6.1).

By stating that unplanned processes occur, the definition draws attention to this potentially potent source of variations in intervention outcomes. In stressing that unintended outcomes occur, the definition helps minimize the chance that unintended negative outcomes and positive side effects are ignored. Inclusion of the phrase "nonproblematic conditions" helps avoid interpreting the term with a pathological bias. And specifying a focus on environments highlights the fact that the term applies to activity involving behavior settings, organizations, and societal institutions. (With respect to processes, we should also note that activities such as assessment, diagnosis, and referral often are contrasted to "intervention." This distinction inappropriately limits use of the term and is unnecessary since the activity fits most definitions of intervention.) All intervention is potentially life-shaping. The term's definition

Figure 6.1
Essential Features of a Definition of Intentional Intervention and Potential Combinations of Means and Ends

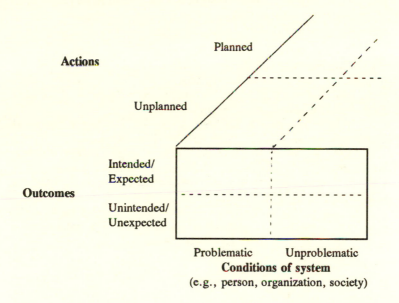

Actions

Planned

Unplanned

Outcomes

Intended/
Expected

Unintended/
Unexpected

Problematic   Unproblematic
Conditions of system
(e.g., person, organization, society)

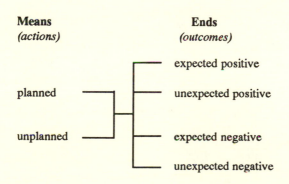

Means
(actions)

Ends
(outcomes)

planned

unplanned

expected positive

unexpected positive

expected negative

unexpected negative

plays a key role in intervention planning, implementation, and evaluation and how the phenomenon is studied and understood. Thus, one's formulation or choice of definition is not a trivial matter. The following discussion approaches each topic from the perspective of the broad working definition outlined above.

NOTES

1. N. Hobbs (1975). *The future of children: Categories, labels, and their consequences*. San Francisco: Jossey-Bass.

2. B.G. Suran & J.V. Rizzo (1979). *Special children: An integrative approach*. Glenview, IL: Scott, Foresman.

3. F.H. Kanfer & A.P. Goldstein (1991). *Helping people change: A textbook of methods* (4th ed.). New York: Pergamon Press.

4. W.C. Rhodes & M.C. Tracy (1972). *A study of child variance: Intervention*. (Vol. 2). Ann Arbor: University of Michigan Press.

5. L. B. Schorr with D. Schorr (1988). *Within our reach: Breaking the cycle of disadvantage*. New York: Doubleday.

6. I. Illich (1976). *Medical nemesis*. New York: Pantheon Books. T.S. Szasz (1969). Psychiatric classification as a strategy of personal constraint. In T.S. Szasz (Ed.), *Ideology and insanity*. New York: Doubleday.

7

Purposes

If you don't care where you're going, it doesn't matter which way you go.

Anonymous

Or, in the words of Yogi Berra: You have to be very careful when you don't know where you are going or you might never get there.[1]

Intervention is undertaken to accomplish desired ends. Formulation of the intended purposes of the intervention, therefore, is a primary element of an underlying rationale. A statement of purpose is primary because it is the essential referent for planning how to get from here to there. Purposes may be assigned or adopted.

Several concerns must be addressed in stating intended outcomes. There is the matter of bias in decisions about the focal point for intervention. There are problems of translating long-range, abstract aims into immediate objectives and of accounting for unintended outcomes. Fundamental to addressing these concerns is an understanding of potential conflicts between societal and individual aims and the problem of who decides which perspective prevails when there is conflict over intervention purposes. Each of these topics is discussed to illustrate the issues and problems that arise with respect to stating purpose in formulating an underlying intervention rationale.

FOCUS OF INTERVENTION

Given how many definitions of intervention are person-centered, it is not unexpected to find person centered models dominating professional thinking. For instance, most of what is written about psychological and educational intervention stresses strategies for changing individuals. This state of affairs contributes to the limited focus of intervention.

Individuals, environments, or both? Overemphasis on individual intervention raises many concerns. For example, focusing only on individuals when addressing problems colludes with limited assumptions about what may need to change. We are not suggesting a lack of awareness about problems of individuals that may arise, for instance, because the environment (home, school, society) applies inappropriate standards or restricts choice. We are saying that, despite this awareness, a tendency exists to focus planning on outcomes related to individuals. Ironically, many interventions that address the environment mainly stress manipulating reinforcers to control and reshape the behavior of specific individuals.

When individuals manifest problems, interventions designed with person outcomes as the primary focus may be the most appropriate choice. Sometimes, however, a primary focus on changing the environment is more appropriate (e.g., when the environment is changed to accommodate individuals or groups). Such environmental modification should not be confused with altering the environment as an indirect way of producing person outcomes.

Because the distinction is so important, it is worth underscoring the difference between manipulating the environment to change persons and changing the environment per se. Instructing interveners to be more discriminating in their use of reinforcement contingencies is meant as an indirect way of modifying the behavior of the reinforced individuals. Such an approach is in marked contrast to helping interveners make appropriate changes in their own and others' socializing practices through transformed understanding and expectations about what constitutes acceptable behavior, performance, and rates of progress. For example, teaching a mother behavior control strategies is not the same thing as helping her see implications of offering additional options to her children whenever appropriate and feasible. This latter option includes extending the range of choice in what the children are allowed to do and how they are allowed to do it.[2]

The point is: When the cause of a problem is in the environment, the most appropriate intervention, if feasible, involves changing the environment. This includes altering situations hostile to individual well-being so that they accommodate either a specific individual or a wider range of individual differences. Such changes can be preventive in the full sense of the term. And, as discussed subsequently, they also are in harmony with the principle of using the least intervention needed—at least as viewed from the perspective of an individual who is no longer the focus of intervention.

To reemphasize, the point is that the primary focus of intervention may be on the person, the environment, or both. In each case, different areas and levels may be addressed separately or in combination.

As represented in Figure 7.1, the focus on the individual may be direct or indirect and aimed at maintaining, changing, or transforming one or more functional domains (i.e., biological, psychosocial/cognitive). Environmental interventions are designed to accommodate an individual or group or to maintain, change, or transform one or more environmental systems and subsystems. When the focus is on both the person and the environment, any combination of the above may be involved. Furthermore, in addressing any system, interveners may aim at a macro (observable behavior) or micro (underlying structures and functions) level. For example, with respect to the environment's transacting layers, the focus may be on first level systems such as home, worksite, and classroom, second level systems such as neighborhood, work organization, and school, or third level systems such as city, state, society, and culture.[3] At each level, subsystems of interest include mechanisms for governance, planning, and administration and implementation.

From a holistic perspective, of course, the focus is on the totality. Such a perspective fosters appreciation of relationships among system parts and systems. Understanding of these relationships is central to designing interventions to maintain or change how subsystems communicate, coordinate, and integrate with each other.

Maintenance, Change, or Transformation?

To illustrate how divergent intervention purposes can be, it is useful to contrast them with respect to whether the primary aim is

Figure 7.1
Focus of Intervention

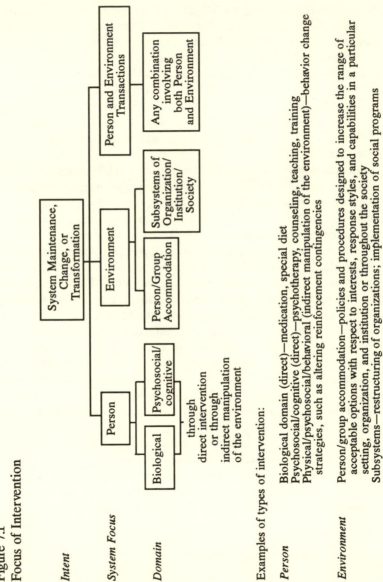

Intent

System Focus

Domain

Examples of types of intervention:

Person   Biological domain (direct)—medication, special diet
            Psychosocial/cognitive (direct)—psychotherapy, counseling, teaching, training
            Physical/psychosocial/behavioral (indirect manipulation of the environment)—behavior change
            strategies, such as altering reinforcement contingencies

Environment Person/group accommodation—policies and procedures designed to increase the range of
               acceptable options with respect to interests, response styles, and capabilities in a particular
               setting, organization, and institution or throughout the society
               Subsystems—restructuring of organizations; implementation of social programs

to maintain, develop, improve, or transform systems. Supportive psychotherapy and many school and other organizational programs are examples of instances when the purpose of an intervention is to maintain homeostasis (e.g., prevent problems from becoming worse or institutionalize the status quo).

Efforts to develop and improve systems are well illustrated by trends aimed at reforming current psychological and educational practices. They ask questions such as "What is wrong with the system and how can we improve it to make it more effective and efficient?"

In contrast, transformational thinking asks such questions as "What is the current nature of the age in which we live, and what implications does this have for redesigning the content, processes, and outcomes associated with psychological and educational interventions?" In research, such thinking is reflected in what is called the transformational experiment.

An example of improving/correcting versus transforming systems is offered by Banathy in discussing educational reform. Influenced by Alvin Toffler, Banathy sees such efforts as coming in three waves. The first was school improvement—with its focus on doing more of the same but doing it more effectively and efficiently. The second, seen as still in motion, involves school restructuring—reorganizing the system's components and realigning distribution of responsibilities. The focus of both the first and second waves has been on making adjustments in the existing system. The third wave that seems to be emerging advocates a fundamental transformation of the system—starting with new operating assumptions and rebuilding from the ground up.[4]

Socialization, Helping, or Both?

Divergence of purposes is further illustrated by contrasting interventions whose primary aim is to prepare clientele to function appropriately in a given society with those aimed at helping specific clients pursue their own best interests. This contrast arises because those who make decisions about intervention aims (e.g., client, intervener, society) frequently have different interests. In psychology and education, for instance, practitioners may intervene based on professional, societal, personal, or client perspectives of what should be accomplished. Even when client perspectives are used, the question can arise: Who is the client? Is it the entity underwriting the intervention (e.g., taxpayers through their legislative bodies, family members, insurance companies), or is it the system that is the focus of intervention (e.g., a student, a patient, an organization)?

The perspectives of interested parties, of course, may be compatible. But conflicts of interest are common. One way to understand such conflicts is to draw on social philosophical and political-economic ideas to differentiate between *helping* and *socializing* interventions.

Responsibility for socialization includes intervening to ensure that clients manifest the knowledge, skills, attitudes, and actions required of contributing members of society. Responsibility for helping encompasses intervening to maximize the best interests of a client even when the society's current agenda devalues or gives precedence to other interests.

When the best interests of a client conflict with society's, those of the client often are suppressed. Whether this occurs depends on who makes the decisions. For instance, one of the reasons society establishes schools is to socialize the young. Teachers are hired to carry out this agenda. Such an agenda may or may not be in the best interests of a given student. To ensure that the "right" decisions are made (i.e., those in society's best interests), school personnel control decision-making processes. In this way, the school's socialization agenda is asserted. By understanding that schools are socialization agencies, it becomes clear why schooling is compulsory, why grades are used to control more than to inform, and why school decision-making processes are so one-sided.[5]

The example of Jesse is illustrative of how a school's socialization agenda can conflict with helping an individual:

> Jesse was constantly fighting. The behavior had been diagnosed as stemming from frustration and anger related to a history of school failure and lack of caring and guidance at home. At school, his teacher, Ms. Johnston, understood all this and set out to get close to Jesse and involve him in ways designed to minimize frustration and maximize success.
>
> Unfortunately, Jesse's altercations with others did not abate quickly.

Several concerned parents complained to the principal. Ms. Johnston was told she had to stop Jesse from hitting others. "If he learns nothing else, he has to understand that such behavior is unacceptable," she was informed, "And the way to do it is to stop coddling him and to crack down."

Ms. Johnston did as she was told. Jesse's behavior got worse. He started cutting school. The more she "cracked down," the more he acted out. It was frustrating and disappointing for both of them.

At a meeting with Jesse's parents, the guidance team thought the youngster should be tested for possible placement in a special education program. The parents acquiesced.

When a student has a problem, teachers often are caught in a dilemma. They want to help the student overcome the problem. But because schools are socializing agencies, teachers are expected to institute a helping agenda only when it does not conflict with socialization aims. The result often is that the student receives no help, and indeed, the student's problem may be exacerbated because of increased avoidance motivation and related negative reactions. In addition, the teacher may experience extreme frustration contributing to burnout.

As outlined in Figure 7.2, the defining characteristics of helping as contrasted with socialization interventions involve consideration of (1) whose best interests are served, (2) how consent is determined, and (3) how ongoing general decisions about goals and processes are made. A helping intervention requires putting the client's interests first. It may involve setting temporary goals and trying procedures that deviate from society's socialization agenda in order to maximize pursuit of the client's interests.

Capabilities, Attitudes, or Both?

Motivation as a process concern is widely discussed because of the role it plays in intervention success or failure. Yet a significant number of underlying rationales appear not to address motivation systematically. Moreover, relatively little attention is paid to attitudes and interests as outcomes. Instead, the primary focus of underlying rationales, as reflected in discussions of intervention outcomes and processes, is biased toward maintaining, changing, or

Figure 7.2
Helping and Socialization Interventions

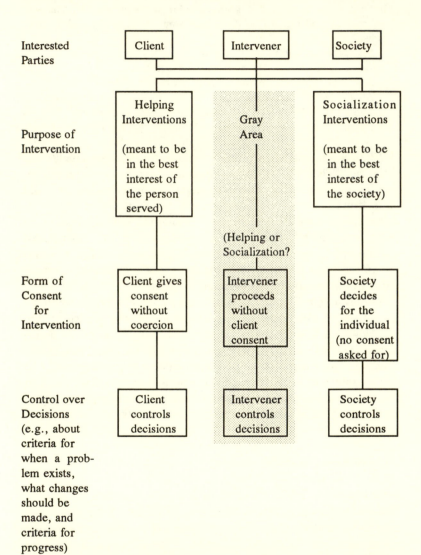

Interested Parties	Client	Intervener	Society

Purpose of Intervention	Helping Interventions (meant to be in the best interest of the person served)	Gray Area (Helping or Socialization?)	Socialization Interventions (meant to be in the best interest of the society)
Form of Consent for Intervention	Client gives consent without coercion	Intervener proceeds without client consent	Society decides for the individual (no consent asked for)
Control over Decisions (e.g., about criteria for when a problem exists, what changes should be made, and criteria for progress)	Client controls decisions	Intervener controls decisions	Society controls decisions

Source: H.S. Adelman and L. Taylor (1988). Clinical child psychology: Fundamental intervention questions and problems. *Clinical Psychology Review, 8*, 637–665. Reprinted with permission.

transforming specific capabilities.

Capabilities certainly are a central concern of any intervention. But so are attitudes and interests. Attitudes and interests are a primary consideration in systematically addressing intervention readiness and maintaining involvement. Toward understanding motivation with respect to such intervention process concerns, the cognitive-affective literature on motivation has much to say about the role of expectations and values.[6]

With respect to outcomes, implicit in many interventions is the intent to eliminate or reduce negative attitudes and interfering interests and enhance and expand positive interests and attitudes. Such outcomes require explicit articulation if they are to receive the attention and resources they warrant.

The First Question is, Who or What Is the Focus?

The above discussion underscores that one of the first decisions an intervener must make involves answering the question, Who or what should be the focus of intervention?

Of course, answering this question is enmeshed with the question: What are we trying to accomplish? That is, what is our intent with respect to the substance or content focus of the intervention? Debates about this are endless. In education, the debate centers around the nature and scope of the curriculum. Those concerned with psychological problems argue about when the content focus should be limited to correcting specific problem behaviors and when interveners should comprehensively deal with underlying attitudes and capacities (e.g., related to self-determination, competence, and relationships with others). Similarly, decisions about the appropriate focus for organizational interventions range from specific areas of functioning, such as improving communication, to comprehensive restructuring or transformation of the system. Moreover, in each instance, answers to questions about focus and intent clearly also involve debate about specific content, including domains and levels of focus.

Clearly, concerns about the focus of intervention warrant careful consideration by every intervener. And any analysis of underlying rationales should explore how these concerns are addressed.

DISTINGUISHING AIMS, GOALS, AND OBJECTIVES

After deciding on the focus and general intent of intervention, it is time to delineate desired outcomes. In discussing outcomes, one must distinguish between abstract, long-range aims and concrete, immediate objectives. Without such a distinction, the substance of intended purposes can be lost in the day-by-day emphasis on formulating and measuring the attainment of immediate objectives. We distinguish between *aims* (abstract statements of purpose—usually long-range outcomes), *goals* (the less abstract components of a particular aim), and *objectives* (specific and sometimes operationally stated components of a particular goal). In articulating an intervention's rationale, the emphasis is on formulating general aims, not delineating lists of specific objectives.

To illustrate the distinction, one aim of psychological interventions is to promote mental health; a major aim of formal schooling is to prepare economically self-sufficient citizens.[7] It is from such extremely abstract statements of purpose that somewhat less abstract goals are formulated, and, in turn, less abstract and more immediate objectives are articulated (see Figure 7.3). The translation process is analogous to operationally defining highly abstract psychological concepts, such as intelligence, in order to clarify subconcepts and corresponding sets of related observable variables. A key difference, however, is that in specifying objectives relevant to an intervention's aims many are not readily translated into observable behavior.

The distinction among aims, goals, and objectives is important even for interventions where the intent is only to accomplish short-range *outcomes*. Crisis interventions are a dramatic example. Although the time frame is short, the intended outcomes almost always are abstract aims (e.g., restoration of equilibrium) from which concrete objectives are derived.

Short-Range Objectives

Because of the increased interest in accountability, short-range *objectives* stated in measurable terms assume a central role in intervention planning. The benefits of measuring the attainment of

Figure 7.3
Translation of Long-Range Aims into Goals and Objectives

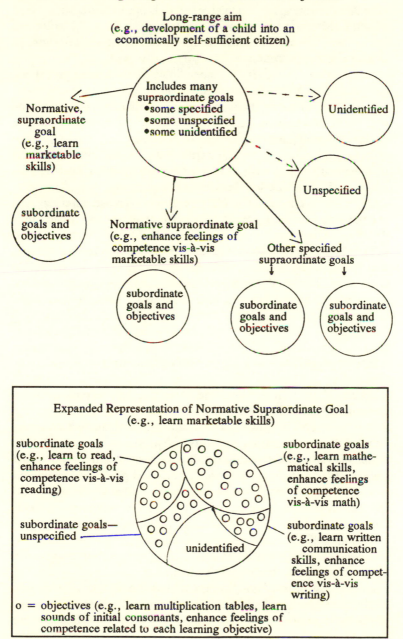

intended outcomes are undeniable. This is not to say, however, that all intended outcomes are readily measured, or that the ability to specify objectives is the same thing as identifying the appropriate direction for intervention.

Many more objectives are specifiable than can or must be achieved through intervention. Furthermore, short-range objectives are not ends in themselves; they are a small part of a particular goal and aim and sometimes are prerequisites for moving on to a goal. We must not lose sight of the fact that many specific objectives are relatively small, unrepresentative, and often unimportant segments of the most valued aims society has for its citizens—and that citizens have for themselves.

Unfortunately, as accountability pressures increase, interventions may be guided more by evaluation needs than by long-range aims. That is, demands for immediate accountability can reshape intervention practices so that the emphasis shifts to immediate and readily measured objectives and away from fundamental purposes. Over time, this can inappropriately lead to radical revision of intervention rationales. (We have more to say about this concern in Parts III and IV.)

Intervention Rationales and Intended Outcomes

In articulating an intervention rationale, the emphasis is on formulating general aims and supraordinate goals, not delineating lists of specific objectives. To illustrate the point, two common aims of psychological and educational programs are to promote social and emotional functioning. It is from such extremely abstract statements of aim that somewhat less abstract goals are formulated (e.g., to promote feelings of competence, personal direction, and relatedness to others), and, in turn, less abstract and more immediate objectives are articulated (e.g., to promote ability to approach tasks with self-assurance, make accurate self-evaluations, plan and implement learning activities with initiative, work cooperatively with others in pursuing common objectives).

The process of translating program aims is analogous to defining highly abstract psychological concepts, such as intelligence, in order to clarify subconcepts and corresponding sets of related observable variables. A key difference, however, is that in specifying objectives relevant to an intervention's aims many are not readily translated into observable behavior. The concepts we are dealing with are "wholes" that intervention developers and those concerned with evaluation and outcome-accountability conceptually break apart for convenience. But this is done at the risk of committing a major disservice to the whole.

Standards, Norms, and Benchmarks

Calls for high standards and the delineation of benchmarks often are raised when intervention rationales are discussed. In education, for example, there has been a call for adopting world class standards. The term *standards* refers to the use of values (a philosophical and theoretical idea) or some empirical basis as criteria for making judgments about intervention outcomes. Standards may be absolute or relative. Absolute standards are ideals that usually can be only approximated. Relative standards may be formulated based on norms related to the functioning of comparable others or to a system's own previous functioning.

Norms are empirical standards (e.g., the individual is above or below the mean on a test, a group is above or below another group of similar age or background). Because norms are not value statements, values must be used as criteria to make judgments after norms are applied. For example, how much below the mean must an individual or program be before we decide that there is a significant problem requiring additional intervention? If an individual or program starts off well below the mean, what criteria should be used to judge progress over a given period?

Benchmarks reflect ongoing (formative) evaluation of progress toward outcomes. That is, data are gathered on samples of specific objectives at designated times, then standards are applied to judge progress. The formulation of benchmarks entails (1) deciding on intervention objectives for the system, (2) choosing which will be the focus of data gathering, (3) designating measures, (4) designating when measures will be used, and (5) deciding on criteria for judging how close to the benchmark the system comes.

The notion of holding individuals or programs to "high standards" or "standards of excellence" suggests that there is some ideal to be approximated. This raises the problems of agreeing on the ideal and formulating the criteria for judging how well it is approximated. These problems have both a value and a political component. (What ideals and criteria should be considered? Whose ideals and criteria are to prevail?) We shall address the problem of who decides about such matters after we underscore concern about unintended outcomes.

Unintended Outcomes

As our working definition stresses, interventions produce not only intended but *unintended* outcomes—some positive, some negative. For example, on the negative side, by their very nature most intervention processes have the potential to produce dependency, distorted views of personal competency and interpersonal relationships, and inappropriate stereotyping. The fact of unintended outcomes is well established (i.e., the law of unintended consequences), but the tendency is to view them as minor side effects rather than as potentially major outcomes.[8]

Given that they may be as significant, and perhaps more significant than what is intended, awareness of potential major negative consequences and positive side effects is highly desirable in intervention decision making. Thus, articulation of the possibility of such outcomes is another basic aspect of formulating a sound underlying rationale.

WHO DECIDES? THE POLITICS OF INTERVENTION

Interveners tend to make decisions for clients—except when a client's decisions are those with which they agree or see as not very important. After all, the thinking goes, additional years of experience or special training or both make for better judgments. Interveners tend to feel more competent than clients and often prefer to or are expected to make the major intervention decisions. Moreover, interveners usually have the legal power to control decision-making processes.

It is perhaps natural for interveners to want to believe that they operate in a client's best interests (e.g., nurturing unique potential and qualities, ensuring freedom of inquiry and rights to learn and know). The degree to which interveners actually make the best decisions is a matter as yet unclarified by researchers. In the meantime, as highlighted below, plenty of philosophical, legal, and political issues are tied up in all this that should not be ignored.[9]

When the objectives of the client are compatible with other involved parties, who decides may be of little concern. The politics of decision making becomes a major issue when ideas and interests conflict.

One reason conflicting interests raise concern is because of society's ability to exercise control through psychological and educational interventions. With respect to problems, for instance, it is well not to forget that society defines what is exceptional or deviant, and interventions are designed as much to protect society as to help a client. To paraphrase Hobbs, "to take care of them" has two meanings: one is to help clients; the other meaning encompasses the many ways society can eliminate what it disapproves of—including removing individuals from the community.[10]

At one extreme, it is argued, there are times when society must put its needs before individual rights and mandate interventions designed to maintain itself, such as compulsory education and diversion programs. At the other extreme, it is argued that interventions that jeopardize individual rights, such as coercion and invasion of privacy, are never justified. For many concerned citizens, however, neither extreme is acceptable.

Without agreeing or disagreeing with a particular position, one can appreciate the importance of the debate. Specifically, it heightens awareness that

- no society is devoid of some degree of coercion in dealing with its members (e.g., no right or liberty is absolute); and such coercion is seen as especially justified with minors and those with problems
- interventions are used to serve the vested interests of some at the expense of other subgroups in society (e.g., minorities, those with disabilities, the poor, females, and legal minors have been deprived of freedoms and rights)
- informed consent and due process of law are central to protecting individuals when there are conflicting interests (e.g., issues about who or

what caused a problem, issues about who or what should carry the brunt of corrective measures)

This awareness and greater sensitivity to conflicts among those with vested interventions interests are essential to protect clients adequately from abuse by those with power to exercise control over them.

Again, the situation in intervening with minors is instructive. As emphasized by Mnookin, society has broad authority to make a wide range of life-shaping decisions "in the best interests of children."[11] Minors under certain statutory age limits are not entitled to many options available to adults; for example, they can't hold certain jobs, obtain a license to drive a car, or receive confidential health services. Moreover, the society and their parents have legal power to make minors do things they may not wish to do, such as stay in school until a given age or experience unwanted treatment regimens. Reformers argue that minors should have broader legal rights in making a greater range of decisions independent of their parents' desires. Some also are concerned that society and parents are not adequately pursuing the best interests of young people and want government programs expanded to serve and protect minors.

Usually, control of decision making is maintained by those with greatest authority in a situation. This is a questionable practice when those in authority have no legitimate basis for assuming power or have interests that conflict with those of other involved parties. The former circumstance includes instances when practitioners assess and prescribe in areas outside their competence or where the state of knowledge precludes anyone having sufficient expertise; it also includes cases where consent to intervene is inappropriately assumed. Conflicts of interest encompass instances where professionals' values or financial involvements clash with those of clients and when society pursues its rights and responsibilities at the expense of the rights and liberties of individuals.

When ideas and interests conflict, the "political" facets of intervention are underscored. Interventions are fraught with power conflicts and imbalances that result in circumstances inappropriately detrimental to the interests of one or more participants. Examples appear whenever the vested psychological, social, political, or economic interests of those with authority are enacted into decisions that those without authority dislike.

Authority stems from psychological and socio-political-economic factors that may or may not be institutionalized and legitimized. Therefore, political facets of intervention are not limited to power stemming from legislated authority. Overt political facets of intervention are seen in mandated activities of governments, schools, industries, and other organizations; a widespread example is the gathering and use of assessment data for planning, evaluating, and policy making purposes. Covert political facets are potentially present in all other intervention activity.

As noted, political concerns arise regarding the decision making role of clients. This is especially the case for minors and those presumed less than competent, such as individuals with emotional, behavioral, or learning problems. The role for such persons and their advocates in decision making increasingly is debated in legal and professional circles. Efforts to ensure protection of those denied a decision-making role are reflected in court cases and advocacy programs. For example, in October 1992, a Florida judge ruled in favor of a minor who asked for a "divorce" from his mother so that he could remain with foster parents. As courts expand the decision-making arena of previously denied groups, improved guidelines should emerge clarifying both the legitimate bases for denying decision-making power and the protections for individuals when others have authority to decide. (We have more to say about this in a subsequent section.)

Because overt and covert power imbalances appear inevitable, stringent protection of the rights of those who are the focus of intervention is essential. Therefore, ethical and legal analyses of rights emerge as fundamental concerns in working on the underlying rationale problem.[12] Ultimately, every intervener must personally come to grips with what is morally proper in balancing the respective rights of involved parties.

NOTES

1. R. Blount, Jr. (April 2, 1984). "Yogi," *Sports Illustrated, 60*, no. 14, p. 84.

2. It is well documented that there are many cases where environments (home, school, workplace, society) apply inappropriate standards and limit choices in ways that cause individuals to behave deviantly and deviously. See the following: H.S. Adelman & L. Taylor (1986). Children's reluctance regarding treatment: Incompetence, resistance, or an appropriate response? *School Psychology Review, 15,* 91–99. L. Bond & B. Compas (Eds.) (1989). *Primary prevention and promotion in the schools.* Newbury Park, CA: Sage. N. Garmezy & M. Rutter (Eds.) (1983). *Stress, coping, and development in children.* New York: McGraw-Hill. K. Heller (1990). Social and community intervention. *Annual Review of Psychology, 41,* 141–168.

3. Bronfenbrenner envisions the environment surrounding and affecting individual functioning as an arrangement of encircling and widening contexts. Our use of the terms first, second, and third level systems is roughly equivalent to what he calls the microsystem, the exosystem, and the macrosystem.   He describes the microsystem as the immediate physical surroundings, the exosystem as the broader formal and informal social structures (including neighborhood, local agencies of government, communication and transportation facilities), and the macrosystem as encompassing such abstract concepts as overarching cultural and subcultural patterns of which the lower level systems are concrete manifestations.   Holahan has further subdivided these systems to form additional encircling contexts. See U. Bronfenbrenner (1976). The experimental ecology of education. *Educational Researcher, 5,* 5–15; U. Bronfenbrenner (1977). Toward an experimental ecology of human development. *American Psychologist, 32,* 513–531; C.J. Holahan (1982). *Environmental psychology.* Random House: New York.

4. B.H. Banathy (1991). *Systems design of education: A journey to create the future.* Englewood Cliffs, NJ: Educational Technology Publications, p. 60.

5. Even as a socializing force, education functions differently depending on the student, the parents, the teacher, the school, the society. The goals of education for some students are extremely limited—to minimize the student's antisocial behavior and teach basic literacy and vocational skills. For others, the intent is to maximize the student's usefulness to society with respect to maintaining what the society values, overcoming problems that interfere with the society's aspirations, and improving the human condition. Futurists want to transform education so that the aims are consistent with a rapidly changing world in which members of society must be equipped to deal with rapid changes and shape social evolution.

6. An excellent application to intervention of cognitive-affective thinking about motivation is seen in E.L. Deci & R. Ryan (1985). *Intrinsic motivation and self-determination in human behavior.* New York: Plenum Press.

7. An example of abstract statements of aim is seen in five of the following six national "goals" for education that emerged in 1990 based on deliberations involving the President of the United States and the Governors from each state. Each is to be accomplished by the year 2000 for persons residing in the United States. The desired ends in each of six areas are: (1) Readiness for School: all children will start school ready to learn; (2) High School Completion: the rate will increase to at least 90 percent; (3) Student Achievement and Citizenship: students will leave grades 4, 8, and 12 having demonstrated competency in challenging subject matter including English, mathematics, science, history, and geography, and every school will ensure that all students learn to use their minds well, so they may be prepared for responsible citizenship, further learning, and productive employment in our modern economy; (4) Science and Mathematics: students will be first in the world in science and mathematics achievement; (5) Adult Literacy and Lifelong Learning: every adult will be literate and will possess the knowledge and skills necessary to compete in a global economy and exercise the rights and responsibilities of citizenship; (6) Safe, Disciplined, and Drug-Free Schools: every school will be free of drugs and violence and will offer a disciplined environment conducive to learning. For a discussion of implications related to these aims, see L. Cuban (1990). Four stories about national goals for American education. *Phi Delta Kappan, 72*, 270.

8. Ivan Illich argues that the iatrogenic effects of institutionalized intervention are so profound that they reshape cultural thought in ways that interfere with the capacity of large segments of society to cope with problems and aid each other. See I. Illich (1976). *Medical nemesis*. New York: Pantheon Books.

9. As discussed by Carl Rogers: "Politics in present-day psychological and social usage has to do with power and control: with the extent to which persons desire, attempt to obtain, possess, share, or surrender power and control others and/or themselves. It has to do with the maneuvers, the strategies and tactics, witting and unwitting, by which such power and control over one's life and others' lives is sought and gained—or shared or relinquished. It has to do with the locus of decision-making power: who makes the decisions which, consciously or unconsciously, regulate or control the thoughts, feelings, or behavior of others or oneself." C. Rogers (1977). *On personal power: Inner strength and its revolutionary impact*. New York: Delacorte Press, p. 4.

10. N. Hobbs (1975). *The future of children: Categories, labels, and their consequences*. San Francisco: Jossey-Bass.

11. R.H. Mnookin (1985). *In the interest of children: Advocacy, law reform and public policy*. New York: W.H. Freeman.

12. Coercive interventions provide some of the most dramatic examples

of the politics of decision making. In the 1980s, the problem of coercive treatment of minors was the focus of a series of court cases. As summarized by Melton and Davidson (1987):

> In the case of *Milonas v. Williams* (1982) involving the Provo Canyon School in Utah, youth sent to the school were required to take polygraph examinations to prove that they were obeying, among other rules, avoidance of "negative thinking," including a mere intent to say bad things about the school. Refusal of the polygraph examination resulted in punishment and failure to advance in the program or leave the school. Students' ongoing mail was censored, boys were required to rewrite "negative" letters, and therapists wrote comments like "manipulative" in the margins.
>
> Other programs intended to "resocialize" troubled or troubling youth sometimes have resorted to holding youth incommunicado (see, e.g., *Doe v. Public Health Trust of Dade County*, 1983, on "no-communication therapy"), refusing to allow them to wear street clothes (see, e.g., *Wheeler v. Glass*, 1983), or keeping them in isolation for prolonged periods (see, e.g., *Mary & Crystal v. Ramsden*, 1980; *Santana v. Collazo*, 1983), or forcing them to wear self-derogatory signs, engage in other humiliation rituals (e.g., cleaning floors for hours with toothbrushes; see *Stare ex rel. K.W. v. Werner*, 1978), or submit to intense and prolonged group confrontation.

See G. Melton & H.A. Davidson (1987). Child protection and society: When should the state intervene? *American Psychologist, 42*, 172–175 (p. 174).

Not only do the court cases illustrate coercive and repressive intervention, the rulings provide some guidelines as to the limitations on interveners. At the same time, judicial cases raise concerns about the dangers involved in determining public policy and professional practice through litigation. Mnookin discusses such dangers and goes on to caution that policymaking "requires difficult predictions and troubling value choices. Whether policy is made in the legislature or in the courtroom, [many individuals] can neither define nor defend their own best interests. Nor can they control their own advocates." Mnookin, *In the interest of children*, p. 516.

Indications of the impact of advocacy for client rights in general and minors' rights in particular are seen in legislative guidelines related to intervening with individuals with disabilities and the various documents that have appeared in recent years with titles such as "Clients' Bill of Rights" and "Rights of Minors."

8

Processes

I hear, and I forget;
I see, and I remember;
I do, and I understand.
                    Chinese Proverb

Psychologists and educators are enmeshed in a great variety of intervention approaches, each of which can appear almost unique. Fortunately, as noted in the introductory chapter, some cross-system analyses of interventions have begun to clarify commonalities and critical differences.

What follows is a brief presentation of frameworks, concepts, and concerns relevant to a generic understanding of intervention processes. First, we highlight variations associated with intervention collaboration and outline major intervention phases and tasks. Then we explore underlying rationale concerns about process in terms of how much intervention is needed, sequential and hierarchical approaches, contrasting orientations, and eclecticism.

INTERVENTION COLLABORATION

As was indicated in Figure 7.1, interventions vary with respect to their focus. Figure 8.1 reiterates variations in system focus and highlights two other important variations. One underscores the fact that interventions are planned and carried out by one or more individual practitioners, the staff of one or more organizations, or some combination of both. The second dimension stresses that, when more than one agent is involved, the multiple interventions may be planned and implemented in ways that arc (1) uncoopera-

Figure 8.1
Variations in Intervention Focus, Agent, and
Degree of Collaboration

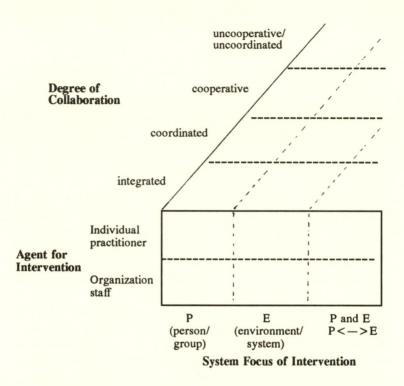

tive/uncoordinated, (2) cooperative, (3) coordinated, or (4) highly
integrated.

Despite considerable agreement about its value, collaboration is
not widely practiced in psychology and education. Indeed, the
evidence suggests that few intervention rationales substantively
address the topic.[1]

Simply stated, the purpose of collaboration is to counter inappropriate fragmentation of intervention efforts. Varying degrees of
collaboration are accomplished through cooperation, coordination,
or integration.

Concerns that arise include a host of philosophical, socioeconomic, and political considerations that shape the degree of collaboration pursued. Also, the processes by which existing independent programs can develop collaboration are poorly understood. For example, should efforts proceed in stages starting with cooperation, moving on to coordination, and then transforming into an integrated model? What mechanisms are needed?

Another concern about working against fragmentation involves not confusing coherence with consistency. Although the two concepts resemble each other, a critical difference exists. As delineated by Buchman and Floden, consistency specifies logical relationships and tries to rule out contradictions. Coherence "allows for many kinds of connectedness, including associations of ideas and feelings, intimations of resemblance, conflicts and tensions, and imaginative leaps. Coherence—but not consistency—is hospitable to change and imagination." From this perspective, efforts to collaborate should be guided more by the concept of coherence than by that of consistency.[2]

INTERVENTION PHASES AND TASKS

Collaboration may be facilitated by greater understanding of process concepts that cut across intervention activity. However, even if this proves not to be the case, such understanding certainly will aid in formulation of underlying rationales and comparative studies of interventions. An appreciation of generic steps, phases, and tasks represents a useful starting point.

A common generic way to think about interventions that focus on problems is to conceive the process in terms of problem solving steps and tasks. Such a conceptualization is seen in Figure 8.2.

A complementary approach involves conceiving intervention in terms of major programmatic phases and activities. Figure 8.3 graphically outlines intervention conceived as seven interrelated phases: (1) formulation of an underlying rationale, (2) normative planning, (3) administrative planning, (4) specific planning of daily practices, (5) evaluation planning, (6) implementation of daily plans, and (7) implementation of the evaluation plan. Discussion throughout Part II illustrates concepts and concerns relevant to

Figure 8.2
Key Steps and Tasks in Problem-Solving Intervention

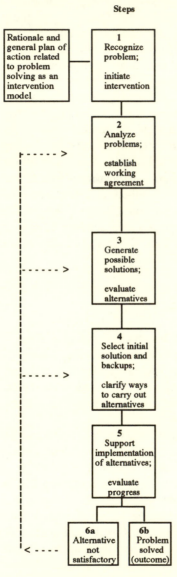

Steps   **Tasks**

Rationale and general plan of action related to problem solving as an intervention model

1
Recognize problem;

initiate intervention

(a) Be aware of the problem
(b) Decide intervention is needed
(c) Initiate intervention tentatively
(d) Build relationship (e.g., trust/respect)
(e) Deal with emotional charge (e.g., fears, anger)
(f) Become aware of mutual expectations related to intervention

2
Analyze problems;

establish working agreement

(a) Mutually assess the problem
(b) Come to a shared understanding of the problems, including diagnostic classification if needed and cause-effect (functional) analyses if feasible
(c) Work through to shared understanding of expectations for working together
(d) Develop attitudes toward effective problem solving (e.g., openness to innovative solutions, deferring judgments)

3
Generate possible solutions;

evaluate alternatives

(a) Come to a shared understanding of alternatives for solving the problem, deferring judgment as much as is reasonable
(b) Use new information arising from process to further clarify the problem
(c) Develop criteria for evaluating pros and cons of alternatives
(d) Apply criteria

4
Select initial solution and backups;

clarify ways to carry out alternatives

(a) Come to a shared understanding of proposed solution (e.g., implications and subtleties)
(b) Evaluate additional alternatives that arise
(c) Choose primary and backup solutions
(d) Develop plan for achieving selected alternatives (e.g., identify support/skill needs)
(e) Develop needed skills
(f) Develop criteria for deciding whether problem is resolved or whether to adopt backup

5
Support implementation of alternatives;

evaluate progress

(a) Deal with emotional charge
(b) Continue development of needed skills
(c) Make formative evaluation
(d) Apply criteria to decide whether to shift to backup solution

| **6a** Alternative not satisfactory | **6b** Problem solved (outcome) |

(a) Make formative and summative evaluations (outcomes provide data for decisions)
(b) Apply criteria regarding need for other alternatives
(c) If alternative has not been satisfactory, analyze feedback to determine whether information suggests additional alternatives (e.g., alternatives not previously realized or perspectives of the problem that were not previously understood and that may lead to new alternatives)

Figure 8.3
Programmatic Phases of Intervention

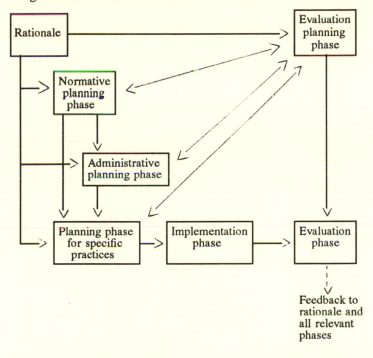

Source: H.S. Adelman and L. Taylor (1993). *Learning problems and learning disabilities: Moving forward*. Pacific Grove, CA: Brooks/Cole. Reprinted with permission.

formulating an underlying rationale; Parts III and IV highlight the other six phases. At this point, we just want to outline the phases and their relationship to each other.

Activity during the seven phases is conceived in terms of five basic tasks (usually translated into specific programs or services). As represented in Figure 8.4, these tasks are labelled with respect to the general processes involved, namely: (1) assessment, (2) decision making, (3) transition-in facilitation, (4) facilitation toward outcomes, and (5) transition-out facilitation. In keeping with our working definition of intervention, the focus for each task (and related program or service) may be on the environment, a person,

Figure 8.4
Major Intervention Tasks

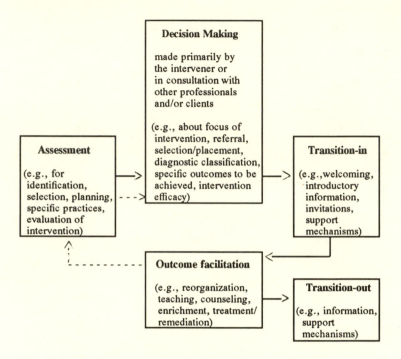

All tasks are based on a rationale and require planning for appropriate
implementation and evaluation of designated programs and services.

or both and may be concerned with nonproblematic functioning or
preventing/treating problems. And because each is an intervention
unto itself, appropriate implementation and evaluation are based on
some rationale and require systematic planning.

In general, then, the above frameworks outlining steps, phases,
and tasks provide templates for planning intervention. They also
are potential aids in analyzing underlying rationales—particularly
such questions as, Are the various phases and tasks addressed?
How? How well?

HOW MUCH INTERVENTION IS NEEDED?

An underlying rationale also must address the problem of providing as much but no more intervention than is necessary. In doing so, a balance must be struck between two complementary principles. As a generality, complex changes require comprehensive and integrated programmatic interventions that are both available and accessible. Thus, one principle for good practice is to ensure that a comprehensive and integrated set of programs is used. At the same time, because interventions are costly, financially and in terms of potential negative consequences, another principle for good practice is to intervene only to the degree that is absolutely necessary.

Comprehensive and Integrated Programs

As an example, a continuum of interventions for addressing psychosocial and educational problems is outlined in Figure 8.5. The continuum ranges from programs for primary prevention and early-age intervention, through those for addressing problems soon after onset, on to treatments for severe and chronic problems. With respect to *comprehensiveness*, the continuum highlights that many problems must be addressed developmentally and with a range of programs—some focused on individuals and some on environmental systems. With respect to concerns about *integrating* programs (e.g., to avoid piecemeal approaches), the continuum of community and school interventions underscores the need for concurrent interprogram linkages and for linkages over extended periods of time.

It is easy to conceptualize a comprehensive package of interventions. It is excruciatingly hard to (1) establish such a range of programs, (2) integrate those that are in operation, and (3) conduct the type of research that advances understanding. The picture that emerges from the literature on psychological, educational, health, and social interventions illustrates the difficulty.

Given the difficulty in establishing comprehensive, integrated programmatic efforts, it is not surprising that research on this topic is almost nonexistent. Available descriptions suggest that poor

Figure 8.5
From Prevention to Treatment: A Continuum of Programs for
Ameliorating Learning, Behavior, and Socioemotional Problems

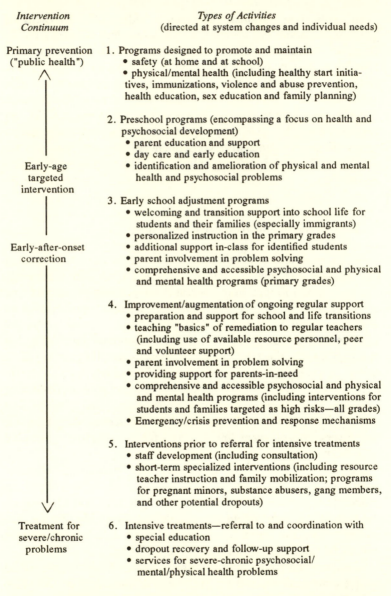

Intervention Continuum	*Types of Activities* (directed at system changes and individual needs)
Primary prevention ("public health")	1. Programs designed to promote and maintain • safety (at home and at school) • physical/mental health (including healthy start initiatives, immunizations, violence and abuse prevention, health education, sex education and family planning)
Early-age targeted intervention	2. Preschool programs (encompassing a focus on health and psychosocial development) • parent education and support • day care and early education • identification and amelioration of physical and mental health and psychosocial problems
Early-after-onset correction	3. Early school adjustment programs • welcoming and transition support into school life for students and their families (especially immigrants) • personalized instruction in the primary grades • additional support in-class for identified students • parent involvement in problem solving • comprehensive and accessible psychosocial and physical and mental health programs (primary grades)
	4. Improvement/augmentation of ongoing regular support • preparation and support for school and life transitions • teaching "basics" of remediation to regular teachers (including use of available resource personnel, peer and volunteer support) • parent involvement in problem solving • providing support for parents-in-need • comprehensive and accessible psychosocial and physical and mental health programs (including interventions for students and families targeted as high risks—all grades) • Emergency/crisis prevention and response mechanisms
	5. Interventions prior to referral for intensive treatments • staff development (including consultation) • short-term specialized interventions (including resource teacher instruction and family mobilization; programs for pregnant minors, substance abusers, gang members, and other potential dropouts)
Treatment for severe/chronic problems	6. Intensive treatments—referral to and coordination with • special education • dropout recovery and follow-up support • services for severe-chronic psychosocial/mental/physical health problems

Source: H.S. Adelman and L. Taylor (1993). *Learning problems and learning disabilities: Moving forward*. Pacific Grove, CA: Brooks/Cole. Reprinted with permission.

interface is characteristic of most intervention activity related to behavioral, emotional, and learning problems. In particular, lack of connection between efforts to address functioning in biological and psychosocial/cognitive domains is of increasing concern. Physical and mental health programs, for example, rarely are coordinated with each other or with social service, educational, and vocational programs, and thus are widespread illustrations of the problem of piecemeal and fragmented intervention.

For instance, the problems of illiteracy, substance abuse, suicide, unwanted pregnancy, sexually transmitted diseases, school and societal dropouts, all require more than one type of intervention; they may require similar types of programs, and services should be developed and function in an integrated way over a significant period of time. For the most part, however, programs for each type of problem are developed and function separately. An individual identified as having several problems may be involved in counseling with several professionals working independently of each other (sometimes within the same agency).   Similarly, a youngster identified and treated in early education programs who still requires special support may not receive systematic help in the primary grades. And so forth. Moreover, in many locales, programs are available only at relatively distant geographic sites, and some essential programs are so underfunded that they are functionally inconsequential.

Funding naturally fluctuates with economic conditions. However, even in the best of times, resources are not provided to underwrite a comprehensive set of programs in many catchment areas. Within even relatively large catchment areas, only a limited range of needed programs usually is available, and most operate in relative isolation of each other.   Interface clearly is handicapped when programs are difficult to access; interface is irrelevant when programs are unavailable.

Deficiencies related to comprehensiveness and interface are attributable in significant measure to the way interventions are conceived and organized and the way professionals understand their roles and functions. Conceptually, intervention rarely is presented comprehensively.   Organizationally, the tendency is for policy makers to mandate, and for planners and developers to focus on, specific programs. Functionally, most practitioners and intervention researchers spend the majority of their time working directly with specific interventions and samples and give little thought or time to comprehensive models of mechanisms for program development and collaboration. In terms of policy, psychological and educational interventions are not as high a priority as maintaining society's financial security and the basic physical health and safety of its citizens.

Concern about the current state of affairs naturally stems from awareness that noncomprehensive and piecemeal approaches limit efficacy and work against cost efficiency. Limited efficacy seems inevitable as long as a reasonably full continuum of necessary programs is not available; limited cost effectiveness seems inevitable as long as related interventions are carried out in isolation from each other. From this perspective, many doubt that major intervention breakthroughs can occur without a comprehensive and integrated programmatic thrust.[3]

Availability and accessibility of a comprehensive, integrated set of programs are high priority items among policy advocates and warrant discussion as part of intervention rationales. To redress concern over piecemeal programs, greater commitment is needed with respect to, first, developing a comprehensive continuum and, second, establishing the type of mechanisms that ensure that programs remain mobilized and are at least coordinated. We discuss such mechanisms in a subsequent section.

Least Intervention Needed

Availability and accessibility do not mean that an intervention should be used. Interventions must also be necessary, beneficial, and cost effective. The desire to meet needs in ways that ensure that benefits outweigh costs (financial and otherwise) makes the principle of "least intervention needed" another fundamental intervention concern.

As the phrase states, the intent is to do no more than is needed. The adjective "least" reflects concerns that intervention (1) is an interference into the affairs of others (can be intrusive, disruptive, restrictive), (2) consumes resources, and (3) may produce serious negative outcomes. Translated into a guideline for interventions that affect people, the concept can be stated as follows: *Do not interfere with people's opportunity for a normal range of experiences more than is absolutely necessary.*

The notion of using the least intervention needed and the related concept of placement in the least restrictive environment find support in "the principle of normalization"—which is associated with antilabelling, mainstreaming, and deinstitutionalization policies.[4] In psychology and education, the broadest applications of these ideas are found with respect to problem-focused intervention.

In making general decisions about intervening for problems, most professionals agree that activity should be kept to the necessary minimum. For example, if an individual with emotional problems can be helped effectively at a community agency, this seems better than placing the person in a mental hospital. For special education populations, when a student with learning or behavior problems can be worked with effectively in a regular classroom, placement in a special education program is inappropriate. Indeed, laws exist to protect individuals from removal from the "mainstream" without good cause and due process. Such legislation and associated regulations reflect concern that disruptive or restrictive interventions produce negative effects, such as poor self-concept and social alienation; in turn, these effects narrow immediate and future options and choices, thereby minimizing life opportunities.

The example of placing youngsters with problems in special settings illustrates the difficulty in applying the principle of least intervention needed. By law in the United States, schools must have a continuum of alternative placements for students with disabilities. Legislative regulations also call for placement in the least restrictive environment. As a conceptual aid, placements are listed in terms of a continuum ranging from least to most restrictive (see Figure 8.6). By consensus, the least restrictive placement is described as keeping people in normal situations and using special assistance only to the degree necessary. Placement in a special class is listed as somewhat more restrictive than keeping the individual in a regular class. A full-day placement in a special class is viewed as even more restrictive. Assignment to a special school or institution is described as the most restrictive placement.

Considerable support exists for models that describe placements on a continuum from least to most restrictive. There are, however,

Figure 8.6
Continuum of Placements Ranging from Least to
Most Restrictive

Least restrictive	•regular class—ongoing teacher education and support to increase range of individual differences accommodated (prevention and mainstreaming)
	•regular class— consultation for teacher provided as needed (prereferral interventions and mainstreaming)
	•regular class—resources added—such as materials, aides, tutors, specialist help on a regular basis
	•special class—partial day (specialist or resource room)
	•special class—entire day
	•special school—public or private
Most restrictive	•special institutions—residential homes, hospital programs

interpretative and administrative problems related to such listings. A designated least restrictive setting may be the most restrictive in the long run if it cannot meet the needs of the individual placed there. The assumption often is made that the least restrictive environment is also the most effective. However, a short stay in a more restrictive placement may be more effective than a long stay in a minimally restrictive but less effective program. Thus, for the relatively small number of individuals with extremely severe problems, more restrictive placements may be most appropriate initially.

Another concern in applying the least restrictive environment guideline arises because administrative factors such as financial support and program availability play significant roles in intervention decisions. At times, for example, psychological and educational placements are approached as an administrative rather than a treatment arrangement. When this occurs, individuals are shifted from one setting to another without significant attention to whether the new setting can provide appropriate treatment or remediation. In particular, efforts to return individuals from special placements to community and regular school programs often are not paired with improved capability of regular settings to meet the individuals' special needs. When this occurs, the emphasis is on providing *least intervention*, but without ensuring that *needs* are met.

In sum, answering the question about how much intervention is needed involves addressing comprehensiveness and use of the least amount of intervention necessary. Thus, a rationale must specify both a full continuum of programs that may be needed and criteria for determining need in a particular instance.

SEQUENTIAL AND HIERARCHICAL APPROACHES

Thinking about intervening sequentially and hierarchically provides a helpful perspective for balancing use with need. For example, in keeping with the principle of least intervention needed, a logical first step calls for ensuring that the best general practices are applied. This is essential because a system (organization, person) may not have had appropriate opportunities to function up to capability. Stated differently, if the environment is a potential cause or is causing problems, efforts to eliminate causal conditions and/or enrich the environment should be made first.

After this step is well implemented, specialized practices can be added as necessary. That is, special processes and settings are appropriate only if the system still manifests specific needs warranting attention—and these are used only for as long as necessary. Figure 8.7 illustrates this two-step sequence and outlines a hierarchical and sequential approach for pursuing each step.

As illustrated in the figure, a three-tier hierarchy seems minimal. Intervention at the top tier (Level A) focuses on observable, surface level factors required for performing contemporary tasks (e.g., observable functions directly related to the task). At the second tier (Level B), the focus is on prerequisite factors required for surface level functioning (e.g., areas of "readiness"). The lowest tier (Level C) is concerned with underlying factors (e.g., motivation, functional mechanisms).

The sequence in which each level becomes the focus of intervention varies based on the observed impact of preceding strategies. For instance, as indicated above, the intent of the first step is to ensure that conditions are established that enable the system (organization or person) to function as optimally as feasible. This

Figure 8.7
Sequences and Levels in Providing a Good Match and
Determining Least Intervention Needed

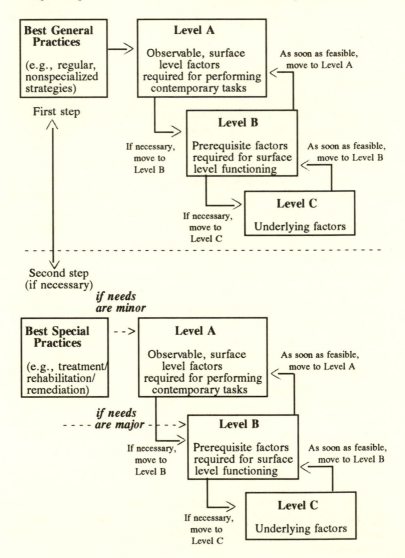

involves use of best general practices and starts by addressing observable factors (Level A).

Some systems, however, lack certain prerequisite knowledge, skills, or attitudes for performing designated tasks. This becomes apparent as Level A is pursued. In such cases, best general practices are continued but the level of focus shifts to facilitating development of prerequisites (Level B). That is, the focus drops down a level to address such prerequisites as lack of skill for ordering and sequencing events or following directions, lack of motivational readiness to learn, and so forth. Once specified prerequisites are developed, the focus shifts back to Level A so that the system can acquire surface level functions for performing contemporary tasks.

If a system is still not functioning appropriately even after prerequisites are addressed, it seems reasonable to consider underlying factors (Level C). Such factors are grouped into three categories: (1) motivational factors (e.g., values and expectations), (2) mechanisms (e.g., underlying structures and their functioning), and (3) interfering activity (e.g., any acts that are incompatible with pursuing system tasks). At Level C, strategies are designed to deal with a range of possible disruptors of desired functioning. As soon as feasible, the intervention shifts back to prerequisite and surface levels.

If none of the above works, Step 2 is introduced. This involves use of specialized rehabilitative, remedial, and treatment practices. When problems are minor, intervention begins by directly addressing observable deficits (Level A). For example, if an organization is not performing a function, the emphasis is on special practices that lead directly to establishing the function. Similarly, if a person is not able to perform a task, direct strategies are used to teach and reteach the knowledge and skills associated specifically with the task. When problems are pervasive and severe, the sequence begins with prerequisites (Level B), and if this is insufficient, the focus drops to Level C. A shift back to the higher levels is made as soon as feasible.

Two case examples are offered for further clarity. We turn again to the school context and discuss Juan, a student experiencing minor reading difficulties, and Beth, whose problem is somewhat more severe.

Ms. Johnston's first efforts to help Juan improve his reading skills involved a variety of reteaching strategies. The activity focused on current reading tasks in which he was interested. The reteaching strategies were not simply a matter of trying more of the same—more drill, for example. The teacher introduced alternative approaches including commonly used explanations, techniques, and materials (such as another example or analogy, a concrete demonstration, a memorization strategy). After working on this level for a week, it became clear that Juan had not learned many prerequisites (i.e., reading-readiness skills). For example, he had difficulty following directions involving more than one point at a time, and he had problems ordering and sequencing events described to him. He also seemed to have little awareness of the relationship between the spoken and the printed word. In other cases, Ms. Johnston had found that once the missing prerequisites were acquired, students had little problem learning basic reading skills. This turned out to be the case with Juan.

Beth's situation proved more difficult. Because her problem was more severe, Ms. Johnston focused from the start on absent reading prerequisites. At first, Beth was hesitant to try things that she had failed at previously. Ms. Johnston did not push. She followed Beth's lead and, at the same time, increasingly encouraged her to risk exploring new things. As she worked with her over a period of several weeks, she found that Beth had trouble learning most of the prerequisites and retained only a small amount of what she seemed to learn. It became clear that Beth was having widespread difficulty discriminating sounds, and this was seen as a possible indicator of an underlying factor interfering with learning. Rather than have her continue to experience failure, Ms. Johnston shifted to a lower level of instructional focus and worked with her using techniques that stressed multisensory involvement. To improve Beth's retention, amounts to be learned were reduced, and a variety of interesting activities for immediate application and practice were identified.

It should be noted that an important goal was to help Beth increase her feelings of competence. Unfortunately, the girl's initial reaction was the common one of perceiving the special help as another sign of her lack of competence, and this made her feel worse. Eventually, she began to have sufficient success to counter such perceptions and feelings, and while overall reading progress was slow, it was steady.

One further complexity should be noted about adopting a sequential and hierarchical approach. When an intervention is designed to address all facets of a system, it is necessary to use both steps and work at several levels at the same time. Beth, for instance, required special strategies addressing underlying factors to improve her reading. She was, however, functioning satisfactorily in several other subjects, and in these areas the teacher used general practices and stayed at Level A.

Before moving on to the next topic, we want to underscore that the sequential and hierarchical model outlined above provides an *in situ* strategy for ongoing "needs assessment." As such, it also can aid in detecting diagnostic errors. For instance, diagnoses denoting underlying dysfunctions or pathology as the cause of a system's difficulties seem in error when problems are corrected through interventions at Levels A and B.

CONTRASTING ORIENTATIONS

The level of intervention focus chosen is influenced by the intervener's view of how outcomes can and should be accomplished. Among psychological and educational practitioners different models or "orientations" can be delineated. To illustrate the point, we contrast two fundamentally different ways of thinking.

One view is that ends can and should be attainable through what we have described above as best general practices focused on observable and prerequisite factors. This includes use of general processes to establish new organizational functions, redirected use of existing skills, teaching or reteaching nonacquired skills to improve group or individual functioning, and so forth. In emphasizing best general practices, this view also actively downplays use of specialized practices.

The contrasting view is characterized by its emphasis on specialized practices focused on underlying factors. This includes, for example, strategies designed to compensate for dysfunctions in fundamental organizational structures and therapeutically oriented approaches designed to address the social, emotional, and motivational underpinnings of human functioning. While stressing specialized practices, advocates of this view also find general practices appropriate in some instances.[5]

These contrasting orientations permeate interventions. To illustrate, we offer a brief conceptual look at processes for treating psychological and educational problems and at general models of teaching.

Processes for Treating Problems

Treatment and remedial approaches in psychology and education have been described extensively in books and journals. One reads about counseling, behavior modification, psychodynamic therapy, remedial techniques, rehabilitation, metacognitive strategies, and so forth. And there are some works devoted to analyzing commonalities and differences in practices. As suggested above, one useful distinction that emerges is that treatment approaches can be dichotomized by identifying their chosen level of focus. That is, they can be contrasted as reflecting an orientation to underlying or observable factors (see Table 8.1).

Table 8.1

Contrasting Orientations to Treatment and Remediation

	UNDERLYING FACTORS ORIENTATION	OBSERVABLE FACTORS ORIENTATION
PRIMARY OVERALL CONCERN	Motivational and developmental differences and disabilities that disrupt desired functioning	Unlearned skills and interfering behavior
	Specific Areas of Concern	
	Motivation •reactive motivation problems •proactive motivation problems Development •perceptual problems •motor problems •cognitive problems •language problems •social problems •emotional problems Knowledge, skills, and attitudes to compensate for disabilities	Knowledge and skills relevant for performing life tasks •readiness needs •contemporary task needs •general life adjustment needs
SECONDARY CONCERNS	Enhancing intrinsic motivation Knowledge and skills relevant for performing life tasks	Interfering behaviors (e.g., poor impulse control, lack of sustained attention)

(cont.)

Table 8.1 (cont.)

TERTIARY CONCERNS	Interfering behaviors	

Assessment

PROCESS COM- PONENTS	Construct-oriented assessment of developmental and motivational functioning as a basis for program planning and evaluation	Task-based assessment of knowledge and sequential skills as a basis for program planning and evaluation

Form of Objectives

Nonbehavioral, as well as behavioral and criterion-referenced objectives	Behavioral and criterion-referenced objectives

Treatment/Remedial Rationale and Methods

Therapeutic-oriented interventions (primary emphasis on establishing rapport through interpersonal dynamics and use of a variety of intervention models)	Behavior change interventions (primary emphasis on establishing control over behavior through manipulation of reinforcers and use of cognitive self-direction and monitoring)
•counseling and psychotherapy	
•expanded life task options and choices	•direct instruction to teach missing skills and information
•minimized coercion	
•enhanced interpersonal option	
•accommodation of a wide range of motivational and developmental differences	•behavior management to reduce interfering behaviors
•exercises intended to correct developmental anomalies and accelerate lagging development	
•eclectic instruction related to compensatory strategies	
•eclectic strategies for reducing interfering behaviors	

The *underlying factors orientation* is based on the assumption that many problems in functioning are symptoms of an underlying problem. As outlined in Table 8.1, practitioners adopting this orientation hypothesize and attempt to address motivational and developmental differences and disabilities seen as disruptive of functioning.

The roots of the orientation are found in medical, psychotherapeutic, and educational concepts. For instance, cognitive deficits or emotional distress often are identified as underlying a behavior or learning problem. In turn, the cognitive deficits and related emotional distress are seen as psychologically or biologically based.

An example is seen in discussion of the causes of learning disorders. The subtype of learning problems designated as learning disabilities is posited as stemming from biological underpinnings. That is, a relatively minor underlying CNS dysfunction is postulated as interfering with psychological processes needed for effective and efficient learning, such as short-term memory and selective attention. Over time, this state of affairs is viewed as affecting development by slowing it down or producing anomalies; in turn, this is seen as interfering with acquisition of certain prerequisites involved in learning to read and write, such as visual and auditory perceptual discriminations. Consequently, the foundation is laid for a range of learning and performance problems.

Anorexia nervosa provides another illustration of pathology hypothesized as caused by underlying factors; in this case the underpinnings usually are seen as psychological. That is, the problem is seen as stemming from severe anxiety related to sexuality and/or a family relationship where a domineering parent fosters both overdependence and rebelliousness.

Corrective interventions emerging from the underlying factors orientation usually are built on construct-focused assessment. These include assessments designed to analyze areas such as perceptual, motoric, cognitive, language, social, and emotional functioning. In addition, psychoneurological or neurological testing may be done to aid diagnosis. Intervention objectives generally are stated in nonbehavioral terms, but use of behavioral and criterion-referenced objectives is not uncommon. Intervention strategies draw on psychotherapeutic principles and a variety of teaching models. Examples are application of broad-based learning and psychodynamic principles, use of social interaction and modeling, rapport building to reduce anxiety and increase positive involvement, and so forth. When underlying factors appear resistant to treatment, interveners teach individuals ways to compensate for their problems. And although the primary overall concern is with underlying factors, intervention rationales may also designate provision of support for ongoing growth and learning.

In contrast, interveners adopting an *observable factors orientation* see no value in assumptions about underlying factors (see Table 8.1). Instead, individuals with problems are seen as not yet having learned necessary skills or as having acquired interfering behaviors.

The conceptual roots of the observable factors orientation are in behaviorism (operant and cognitive behavior modification). Proponents of this approach assess knowledge and skills directly associated with daily life tasks. Performance below prevailing standards for an individual's level of development is seen as indicating missing capabilities. Behavioral objectives are formulated to teach these missing capabilities and to address any interfering behaviors. Direct intervention approaches are stressed, such as eliciting and reinforcing specific responses and instruction in cognitive self-direction and monitoring. That is, corrective strategies emphasize direct and systematic teaching and behavior management drawing on behavior change principles.

In approaching reluctant clientele, adherents of both orientations must contend with motivational and behavior problems that interfere with intervention. (Such clients often are inattentive and argumentative.) As would be anticipated, practitioners generally approach these problems in ways that are consistent with their orientation. Some interveners who think in terms of underlying factors, however, do indicate that they use direct behavior change strategies, at times, to control interfering behavior.

Because neither orientation is sufficiently effective over the long run, proponents in each camp have looked to contemporary cognitive concepts and methods in evolving their approaches. Essentially, they have incorporated instruction of efficient strategies for planning, self-direction, remembering, self-monitoring, problem solving, and so forth. Currently, *metacognitive strategies* are widely used in both camps. Proponents of the two prevailing orientations adapt such strategies to fit in with their own views. That is, those with an underlying factors orientation view metacognitive strategies as an underlying ability or as a way for an individual to compensate for an area of dysfunction. Advocates of observable factors see metacognitive strategies as another set of skills clients should acquire through direct instruction.

Examples of efforts to integrate the above contrasting orientations are found in the literature on psychotherapy integration. However, as reviewers have noted, these efforts have generated more discussion than systematic theorizing and research.[6]

Models of Teaching

Despite the long history of formal schooling, no comprehensive and widely accepted theory of instruction exists. Many efforts have been made to weave ideas about learning and teaching into conceptual frameworks and models. A landmark piece of work appeared in 1966 when Jerome Bruner published *Toward a Theory of Instruction*. Since then, interest in the development of such a theory has increased, but the problems related to understanding learning make the task exceedingly difficult.[7]

With respect to actual approaches to classroom instruction, Joyce and Weil group twenty separate (but not mutually exclusive) teaching approaches or "models" into four contrasting "families." They agree with Dewey that, at its core, the process of teaching involves the arrangement or creation of environments with which the learner is to interact. This idea is elaborated as follows: "A model of teaching is a plan or pattern that we can use to design face-to-face teaching in classrooms or tutorial settings and to shape instructional materials—including books, films, tapes, and computer-mediated programs and curriculums (long-term courses of study). Each model guides us as we design instruction to help students achieve various outcomes."[8] Thus, the approaches adopted as part of an intervention rationale say a great deal about what is intended to happen in a teaching situation and what kinds of life-views are likely to emerge.

Teaching methods are clustered into "families" by Joyce and Weil based on whether an approach emphasizes (1) behavioral systems, (2) information processing, (3) personal functioning, or (4) social functioning. In terms of the contrasting orientations discussed above, behavioral systems approaches reflect an observable factors orientation. Information-processing approaches also have roots in this orientation but are amplified by views about metacognitive strategies. Personal and social approaches address underlying factors. A brief abstract of Joyce and Weil's description of each model follows.

Behavioral systems approaches stress processes by which human behavior is shaped and reinforced. Their roots are in behavior modification, behavior therapy, cybernetics, and social learning theory. They reflect a view of human beings as self-correcting communication systems who modify behavior in reaction to feedback. Thus, the emphasis is on organizing clearly defined tasks and methods for communicating feedback to make it easier for individual self-correction to take place. The intent is to change visible behavior rather than underlying psychological structure. Among the specific behaviors addressed are basic academics, social and athletic skills, and relaxation to cope with anxiety. Common to behavioral models are strategies to turn learning tasks into a series of small, sequenced behaviors. Most rely on teacher control, but a few are based on the premise of self-directed learning. Four models are included in this group: (1) mastery learning, direct instruction, and social learning theory, (2) learning self-control, (3) training for skill and concept development, and (4) assertiveness training.

Information processing approaches are designed to enhance capacities for acquiring and organizing data, sensing problems and generating solutions, and developing concepts and language to convey them. The approaches vary in emphasis: some provide information and concepts; others stress concept formation and hypothesis testing; a few focus on creative thinking; and a few others are meant to enhance general intellectual ability. All intend to help individuals improve capabilities for acquiring and using information and thinking effectively. Many may be useful in studying self and society in order to foster the personal and social goals of education. Seven models are grouped under this category: (1) concept attainment, (2) inductive thinking, (3) inquiry training, (4) advance organizers, (5) memorization, (6) the developing intellect, and (7) scientific inquiry.

Approaches to *personal* functioning are oriented to the individual's capacity to become an integrated personality. They stress learning to understand oneself (for example, how one constructs and organizes unique reality); and they encourage individuals to learn how to take responsibility for their own learning. They also encourage reaching for high-quality lives through self-understanding, continuing growth, self-esteem, sensitivity, creativity, and productive relationships with their environments. Personal approaches pay great attention to individual perspectives and encourage productive independence in order to increase self-awareness and responsibility. At the same time, the intent is to produce positive interpersonal relationships and more effective information-processing capabilities. Four models are included in this group: (1) nondirective teaching, (2) synectics, (3) awareness training, and (4) the various forms of classroom meetings.

Social approaches are oriented to people working together and generating collective energy or synergy. The emphasis is on cooperative study (working together on tasks, joint rewards) to enhance learning about and relating to others as individuals, groups, and members of society. Processes are used by which reality is socially negotiated. Along with social relations, there is concern for cognitive development in areas such as information acquisition and concept formation, and for personal growth. Five models are grouped in this category: (1) group investigation (emphasizing democratic processes as a source), (2) role playing (studying social behavior and values), (3) jurisprudential inquiry (clarifying public issues), (4) laboratory training (T-group model), and (5) social science inquiry.

ECLECTICISM: THE ONGOING SEARCH FOR BETTER PRACTICES

Which orientation or approach is best? Currently, no one model is viewed as superior for all purposes or as the best way to achieve a given objective. Increasingly, when asked their orientation, professionals in psychology and education seem to answer "I am eclectic." ("I use whatever works.") With respect to models of teaching, for example, Joyce and Weil advocate matching approaches to different goals and adapting them to a student's styles and characteristics. In their words, effective teachers "need to master a range of models and prepare for a career-long process of adding new tools and polishing and expanding their old ones. . . . combinations of models can have a more dramatic effect on learning than any one could have alone."[9]

In discussing approaches to psychotherapy and behavior change,

Garfield and Bergin stress: "The fact that a large number of psychotherapists have chosen an eclectic approach . . . is a finding of some significance. We believe it indicates a certain dissatisfaction with following or limiting oneself to a particular orientation."[10]

Eclecticism can be very healthy. Certainly, given that mucking around in the lives of others is not a benign process, blind dogmatism is contraindicated—especially in psychology and education, where there is so much to learn. But an eclectic rationale is acceptable only if it is not naive.

Naive eclecticism stems from a tendency among some practitioners simply to keep their eyes open for every new idea that pops up. If it appeals to them, they adopt it with little concern for whether it is valid or consistent with other practices they use. This casual and undiscriminating approach probably stimulates fads and certainly contributes to the negative image of eclecticism.

A more acceptable rationale is built on what we call *applied eclecticism*. That is, after years of applied work, some interveners find that certain practices don't work and should be avoided and that other procedures are useful in select situations under specific conditions. Thus, over the years, they develop a repertoire of approaches and a rationale for their use.

Scholarly eclecticism represents an even higher level. Rationales formulated through this process incorporate systematic theoretical and philosophical analyses, related empirical activity, legislation, and judicial decisions. What emerges is a comprehensive and integrated set of procedures that undergoes continuous modification in a never-ending and endlessly controversial search for better ways.

An example of efforts to move toward scholarly eclecticism is seen in applications of *systems design* to intervention. As discussed by Banathy, systems design views intervention as encompassing ideas that are "interconnected, interdependent, interacting, AND internally consistent." In essence, the approach is holistic; that is, the essential quality of each part is viewed as residing in its relationship to the whole. The emphasis on holism underscores the fundamental importance of coordination and integration in designing interventions. With reference to a social system such as education, Banathy suggests that the design must stem from perspectives of (1) the system itself, (2) its component parts, and (3) its environment. He states, "The system should serve the purpose for which it was designed, it should serve the purpose(s) of people in the system—the learners in our case—and it should serve the purpose of the environment, the larger societal system that created the system."[11]

Applying systems theory to clinical and community psychology, Sundberg, Taplin, and Tyler view system change as underlying all intervention. They stress that "to adopt a systems perspective means to abandon assumptions that a single cause produces a single effect. The question always is: How will this change in one component of the system affect the functioning of all the others?" As an aid for designing intervention, key subsystems of individuals, families, and organizations are delineated as mechanisms associated with (1) decision making (about purposes, priorities, problem solving); (2) boundaries; (3) the functions of perception and feedback; (4) input, central processes, and output; (5) memory (e.g., institutional); (6) formal and informal structures; and (7) linkages to other subsystems and systems.[12]

Whether eclectic or not, as a matter of principle practitioners intend to give the best quality of intervention possible. This involves careful consideration of both means and ends (intended and unintended). Few would argue that any means to a desired end is justified.

Optimal means are congruent (e.g., ethically, theoretically, legally) with desired ends. Optimal means also minimize undesired ends. (As our definition stresses, intervention efforts produce unintended outcomes—sometimes as a by-product of planned processes and sometimes because unplanned processes occur. Indeed, undesired outcomes may outweigh positive ones. And, paradoxically, some means are antithetical to desired ends at least initially; an example is seen in processes that increase client dependency.)

The search for optimal means to desired ends goes on. Perhaps most basic to success in this search is understanding the psychology of clients with specific regard to creating a good person-intervention match. Also enmeshed in this "problem of the match" are numerous ethical considerations—some of which are especially relevant in thinking about the contractual bases for intervention. A conceptual appreciation of these matters provides an essential foundation for improving intervention rationales; therefore, we touch upon each before concluding our discussion of the underlying rationale problem.

NOTES

1. Lack of collaboration is well documented by those calling for corrective policy changes.   See H.L. Hodgkinson (1989). *The same client: The demographics of education and service delivery systems*. Washington, DC: Institute for Educational Leadership, Inc./Center for Demographic Policy. S.L. Kagan, A.M. Rivera, & F.L. Parker (1990). *Collaborations in action: Reshaping services for young children and their families*. New Haven, CT: Yale University, Bush Center on Child Development and Social Policy. W.A. Anthony, M. Cohen, & W. Kennard (1990). Understanding the current facts and principles of mental health systems planning. *American Psychologist, 45*, 1249-1252.   Also see the analysis by the Center for the Future of Children Staff (1992) in *The Future of Children, 2*, 6–18.

2.   M. Buchman & R.E. Floden (1992). Coherence, the rebel angel. *Educational Researcher, 21*, 4–9 (p. 4).

3.   H.S. Adelman (1989). Prediction and prevention of learning disabilities: Current state of the art and future directions. In L. Bond & B. Compas (Eds.), *Primary prevention in the schools*. Newbury Park, CA: Sage, (pp.106–45).   Kagan, Rivera, & Parker, *Collaborations in action*.   Center for the Future of Children Staff, *The Future of Children*.   Hodgkinson, *The same client*.

4.   On deinstitutionalization and the principle of normalization, see N.E. Bank-Mikkelsen (1976). Administrative normalizing. *S.A.-Nyt, 14*, 3–6 and W. Wolfensberger (1972). *The principle of normalization in human services*. Toronto: National Institute on Mental Retardation.

Discussions of mainstreaming and the least restrictive environment are found throughout the literature on special education.   The controversial nature of these topics is seen in the policy debate in the United States about what is called the Regular Education Initiative (REI) or General Education Initiative (GEI).   For a flavor of the debate, see S. Stainback & W. Stainback (1984). A rationale for the merger of special and regular education. *Exceptional Children, 51*, 102–11 and J.M. Kauffman (1989). The Regular Education Initiative as Reagan-Bush education policy: A trickle-down theory of education of the hard-to-teach. *Journal of Special Education, 23*, 256–77.

5.   Dichotomous distinctions among treatment approaches in clinical psychology usually contrast methods in terms of their emphasis on psychotherapy or behavior change strategies.   See S.L. Garfield & A.E. Bergin (Eds.) (1986). *Handbook of psychotherapy and behavior change* (3rd ed.).

New York: Wiley, and M.R. Goldfried, L.S. Greenberg, & C. Marmar (1990). Individual psychotherapy: Process and outcome. *Annual Review of Psychology, 41*, 659–88.

In special education, remedial strategies can be contrasted in terms of approaches focused on underlying abilities as contrasted with direct instruction. See H.S. Adelman & L. Taylor (1993). *Learning problems and learning disabilities: Moving forward.* Pacific Grove, CA: Brooks/Cole.

In each case, the essence of the distinction is rooted in long-standing debates between those who think in terms of internal disorders (assume that many problems in human functioning are symptomatic of internal biological or psychological disorders) and radical behaviorists who see no reason to deal with internal constructs. It should be stressed that nonradical behaviorist practitioners tend to acknowledge the possibility of internal disorders; they just don't think it changes what has to be done to treat a problem. See A.O. Ross (1985). To form a more perfect union. *Behavior Therapy, 16*, 195-204, and P.M.G. Emmelkamp (1986). Behavior therapy with adults. In S.L. Garfield & A.E. Bergin (Eds.) (1986), *Handbook of psychotherapy and behavior change* (3rd ed.). New York: Wiley.

6. B.E. Wolfe & M.R. Goldfried (1988). Research on psychotherapy integration: Recommendations and conclusion from an NIMH workshop. *Journal of Consulting and Clinical Psychology, 56*, 448-51.

7. As Patterson has indicated, foundations for a theory of instruction were laid not only by Jerome Bruner but also by Maria Montessori, Jean Piaget, B.F. Skinner, and Carl Rogers (among others). See C.H. Patterson (1977). *Foundations for a theory of instruction and educational psychology.* New York: Harper & Row.

Robert Gagné's work exemplifies contemporary theoretical efforts. He attempts to weave ideas about essential conditions for learning into a theory of instruction. Using an information-processing model, he conceives of learning as encompassing a set of nine processes: reception, expectancy, retrieval to working memory, selective perception, semantic encoding, responding, reinforcement, retrieval and reinforcement, and retrieval and generalization. To illustrate, he states:

> previously learned material in long-term memory is continually being retrieved to the working memory and to consciousness. There it may be rehearsed, not only in the sense of being repeated, but also *re-encoded* before being again returned to long-term memory. The process of encoding as it occurs in the working memory is continually influenced by inputs whose origins are external to the learner. These inputs have been processed initially by the sensory registers and by the kind of transformation we call selective perception. (P. 243)

Instruction is seen by Gagné as the intentional arrangement of events in a learner's environment for purposes of making learning happen. To do this effectively requires arranging events that provide support to the internal processes of learning. His theory of instruction attempts to relate how the external events affect internal learning processes, resulting in learning outcomes. In the work, he specifies three major themes for his theory of instruction: (1) Learning is conceived as the set of nine internal processes specified above. These transform environmental stimuli into forms of information that progressively establish long-term memory states (i.e., learning outcomes) which, in turn, provide various performance capabilities. (2) Performance capabilities are practically oriented or theoretically based and are grouped into five categories: intellectual skills, cognitive strategies, verbal information, attitudes, and motor skills. "These categories of human capability underlie distinctively different classes of human performance, which means that the effectiveness of the learning which produced them can be differentially assessed." (3) The specific operations involved in the events of instruction are different for each of the five categories of learning outcomes (p. 245).

He also conceives a sequence of nine instructional events to correspond to his formulation of nine internal learning processes. These events, related examples, and corresponding learning processes are:

1. gaining attention (e.g., use of abrupt stimulus change) → reception
2. informing learners of the objective (e.g., telling learners) → expectancy
3. stimulating recall of prior learning (e.g., asking for recall) → retrieval to working memory
4. presenting the stimulus (e.g., displaying the content with distinctive features) → selective perception
5. providing "learning guidance" (e.g., suggesting a meaningful organization) → semantic encoding
6. eliciting performance (e.g., asking learner to perform) → responding
7. providing feedback (e.g., giving informative feedback) → reinforcement
8. assessing performance (e.g., requiring additional learner performance, with feedback) → retrieval and reinforcement
9. enhancing retention and transfer (e.g., providing varied practice and spaced reviews) → retrieval and generalization.

Gagné stresses that his theory states that optimal learning will occur if each instructional event takes the form research shows is most effective (i.e., the form shown to provide the greatest support for the internal learning processes). Moreover, the optimal form for some events—particularly 3, 4, 5, and 9—is viewed as differing for each of the five categories of learning outcomes (i.e., intellectual skills, cognitive strategies, verbal information, attitudes, and motor skills). He also stresses that with older, experienced, learners not all nine instructional events are necessary because self-instruction comes into the picture once they learn how to learn (i.e., acquire learning strategies). Finally, Gagné notes three major assumptions underlying his theory, namely, that (1) the learner spends the necessary time on a task, (2) the learner is motivated to learn, and (3) instructional events take into account individual differences in the learner's prior knowledge and "discourse comprehension" (e.g., ability to comprehend the stimuli presented). R.M. Gagné (1985). *The conditions of learning and theory of instruction* (4th ed). Fort Worth, TX: Holt, Rinehart & Winston.

8. B. Joyce & M. Weil (1986). *Models of teaching* (3rd ed.). Englewood Cliffs, NJ: Prentice-Hall, p. 3.

9. In the introduction to the 1980 edition of their book, Joyce and Weil made a similar point in a somewhat broader context:

Competence in teaching stems from the capacity to reach out to different children and to create a rich and multidimensional environment for them. Curriculum planners need to design learning centers and curricula that offer children a variety of educational alternatives. . . . The existing models of teaching are one basis for the repertoire of alternative approaches that teachers, curriculum makers, and designers of materials can use to help diverse learners reach a variety of goals. . . . We believe the world of education should be a pluralistic one—that children and adults alike should have a "cafeteria of alternatives" to stimulate their growth and nurture both their unique potential and their capacity to make common cause in the rejuvenation of our troubled society. (PP. xxiii-xxiv)

10. S.L. Garfield & A.E. Bergin (Eds.) (1986). *Handbook of psychotherapy and behavior change* (3rd ed.). New York: Wiley, p. 8. These authors provide a brief history of the move toward eclecticism related to psychotherapy and behavior change approaches. Available data suggest that 30–40 percent of psychotherapists in the United States identify themselves as eclectic.

11. B.H. Banathy (1991). *Systems design of education: A journey to create the future.* Englewood Cliffs, NJ: Educational Technology Publications, p. 60. In his articulation of core values and ideas for guiding the design of education systems, Banathy also illustrates one effort to delineate these components of an underlying rationale (see pp. 81–82, 102–03).

12. N.D. Sundberg, J.R. Taplin, & L.E. Tyler (1983). *Introduction to clinical psychology: Perspectives, issues, and contributions to human service.* Englewood Cliffs, NJ: Prentice-Hall, p. 32.

9

The Psychology of Clients and
the Problem of the Match

To help others ... you have to know what they need, and the only way to find out what they need is for them to tell you. And they won't tell you unless they think you will listen ... carefully. And the way to convince them that you will listen carefully is to listen carefully.

David Nyberg[1]

This is not the place to explore all facets of the psychology of clients. Our purpose here is to underscore the importance of the topic as related to creating a good client-intervention match.

What is a good match?[2] Interveners commonly talk about starting "where the client is." This maxim usually is meant to capture the idea that an intervener should establish just the right fit with the client's assimilated way of thinking or responding. However, when articulated in detail as part of an intervention rationale, significant differences emerge with respect to which client characteristics to match and how to approximate an optimal fit.

For instance, the focus may be on intervening in ways that match levels of *development*. Or the focus may be expanded to emphasize matching not only assimilated development but *motivational* factors as well. That is, clients vary not only in their capabilities, but in their approach and avoidance tendencies toward immediate and long-range ends and toward the means by which these are achieved. Thus, the expanded focus requires also matching client attitudes about intended outcomes, processes, and content.

In general, the search for better practices is usefully understood in terms of the concept of the match. Stated in the negative, the poorer the match, the less likely it is that an intervention will lead to outcomes desired by the interested parties. Concern about quality of the match arises at the outset of an intervention and remains throughout.

The problem of the match is viewed broadly as that of creating an appropriate challenge to the *assimilated capabilities and attitudes* and *current states of being* of clients. From an intervention perspective, addressing this problem is the primary function of the intervener. Within limits that usually are unknown, some degree of positive match is always feasible—assuming availability and sound use of appropriate resources. (Note: Resources include intervener assimilated capabilities and attitudes and current states of being.)

The concept of the match can be operationalized using observer or actor viewpoints. For example, the psychological perspective of the intervener may be the sole referent in deciding which client characteristics are considered, which processes are prescribed, and whether a "good" or "appropriate" match is established. In contrast, some interveners work with the psychology of the client and include client perspectives in deciding how to proceed and judging goodness of fit.

The following discussion further clarifies the importance of and the problems associated with creating a good fit. Specifically, we explore the need to account for both motivation and development, and to monitor the client-intervention match continuously.

MATCHING MOTIVATION AND DEVELOPMENT

Whenever we discuss motivation as related to intervention, we are reminded of an old joke:

"How many psychologists does it take to change a light bulb?"
"Only one. But the bulb has to want to change."

The quip has the ring of truth to it. A frequent intervener lament is that some systems (individuals, groups, organizations) aren't motivated to improve their capabilities and overcome problems. At the same time, professionals, family members, friends, and administrators often are advised to motivate and, if necessary, demand better functioning. However, despite general agreement that motivation should be addressed, it often isn't, and when it is, major disagreements arise over how to do it.

Substantial reason exists for addressing individual differences in motivation. Cognitive-affective theories can be interpreted as stressing four broad considerations for designing interventions. First, motivation is a key antecedent condition—a prerequisite to functioning. Poor motivational readiness may be (a) a cause of inadequate and problem functioning, (b) a factor maintaining such problems, or (c) both. Thus, strategies are called for that can result in a high level of motivational readiness (including reduction of avoidance motivation), so that a client is mobilized to participate.

Second, motivation is a key ongoing process concern; processes must elicit, enhance, and maintain motivation, so that the client stays mobilized. For instance, a client may value a certain outcome but may not be motivated to pursue certain processes for obtaining it, and many clients are motivated at the beginning of an intervention but do not maintain that motivation.

Third, it is necessary to avoid or at least minimize conditions likely to produce avoidance reactions. Of particular concern are activities clients perceive as unchallenging/uninteresting, overdemanding, or overwhelming, and a structure that seriously limits a client's range of options or that is overcontrolling and coercive. Examples of conditions that can have a negative impact on client motivation are sparse resources, excessive rules, and a restrictive day-in, day-out emphasis on solving problems.

A client motivated to improve in a particular area of functioning may continue to have negative attitudes about the area and thus use newly acquired knowledge and skills only under duress. Thus, intrinsic motivation becomes a fourth key outcome concern. Responding to this concern requires strategies to enhance stable, positive intrinsic attitudes that mobilize clients ongoing pursuit of desired ends outside the intervention context and after the intervention is terminated.[3] With respect to the psychology of clients, then, motivation is a prime consideration in creating an optimal client-intervention match.

Addressing motivation, however, is difficult without simultaneously matching a client's level of development. System variations in development are manifested as functional differences. Functional differences are accommodated through intervention strategies that match current capacities in each area of development. This means accounting for areas in which development is lagging and those in which development meets or surpasses expectations.

In general, although discussion of specific areas of development is useful, the overall pattern is considered in designing interventions to fit a client. And the observed pattern reflects both accumulated capacities and attitudes.

Psychologists and educators interested in patterns of differences in functioning find it useful for observation and measurement purposes to stress four key performance dimensions: (1) rate—the pace of performance, (2) style—preferences with regard to ways of proceeding, (3) amount—the quantity of produced outcomes, and (4) quality—care, mastery, and aesthetic features demonstrated in performance. As suggested above, rate, style, amount, and quality of performance on a given task and in a given situation not only reflect levels of competence but also are influenced by levels of motivation to perform. Therefore, when previous experiences make a client relatively unmotivated to perform in any area of development, direct measures of these dimensions are of little use in planning how best to fit a client's capabilities.

HOW GOOD IS THE MATCH?

Efforts to create a good match require continuous monitoring. In formulating an underlying rationale, such monitoring can be conceived as a process of evaluation used to identify and modify factors causing a poor match.

Although different fields of intervention use different terms, similar views of evaluation prevail. In medicine and mental health, the nomenclature most commonly used is quality assurance or quality improvement. In education, the term *accountability* is used widely. Essentially, the stated intent in all cases is to accomplish quality control—and by implication to establish and maintain a good client-intervention match.[4]

To these ends, some version of *formative* evaluation is carried out, and findings are used to modify interventions to improve the match. Ideally, the process starts with (1) a definition of an intervention's long-range aims and immediate objectives and (2) clarification of procedures. This is followed by a cycle involving (3) evaluation of what happens, (4) implementation of corrective measures when appropriate, and (5) reevaluation—then back to corrective measures if necessary.

As the above process underscores, improving the match involves more than assessing *outcomes*. Such evaluation also must assess relevant client and intervention *antecedents* (sometimes called inputs or structural conditions) and client-intervention *transactions*. Indeed, decisions about which antecedents and transactions to assess profoundly shape pre- and ongoing intervention planning. For this reason, every intervention rationale must articulate decisions about which to assess.

To elaborate on these points: Prior to implementing any intervention, antecedents must be assessed with a view to modifying normatively planned strategies to fit existing circumstances. Client variations, such as the number of clients and the nature and scope of each client's needs, constitute one significant set of antecedents potentially capable of causing a poor match.   Other critical antecedents are the available material (financial, physical) and human resources and how they are organized and used to accomplish desired ends. Such antecedent conditions determine what can and cannot be done, and how processes are carried out. Ultimately they shape intervention efficacy.

With respect to analyses of transactions, the emphasis is on how resources are actually used and what transpires between involved parties.   This encompasses the ways in which interventions are organized and implemented; also involved are questions about resource utilization, such as whether processes are appropriately used. (Is the system functioning as desired by specified interested parties?   Which resources are needed at this time?   Are the appropriate type and amount of intervention in use?)   The nature and scope of the problem of the match is well illustrated by the range of transactions associated with mental health and special education programs.   In such programs, analyses of intervention organization include concern for staff supervision and support as well as program policies and planning. Analyses of implementation cover procedures used to identify and diagnose problems; receive and make referrals; coordinate and integrate services; maintain records; plan interventions; case manage; consult with others; evaluate progress and immediate and long-term outcomes; respond to legal mandates related to confidentiality and reporting; bill clients; and monitor processes. In monitoring processes, the concern is for both what is and isn't done. More specifically, analyses are made of whether what occurs (and doesn't occur) is consistent with antecedent conditions and intended processes.

Of course, in evaluating the quality of the match, the ultimate referents are outcomes. In the short run, the question is, How well are immediate objectives met? An equally important concern is the nature and scope of unintended negative outcomes. In the long run, the questions are, How much did the client benefit from the intervention? Did the benefits outweigh the psychological, financial, and other costs? (For example, Were desired aims accomplished at a reasonable cost? Was a client's problem ameliorated? Was quality of life improved?)

Whether considering antecedents, transactions, or outcomes, different judgments about the quality of the match may be made by different interested parties. Given the politics of decision making, the concern arises as to whose judgments should prevail: the client's? the intervener's? the society's?

Society, particularly through the accountability demands of intervention underwriters, inevitably makes its judgments felt. Indeed, increasing pressures for accountability are reshaping intervention rationales in ways that often inappropriately give precedence to outcome evaluation. And, as major stakeholders, professionals and their guilds are significant political forces shaping evaluation policies and processes.

Clearly, the judgments of society and interveners cannot be disregarded. Our intent here, however, has been to underscore the central role of client judgments. Cognizance of the psychology of clients and the problem of the match makes it evident that client judgments also cannot be ignored. Client perceptions profoundly shape how procedures are aligned with relevant antecedent characteristics and ultimately how well they produce desired ends. Even when society and interveners take the position that client evaluation of outcomes is a minor consideration, client expectations and values are an essential link to intended outcomes. Consequently, a sound intervention rationale must reflect an appreciation of how to account for such perceptions.

NOTES

1. D. Nyberg (1971). *Tough and tender learning*. Palo Alto, CA: National Press Books. In keeping with the nonsexist intent of the original source, this quote is translated from the singular "he" to the plural "they" (p. 181).

2. Although different terms are used, the concept of the match is found throughout the theoretical writings of leading thinkers who have influenced intervention. For example, the concept permeates the work of Piaget, Bruner, and Vygotsky as applied in psychology and education.

3. Again, we stress the importance of the growing literature discussing cognitive-affective theories of motivation. For example, see E.L. Deci & R.M. Ryan (1985). *Intrinsic motivation and self-determination in human behavior*. New York: Plenum Press.

4. Discussions of quality control and assurance often have a managerial flavor, emphasizing assessment of program staff (e.g., availability, qualifications, assigned functions, and conception of program goals), operating budget, space, equipment, and so forth. A recent trend is toward adopting the term *quality improvement* and emphasizing a client orientation. In this context, the concepts of quality control and quality assurance are expanded to include a focus on (1) appropriateness (providing what's actually needed), (2) equity (ensuring fairness in access), (3) accessibility (minimizing barriers to access), (4) effectiveness (achieving intended benefits), (5) acceptability (meeting the reasonable expectations of clients, providers, and the community), and (6) efficiency (minimizing waste). See the following works for a basic overview of these topics: A. Donabedian (1982). *The criteria and standards of quality*. Ann Arbor, MI: Health Administration Press. R.H. Palmer, A. Donabedian, & G.J. Povar (1991). *Striving for quality in health care: An inquiry into policy and practice*. Ann Arbor, MI: Health Administration Press. G. Stricker & A.R. Rodriquez (Eds.) (1988). *Handbook of quality assurance in mental health*. New York: Plenum Press.

10

Ethical Considerations

The two besetting sins in our prevailing habits of ethical thinking are our ready acquiescence in unclarity and our complacence in ignorance.

William Frankena[1]

Commitment to specific social and moral philosophical positions plays a central role in decisions to intervene and in creating a good person-intervention match. Thus, such positions represent another essential component of underlying rationales.

We have already covered some pertinent social philosophical concerns. In this chapter, we discuss specific ethical considerations. A wide range of topics could be reviewed in relation to intervention rights and responsibilities, such as the ethics of coercion, bases for privacy and confidentiality, obligations to minimize negative consequences, rights to information, and so forth. Our choice here is to highlight ethical considerations about (1) cost versus benefits, (2) fairness, and (3) informed consent; these topics are discussed because of their fundamental role in thinking about the contractual bases for psychological and educational intervention.[2]

COSTS VS. BENEFITS

Professional practices are designed to provide benefits. However, such benefits usually are acquired at a cost—in several senses of the term. That is, every intervention may have negative consequences stemming from mistakes, invasions of privacy, overdependency on interveners, and so forth. Negative effects encompass a wide range of material, psychological, and social costs, such as wasted financial resources, system disruption, reduced sense of self, and reduced social mobility.

Negative effects alone, of course, do not contraindicate use of a practice. Many medications, for example, have side effects, but as long as a drug is viewed as more helpful than harmful and clients are aware of the negative effects, most practitioners conclude that its use is ethical.

How does one know that a practice is more helpful than harmful, however? Often, data on effectiveness and negative effects are sparse. This makes it extremely difficult to specify benefits and costs, let alone determine net gains or losses. In psychology and education, for instance, reviewers find the validity of reported intervention studies to be limited and frequently inconsistent. Claims of positive benefits in such cases are more hope than fact. At the same time, because more than financial considerations are involved, intervention costs also are not readily quantified. Thus, decisions about the relative balance between costs and benefits usually involve weighing potential—but unproved—positive and negative effects.

In trying to correct person problems, for example, decisions to place an individual in a special treatment program or to prescribe medication often must rely on expert opinion in answering basic questions such as, Is the appropriate focus for intervention the person? Will the treatment correct the problem? If so, will the benefits justify the financial expense, discomfort, stigmatization, and other potential negative effects the person may experience upon being labelled and treated as different from others? Comparable questions arise when interventions are designed to restructure organizations such as schools and service agencies.

The complexity of cost-benefit analyses is compounded by the realization that one must go beyond consideration of outcomes for a particular person or organization. Persons from subgroups whose background differs from the dominant culture provide a case in point. Such persons sometimes are classified and treated as deficient primarily because their values and norms, and thus their actions and performance, are different from those of the dominant culture. However unintentional, the labelling and treatment collude with biased attitudes and discriminatory actions against certain subgroups. Court cases dealing with IQ testing in minority populations reflect the concern about such negative effects for subgroups in the society. Some litigants argue that minority populations are inappropriately served by most IQ tests and labelling. Court decisions stress that intelligence testing should be "culture fair," including use of the individual's "home language," and that tests alone should not be the basis for classifying individuals. The courts have even restricted the use of tests because of the costs to persons from minority backgrounds. These cases highlight that a practice's benefits for an individual may be outweighed by its costs to specific subgroups in the society. Of particular concern are interventions that perpetuate racial injustice in the form of additional discrimination, stigmatization, and restriction of educational and socioeconomic opportunities. Given that harmful effects go beyond specific clients, cost-benefits for subgroups and multiple systems also must be weighed.

A broader ethical perspective warns that modern societies are manifesting an ever increasing, distressing, and unnecessary overdependence on professional services. Some writers suggest that the negative effects of this overreliance on professionals are widespread mystification of the public and a general loss of people's ability to cope with their own affairs. These effects are illustrated by the unquestioning acceptance by large numbers of people of diagnoses and related special interventions. For example, with respect to psychological and educational problems, we see widespread uncritical use of labels such as *emotional disturbance* and *learning disabilities* followed by application of unwarranted treatments. Illich calls this state of affairs "cultural iatrogenesis." He argues that professionals must judge the ethics of their activities not only in terms of consequences for specific clients, subgroups, and multiple systems but also with regard to impact on the entire culture.[3] This position, of course, further compounds the complexity of determining whether costs outweigh benefits.

Every intervention rationale reflects conclusions that the benefits of chosen processes and intended outcomes outweigh costs. Ethically, clients are entitled to understand the basis for such conclusions. At the same time, even when benefits seem to outweigh costs, decisions to intervene must not overemphasize this "utility" principle. Consideration must also be given to fairness (equity and justice).

FAIRNESS

Legal emphasis on "right to treatment" and "right of all to an education" highlights the moral obligation to ensure fair allocation of society's resources. Given inadequate budgets to underwrite needed programs, many compete for the same resources. Schools vie with social programs. Enrichment interventions compete with treatment programs. Questions arise such as, Is it fair to help those who have psychological or educational problems by drawing from the limited resources available for regular educational programs? And beyond fair resource allocation, the general expectation is that interventions will be carried out in just and fair ways.

In addressing questions about fairness, a basic problem arises: How do we decide what is fair? Work on this problem requires dealing with such questions as fair for whom? fair according to whom? fair using what criteria and what procedures for applying the criteria? Should everyone be given an equal share of available resources? Should each be provided for according to specific need? Should resources be distributed on the basis that a client has earned them (e.g., societal contribution) or has been denied them previously (e.g., through discrimination)?

Obviously, what is fair for the society or an organization may not be fair for an individual; what is fair for one person may cause inequity for another. To provide special services for one group may deprive another or may raise the taxes of all citizens. To deny services to those who need help is harmful.

Making fair decisions about who should get what and about how rules should be applied requires use of principles of distributive justice. As Beauchamp and Childress underscore, interveners incorporate different principles of distributive justice into their rationales based on whether they subscribe to (1) *egalitarian* theories (emphasizing equal access to the goods in life that every rational person desires), (2) *Marxist* theories (emphasizing need), (3) *libertarian* theories (emphasizing contribution and merit), or (4) *utilitarian* theories (which emphasize a mixed use of such criteria in order to maximize public and private utility).[4]

Clearly, interventions based on rationales adopting different views of distributive justice conflict with each other. In addition, confusion may arise when an intervention rationale incorporates more than one fairness principle.

Decisions based on fairness principles often call for unequal allocation and affirmative action with regard to who gets the resources and how rules are applied. Thus, although justice and fairness are intended, such decisions can be quite controversial, especially when resources are scarce.

Practitioners who see themselves as "helping professionals" lean toward an emphasis on individual need. For instance, they tend to believe that fairness means that those with problems deserve special aid. Indeed, the duty to serve those in need is seen as an ethical reason for diagnostic labelling and other highly intrusive specialized practices.

At the same time, conflicting views exist as to which of many ongoing needs in a society should be assigned highest priority. Are prevention programs more important than treatment programs? Are programs for the gifted more important than programs for students with emotional and learning problems? Should school athletic teams be funded at higher levels than vocational programs? And, beyond resource allocation, interveners consistently are confronted with the problem of fair implementation, especially with regard to applying rules and consequences for infractions. For example, should different consequences be applied for the same offense when those involved differ in terms of needs, problems, stage of development, previous discrimination, potential contribution to society, and so forth?

Some persons try to simplify matters by not making distinctions and treating everyone and every situation alike. (It was said of Coach Vince Lombardi that he treated all his players the same—like dogs!) For instance, professionals working with specific organization or person problems often insist on enforcing rules without regard to the particulars of the case. This approach is seen whenever standard consequences are applied without accounting for an individual's social and emotional problems. In doing so, the position usually is taken that it is unfair to others if the same rule is not applied in the same way to everyone. Unfortunately, while a "no exceptions" approach represents a simple solution, it ignores the possibility that nonpersonalized rule enforcement exacerbates problems not only for the rule breaker but for society, which is unjust.

No underlying rationale and thus no intervention contract can ignore concerns about fairness. In particular, decisions must be made about what constitutes fair allocation of resources, fair rules, and fair rule enforcement. And these decisions require clarity about which principle of distributive justice is used.

CONSENT

Societies that value fairness and personal liberty have a strong commitment to ensuring personal autonomy for everyone. In such societies, consent is a key concept.

The idea that autonomy should be respected has made consent not only a legal but also a major moral concern. The legal and moral mechanism for maintaining autonomy usually is designated "informed consent." Six major functions served by the consent mechanism are the promotion of individual autonomy; the protection of clients or subjects; the avoidance of fraud and duress; the promotion of rational decisions; the encouragement of self-scrutiny by professionals; and the involvement of the public in promoting autonomy as a general social value and in controlling professional practices and research.[5] The desirability of such outcomes seems evident; how to ensure their attainment is less clear.

The problems and issues involved in appropriately eliciting consent have to do with such matters as when is consent needed? When is it justified to offer consent for another? Who decides when consent is needed and when a surrogate can represent another? What information must be given in eliciting consent? How can anyone be certain that consent is voluntarily given? Each question raises significant dilemmas in formulating intervention rationales and contracts.

There was a time not so long ago when practitioners in many professions believed that they knew who needed intervention and what intervention was needed. For them, the decision to intervene was relatively simple; the practitioner simply said what should be done and proceeded to do it. Growing awareness of rights and of potential harmful effects changed the contracting process in fundamental ways.[6] In psychology and education, for example, client involvement has become prominent in decisions about screening, diagnosis, and placement practices. For minors, advocates insist that parents or parent surrogates be involved in any decision that might have a profound effect on the course of a youngster's life.

Over the years, advocacy of client rights has made the concept of informed consent (including minor assent) the keystone in ensuring that client rights are protected. Thus, intervention rationales must incorporate an understanding of and commitment to the basic elements of informed consent, namely, understanding what one is consenting to and freedom from coercion. A brief exploration of each of these elements follows.

Understanding

Among the most basic ethical obligations of practitioners in any field are openness and honesty about the nature of their practices. Few would argue against the idea that the parties entering into a contract should understand the full implications of their agreement. At the same time, few would argue that this is possible or even feasible with respect to most psychological and educational interventions.

Informed consent calls for communicating basic information about the nature and scope of an intervention to clients. Such information includes clarifying purposes, processes, and potential risks, costs, and benefits, as well as providing data on existing alternatives and a clear statement that the client is not obligated to participate.[7] Offering information, of course, is insufficient; it must be communicated in a way that facilitates understanding, and the recipient must have the capacity to understand. This generally means making presentations in a variety of ways. Repeated verbal or written communications, translations, media presentations, question-and-answer follow-ups to evaluate whether information was understood, feedback from other consumers—all may be relevant at times.

Besides providing relevant information as part of specific informed consent procedures, ethical obligations for openness and honesty call for major efforts to avoid deceiving and mystifying others. At the most comprehensive level, this calls for proactive measures aimed at the general public designed to inform, to clarify, and to correct misinformation, that is, *public demystification*.

Widespread use of jargon and failure to clarify the limits, uncertainties, and controversial nature of many practices not only fail to inform but tend to deceive and mystify. Because of these conditions, the general public is quite confused about the nature of a great deal of intervention activity, especially in psychology and education. Indeed, most assessment, diagnostic, and treatment practices are quite a mystery. Even some professionals seem uncertain about what to call individuals who manifest certain behaviors and about how valid some procedures are. Failure to demystify the public probably accounts, in part, for many intervention fads and panaceas that continue to plague society.

Arguments against efforts to take time to explain matters to clients and the general public often stress that nonprofessionals lack the ability to understand professional practices or are not really interested. This argument loses some of its potency given that one of the most frequent formal complaints from clients and consumers is about practitioners who fail to explain the limitations and uncertainties of the procedures they use.

Even without the straightforward ethical matter of honesty, practices that mystify (such as the overselling of expertise) raise concerns because they may undermine the ability of systems to protect and care for themselves. In particular, such practices collude with tendencies toward overreliance on professionals. A large majority of our society believe, for instance, that they are incompetent to deal with problems in certain basic areas of personal and interpersonal functioning (including working relationships) without the services of a professional. This, of course, is good for the intervention business. But serious ethical concerns emerge about self-serving tendencies on the part of interveners and about negative consequences arising from professionals' failure to demystify their activity. In turn, such concerns raise questions about the adequacy of the information upon which intervention contracts are based.

Voluntariness

Information—given and received—is a necessary element of

informed consent, but it does not ensure voluntary consent. As Biklen says of the term: "Consent is a legal concept that has been referred to and implicitly defined in court cases and in legislation. It has three major aspects: *capacity, information,* and *voluntariness*. All three elements are equally relevant to any consent procedure or decision. Simply stated, one must have the *ability* to give consent in order to do so; one must have *adequate information* to do so in a knowledgeable way; and one must be *free from coercion* or any other threat to one's voluntariness."[8]

Informed consent is the prototype of procedural safeguards rooted in the legal concept of due process as established in the Fourteenth Amendment to the United States Constitution. Due process protects people's rights; procedural safeguards are meant to help guarantee that everyone is treated fairly.

Current standards for practice, however, do not extend the concept of informed consent to those seen as lacking competence to consent. This is clearly seen in the case of minors, with a few exceptions spelled out in law. Also exempted are those not specifically designated as clients, even in situations where it is evident that they will be affected by the intervention.

Interest in civil rights in the late 1960s, and the related advocacy of minors' rights in education and mental health, led to greater consideration of the right of all people to participate in making decisions that affect them. One impact is seen in increasing acceptance of the desirability of obtaining minors' assent in addition to parental consent. Concomitantly, long-standing controversies have reemerged about the risks and benefits of people's involvement in intervention decision making and their competence to make appropriate decisions.

Explicitly or implicitly part of the debate over voluntariness are two related concepts: the question of decision-making competence and the problem of paternalism.

Competence. Stated with direct reference to intervention, the question about competence asks, To what degree are potential clients capable of understanding the factors that go into making appropriate intervention decisions? Systems in the early stages of development (e.g., new organizations, minors) and those with problems often are treated in ways that diminish their autonomy. This occurs because of assumptions about their relative lack of competence and wisdom. Even when they are treated autonomously, their decisions may not be respected.

Competence in the context of consent refers to capabilities for understanding and making sound decisions, including the ability to receive and process information and choose from among alternatives. Criteria for deciding about the adequacy of these capabilities are difficult to specify. Usually, very general criteria are established, such as performance, age, and mental status.

Examples abound. Individuals at any age diagnosed as mentally retarded, autistic, or psychotic usually are seen as incompetent in a legal sense and as requiring surrogates such as parents, guardians, and courts to give consent. However, even in these extreme cases, the basis for deciding what constitutes competence and when others should act remains controversial. On a larger scale, minors' consent illustrates just how difficult the problem is. At what age should it be necessary to ask a youngster's consent before involving the minor in a psychological or educational intervention? With regard to certain school assessment activity, the legal answer is that no individual consent or assent is required—often not even from the parents—during the age period when attendance is compelled by the state. With regard to special psychological testing, special class placement, and therapeutic treatments, the common answer is that only parental consent is needed, and in some cases even parental consent is bypassed.

Little in the way of satisfactory research exists on the degree to which individuals at various ages and with various problems are competent to make intervention decisions autonomously. For example, available findings suggest that some minors, even with diagnosed problems, are capable of participating in placement decisions considerably before late adolescence. However, data are limited.[9]

Paternalism. The question of competence is strongly related to the problem of paternalism. Professional paternalism is nicely underscored by Wasserstrom in discussing lawyer-client relationships:

> If there is in fact an area in which one does know things that the client doesn't know, it is extremely easy to believe that one knows generally what is best for the client. . . . In addition there is the fact . . . [that]

the client has a serious problem or concern which has rendered the client weak and vulnerable. This, too, surely increases the disposition to respond toward the client in a patronizing, paternalistic fashion. The client of necessity confers substantial power over his or her well-being. . . . Invested in all of this power both by the individual and the society, . . . the professional responds to the client as though the client were an individual who needed to be looked after and controlled, and to have decisions made for him or her . . . with as little interference from the client as possible.[10]

The problem of paternalism stems from the fact that parents, professionals, and various representatives of society often have special responsibilities for designated others. In carrying out these responsibilities, they are granted the right to make certain decisions. And it comes as no surprise that such persons often have strong opinions as to what is good for those for whom they have responsibility. Such opinions, backed by the power to impose them, may lead to excessive paternalism.[11]

When paternalistic decisions produce little complaint or reaction from those affected or when major health and safety matters are at stake, paternalism is unlikely to be seen as a problem. However, suppose an individual rejects hospitalization for depression; suppose a fourteen-year-old rejects placement in a special class. Suppose those running a poorly functioning organization do not want it restructured? Should they be compelled? If so, what is the justification for doing so? (This brings us back to our discussion of the politics of decision making—see Chapter 7.)

As the above discussion underscores, competence and paternalism are at the heart of most arguments against seeking consent or assent. Those favoring increased involvement of clients in such processes view paternalistic stances as inappropriate and believe that client competence is underestimated. Furthermore, they argue that client participation in decision making can produce major benefits. For one, in contrast to clients who feel they don't have a choice, theory and supporting data suggest that those who feel the choice is theirs have higher levels of commitment and motivation for making the most of a situation. Thus, consent is seen as an important motivational prerequisite to positive participation. Also, if competence to make decisions increases with experience and learning, then participation in the process should help to increase competence for making future decisions. In contrast, not participating in decision making may undermine motivation and competence. We have more to say about these matters later.

NOTES

1. W.K. Frankena (1973). *Ethics* (2nd ed.). Englewood Cliffs, NJ: Prentice-Hall, p. 8.

2. Major discussions of these topics are found in many sources. For example, see T.L. Beauchamp & J.F. Childress (1989). *Principles of biomedical ethics* (3rd ed.). New York: Oxford University Press, and J. Rinas & S. Clyne-Jackson (1988). *Professional conduct and legal concerns in mental health practice.* Norwalk, CT: Appleton & Lange.

3. I. Illich (1976). *Medical nemesis.* New York: Pantheon Books.

4. Beauchamp & Childress, *Principles of biomedical ethics.*

5. A. Capron (1974). Informed consent in catastrophic disease and treatment. *University of Pennsylvania Law Review, 123,* 364–376.

6. Growing awareness of rights has increased attention on the question, When is coercive treatment appropriate? A perspective on this question provides an important counterpoint for appreciating informed consent. A few comments are offered here to clarify the point.

Some practitioners argue that any type of involuntary psychoeducational intervention is unjustifiable. Others argue that various forms of majority disapproved behavior (ranging from illegal acts through immoral and deviant behaviors to compulsive negative habits) produce enough social harm, offense, or nuisance to warrant compulsory treatment. Examples cited with respect to minors include substance abuse, gender confusion, truancy, aggressive behavior toward adults or peers, and low self-esteem. Even when the focus is on the most dramatic psychosocial problems, serious ethical concerns are raised whenever compulsory treatment is proposed to socialize or "resocialize" individuals. When the need for coercive intervention is extrapolated from dramatic cases to less extreme behaviors, such as common misbehavior and attention problems, the ethical concerns seem even more pressing. Ironically, in such instances, the coercive nature of an approach may not even be evident, particularly when the activity is described as in keeping with appropriate socialization goals and as unlikely to be harmful. For behavior that is illegal (or in violation of organizational rules), it is frequently decided to compel or at least "encourage" individuals to enroll in treatment rather than go to jail (or be removed from their positions or expelled from school). When treatment is offered as an alternative to punishment, the choice between the lesser of two evils may seem clear and devoid of coercion. Certainly, many legal offenders can be expected to express preference for a "diversion" program of treatment over incarceration. However, given a third nontreatment alternative they see as more desirable, treatment probably would be chosen to a lesser degree. One moral basis for decisions to allow and pursue involuntary interventions is found in the philosophical grounds for coercion. As Feinberg (1973) suggests, such decisions are informed by principles that address justifications for the restriction of personal liberty. These are: (1) to prevent harm to others, either injury to individual persons (The Private Harm Principle), or impairment of institutional practices that are in the public interest (The Public Harm Principle); (2) to prevent offense to others (The Offense Principle); (3) to prevent harm to self (Legal Paternalism); (4) to prevent or punish sin, that is, to "enforce morality as such" (Legal Moralism); (5) to benefit the self (Extreme Paternalism); (6) To benefit others (The Welfare Principle) (p. 33). J. Feinberg (1973). *Social philosophy*. Englewood Cliffs, NJ: Prentice-Hall.

As Robinson (1974) cogently states:

> None of these justifications for coercion is devoid of merit nor is it necessary that any of them exclude the others in attempts to justify actions against the freedoms of an individual. . . . It is one thing to assert each of these justifications enjoys some merit but quite another to suggest that they are equally valid. And it is manifestly the case that they do not share equally in the force of the law. Yet, while not sharing equally, they have all, on one occasion or another, been relied on to validate a legal judgment. (P. 234)

D.N. Robinson (1974). Harm, offense, and nuisance: Some first steps in the establishment of an ethics of treatment. *American Psychologist, 29*, 233-238.

7. A basic problem is that full understanding usually is not possible before one actually has certain experiences. Thus, informed consent is an ongoing process. As clients gain greater appreciation of intervention processes and impact, some probably will opt out if they truly have a choice. One of the dilemmas involved in explaining possible risks of intervention to potential clients is that the explanation may discourage some from pursuing the help they require. This dilemma is powerfully underscored by Brende and Parson's discussion of what they must tell victims of post traumatic stress disorder (PTSD) before treatment is initiated. Among the major risks they convey are that treatment (1) may result in only partial recovery; (2) often requires long hospitalization or weekly sessions and that the time commitment may play havoc with keeping a job; (3) usually makes emotional problems worse before things gets better (e.g., intolerable psychic pain and fear of psychotic breakdown often accompany catharsis); and (4) may produce changes in personality that cause additional problems related to interpersonal

relationships. J.O. Brende & E.R. Parson (1985). *Vietnam veterans: The road to recovery*. New York: Plenum Press.

8. D. Biklen (1978). Consent as a cornerstone concept. In J. Mearig & Associates (Eds.), *Working for children: Ethical issues beyond professional guidelines*. San Francisco: Jossey-Bass (italics added).

9. Murphy has cautioned: "The vast majority of cases that confront us will be borderline—cases in that greyish area between full competence and obvious incompetence. The real problem that will face us, then, is what to do in the borderline cases. When in doubt, which way should we err—on the side of safety or on the side of liberty? It is vital that we do not adapt analyses of 'incompetence' or patterns of argument that obscure the obviously moral nature of this question." J. Murphy (1979). Incompetence and paternalism. *Archiv fur Rechts-und-sozialphilosophie, 50*, 456–486 (p. 469).

There is evidence that some minors at fourteen years of age and even younger (including individuals manifesting psychoeducational problems) are competent to participate appropriately and effectively in major intervention decisions, such as those made during individual educational planning (IEP). Survey data also indicate that a significant number of parents, professionals, and minors take the position that individuals as young as eight years old should play a greater role in decision making. See L. Taylor, H.S. Adelman, & N. Kaser-Boyd (1985). Minors' attitudes and competence toward participation in psychoeducational decisions. *Professional Psychology, 16*, 226-35 and L. Taylor, H.S. Adelman, & N. Kaser-Boyd (1984). Attitudes toward involving minors in decisions. *Professional Psychology, 15*, 436-49.

For an excellent discussion of the risks and benefits related to increased decision making by those who are seen as less than competent, see G.B. Melton, G.P. Koocher, & M. Saks (Eds.) (1983). *Children's competence to consent*. New York: Plenum Press.

10. R. Wasserstrom (1975). Lawyers as professionals: Some moral issues. *Human Rights, 5*, 1-24.

11. Growing awareness of rights and of the potentially harmful effects of treatment is leading to safeguards. For example, parent organizations and child advocates have insisted that parents be involved in any decision that might have a profound effect on the course of a child's life. With respect to special education, this fact is reflected in the "procedural safeguards" associated with the passage of Public Law 94–142. These safeguards are rooted in the legal concept of due process as established in the Fourteenth Amendment to the Constitution. Due process protects people's rights; procedural safeguards are meant to help guarantee that everyone is treated fairly. The special education procedural safeguards are meant to ensure that parents are involved in decisions regarding testing and placement of their

child. That is, such interventions are not supposed to take place without parental consent. Some of the safeguards spelled out in law are: (1) Parents must be notified whenever the school plans to conduct a special evaluation of their child; (2) parents have the right to refuse consent for such an evaluation (but the school district has the right to a legal hearing to prove that it is needed; should parents want a special evaluation and the school refuses to provide it, parents can seek a legal hearing); (3) parents have the right to (a) review the procedures and instruments to be used in any evaluation, (b) be informed of the results and review all records, and (c) obtain an independent educational evaluation to be considered in any decisions; (4) parents must be notified whenever the school wants to change their child's educational placement, and they have the right to refuse consent for such a change (again, the school district can ask for a legal hearing to overrule the parents' decision; and parents who are unable to convince the school to provide the special placement they want can also seek such a hearing). All notifications and explanations are to be given in the parents' primary language or other primary mode of communication.

11

Improving Intervention Through Transforming Rationales: An Example

If we want to bring . . . quality, equity, and new life to our system—we must trust in a vision and a process of change.

Dwight Allen[1]

Underlying rationales are improved through conceptual refinements and empirical feedback; they are transformed through analyses that lead to insights and inventions (e.g., new models, concepts, and frameworks) that advance research and practice beyond the status quo. To illustrate, we offer an example relevant to both psychology and education drawn from efforts to improve student learning and performance through restructuring schools.

RESTRUCTURING SCHOOLS: WHAT ABOUT SUPPORT SERVICES?

Psychologists and educators long have understood that if schools are to function satisfactorily and if students are to learn and perform effectively, schools must continue to address factors that interfere with students' learning and performance.[2] Thus, proposals for restructuring schools recognize that effective learning and performance at school require appropriate attention to such matters as behavior and emotional problems, school adjustment problems, absenteeism, drug abuse, dropouts, teen pregnancy, violence on campuses, and so forth. In the literature on restructuring schools, this recognition is seen in allusions to the need for support programs and services. When such needs are mentioned, however, better ways to intervene are not examined with the same level of detail found in discussions of new directions for instruction and school management.[3]

In general, despite long-standing and continued emphasis on the importance of schools addressing psychosocial and health problems, there has been little progress in advancing the state of the art. A review of the restructuring literature with respect to support activity primarily finds a renewal of advocacy for such programs (i.e., the view that they are essential to the educational mission). A few analysts have stressed that existing resources are insufficient and hard to access, and that programs are planned and implemented in a fragmented manner. The concern about fragmentation encompasses both the piecemeal way support services are implemented and lack of coordination with community-based health and social service delivery (which also lack cross-agency coordination and integration). In response to such concerns, the primary recommendations are (1) that programs addressing psychosocial and health problems be connected as closely to each school as feasible, and (2) that such programs be evolved into a comprehensive, coordinated, and increasingly integrated package of assistance for students and their families.[4]

A recent, in-depth analysis of one large urban school district illustrates the state of the art. As part of its reform agenda, the district continues to explore ways to revamp what it calls "support services." A blue ribbon commission was formed to assist in the process. As a basis for the commission's work, a research group at a local university analyzed district education support programs.[5] One major question guiding the analysis was, What is the district's commitment to and conception of activity for addressing barriers to student learning and performance?

As a beginning step, various statements of district mission, goals, and guidelines were reviewed. These indicated a substantial commitment to dealing with factors interfering with student learning and performance. For example, in outlining an action plan to end low achievement and establish educational excellence, four of eight policy statements made by the district called for enabling activity and support services. ("Enable students to become full participants in their own academic achievement and social development." "Promote local school opportunities for parent education, involvement, and participation in school governance to empower parents as partners in their child's education." "Provide quality, comprehensive support services at each school." "Reach out to the greater community to coordinate and expand services to support and enrich the child's education.")

Current organization of activity and various statements of purpose found in specific program and project descriptions further underscored the district's commitment to addressing factors interfering with student learning and performance. In addition, district policy makers recently had adopted a task force report emphasizing the importance of linking community-based health and social services to schools. Thus, there could be little doubt about the district's awareness or stated commitment.

At the same time, district policy makers did not behave as if activity to address interfering factors was essential. That is, activity in this area clearly was not assigned the same priority as instructional programs and was among the first considered for reduction in balancing the budget. Moreover, no formal conceptualization was found translating the district's commitment into a cohesive program. Thus, the stated commitment to addressing interfering factors was limited not only by the subordinate status assigned to such activity but also by the absence of an articulated intervention model. A reasonable interpretation of the status assigned such services and programs is that they were viewed and treated as supplementary "add ons" or luxuries. Moreover, observation of practice indicated that the prevailing approach to addressing student and family problems was one of referring individual cases to specific professionals—until resources ran out. And resources always ran out before the vast majority of those in need could be helped. Clearly this represents a weak model for addressing barriers to learning.

Based on the analysis, one of the primary recommendations was that the district make a fundamental transformation in the way it conceived the matter of addressing factors interfering with student learning and performance. A few specific ideas that were formulated are presented here to illustrate the value of transforming an underlying rationale in order to move intervention thinking forward.

A NEW CONCEPT: THE ENABLING COMPONENT

Given the various factors that can interfere with students' learning and performance, a school program committed to the success of all children must be designed to account for learners ranging from those ready and able to benefit from instruction to those who are not.[6] From this perspective, the need for an array of activity to *enable* a school's fundamental teaching mission is well recognized.[7] The general focus of such activity can be conceived as addressing barriers to learning. (Optimally, such activity encompasses efforts to prevent and correct learning, behavior, emotional, and health problems and also can enhance a school's efforts to foster academic, social, emotional, and physical functioning.)

Activity to deal with barriers to learning can be essential (albeit insufficient) in enabling schooling and learning for a significant number of students. In school districts where a high proportion of students are poor or immigrants or both, more than half the students and their families may require school-based and/or linked assistance if they are to succeed.[8] Indeed, as the number in need has increased, policy initiatives have emerged designed to improve access to and integration of necessary medical, mental health, and social services by linking them to the schools.[9]

Unfortunately, in the effort to convince everyone of the importance of these initiatives, certain services have been overemphasized. For example, screening check-ups, individual and family psychotherapy/counseling, and other such activities frequently are touted to the point of sounding like panaceas rather than what they really are—namely, small pieces of an overall enabling approach. By themselves, medical, mental health, and social services are insufficient in addressing the biggest problems confronting schools (e.g., they are not designed to address all the major factors that cause poor academic performance, dropouts, gang violence, teenage pregnancy, substance abuse, racial conflict, and so forth). This is not a criticism of such services. The point is that they must be kept in perspective as necessary but insufficient facets of a comprehensive approach. Moreover, it must be remembered that the long-term efficacy of any service may be undermined if it is not well integrated with others and with the school's efforts to teach.

Concerns about current policy initiatives underscore the need for additional conceptual and applied work related to enabling activity. In particular, models are needed that (1) treat enabling activity as an essential component of a school's efforts to address the full range of learners, (2) outline the nature of program comprehensiveness, and (3) emphasize mechanisms for integrated planning and implementation.

For example, as we have noted, current restructuring in education has been limited primarily to revamping the instructional and management components. Adopting the view that enabling activity is essential leads to a suggestion that school restructuring agendas need to be reconceived as having three primary (essential) and complementary components: an *instructional* component, an *enabling* component, and a *management* component (see Figure 11.1).

As conceived, the *enabling component* encompasses a major *restructuring of school support services*. It does so in ways that *integrates them with school-based and school-linked support programs and teams and special projects* and also *outreaches and links up with community resources* (e.g., health, social, and recreational programs). The aim is to develop a school-based and school-linked

Figure 11.1
Three Major Components to Be Addressed
in Restructuring Education

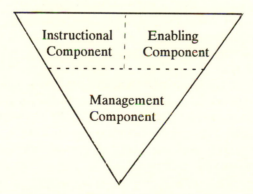

comprehensive, integrated programmatic approach to preventing and ameliorating barriers to learning. (As already noted, efforts to enhance long-term intervention efficacy require the type of comprehensive continuum of interventions for psychosocial, educational, and physical health problems outlined in Figure 8.5.)

THE ENABLING COMPONENT: STARTING AT THE SCHOOL LEVEL

As illustrated in Figure 11.2, the enabling component must address the full continuum of learners who encounter barriers, not just those with mild problems or those with the most serious (and often intractable) problems. In attempting to do so, most schools address student and family problems by referring individual cases to specific professionals, but, as we have noted, this is a weak model because available resources are too limited.

One way to strengthen the approach is to shift the emphasis from specific support services carried out by designated categories of personnel to a model that conceives enabling in terms of a fundamental and interrelated set of collaborative *programmatic needs*. The rationale is that appropriately conceived programmatic needs can better guide development of the range of programmatic activity for addressing barriers to learning. (Such activity can encompass ways to reduce referrals for individual services and augment resources through collaborative efforts, including enhanced home and community involvement.) The shift to an integrated programmatic focus, of course, also has major implications for staff roles and functions and for revamping organizational and operational mechanisms.

The primary challenge at the school level is to conceive and weave existing activity together into an integrated program (including a focus on curricula designed to foster positive social, emotional, and physical development). To address effectively student and related family problems that interfere with learning, a school needs ways to

- help teachers learn an increasingly wide array of strategies for preventing and handling problems in the classroom;

Figure 11.2

Adding an Enabling Component in Order to Address Barriers to Learning

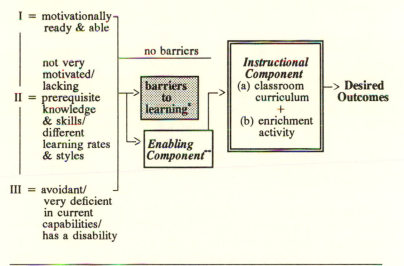

Types of Learners

I = motivationally ready & able

not very motivated/ lacking
II = prerequisite knowledge & skills/ different learning rates & styles

III = avoidant/ very deficient in current capabilities/ has a disability

no barriers

barriers to learning*

*Enabling Component***

Instructional Component
(a) classroom curriculum
+
(b) enrichment activity

-> **Desired Outcomes**

An Enabling Component involves a comprehensive and integrated array of programs to eliminate/minimize/get around barriers to learning.

Examples

*Barriers to learning	**Enabling Component Activity
• negative attitudes toward schooling	• primary prevention
• deficiencies in necessary prerequisite skills	• compensatory intervention
• disabilities	• remediation
• program deficiencies	• staff development for enabling
• lack of home involvement	• parent involvement
• lack of peer support	• peers as interveners
• peers who are negative influences	• volunteers & professionals-in-training
• lack of recreational opportunities	• recreational opportunities
• lack of community involvement	• community involvement/enhancement
• inadequate school support services	• school support services
• inadequate social support services	• social support services
• inadequate health support services	• health support services (physical and mental)

- assist students and families with problems the teacher cannot handle alone (e.g., connecting the student and family with school and community health, human, social, psychological, and special education resources; triage; case management);
- respond to schoolwide crises, minimize their impact, and develop prevention strategies to reduce the number of schoolwide and personal crises;
- facilitate comprehensive home involvement (e.g., to improve student functioning through parent education and instruction in helping with schoolwork; to meet specific parent needs through English as a second language [ESL] classes and mutual support groups);
- facilitate comprehensive volunteer and community involvement, including formal linkages with community-based health and social services, local businesses, and various sources for volunteer recruitment;
- facilitate transitions, including welcoming and providing support for new arrivals, dealing with the transitional aspects of before and after school activity, articulating the move to the next level of schooling, facilitating transitions to and from special education, and facilitating transition to postschool life.

Each of the six areas for programmatic activity listed above is graphically represented in Figure 11.3 and are elaborated upon in Table 11.1. The content of the activity guides program planning, implementation, and evaluation; the broad nature and scope of the activity require each to be seen as involving collaborative effort; the many ways the various activities overlap and interact with each other require that they be integrated. As indicated in the table, specific mechanisms must exist if each area is to be addressed in daily practice and maintained over time. Moreover, the establishment and maintenance of such mechanisms require the support of school governance bodies, and overall coordination and integration require a coordination mechanism.

Conceiving programmatic needs is relatively easy compared to the problems of identifying and deploying committed and able personnel resources. There are a variety of ways to think about personnel to accomplish the collaborative activity described in Table 11.1. Some might be carried out by one individual. Inevitably, some require a team (two or more individuals). For example, some districts have found the mechanisms of a school-based Student Study Team and a Student Guidance Committee of use for students identified as needing something more than can be provided by the

Figure 11.3
Programmatic Focus for School-Based Collaborative Activity
Related to the Enabling Component

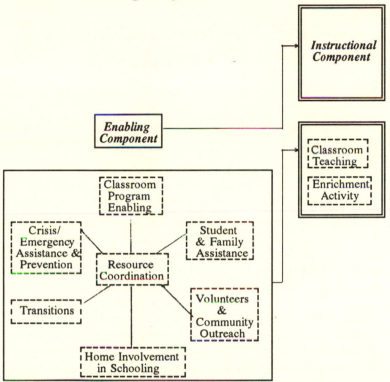

classroom teacher; similarly, school-based Crisis Teams have been useful. In some cases, one mechanism can address more than one area, and for some areas, one mechanism can serve more than one school (e.g., a school cluster level mechanism). Obviously, few schools can establish new mechanisms to address all these areas at one time; the process must go forward in phases.

Early in the process a major challenge involves outreach to other local schools and the community to enhance the school's programmatic activity (e.g., by entering into school complex and cluster collaborations; by establishing formal linkages with community

Table 11.1

Examples of School and Cluster Level Collaboration Tasks

1. **Classroom Program Enabling**—requires a school level mechanism for offering teachers personalized help in increasing their array of strategies for preventing and handling problems encountered in their classrooms.

> That is, when a classroom teacher indicates there are problems in working with one or more youngsters, the first step is to see whether there are ways to address the problem within the classroom and perhaps with added home involvement. As someone helps the teacher explore a variety of options, the teacher learns general ways to address similar problems when they arise in the future. Some problems, of course, cannot be handled by the teacher, thus the task of Student and Family Assistance.

2. **Student and Family Assistance**—requires a mechanism for offering personalized attention for a broad-range of student and family problems.

> The primary focus is on connecting the student and family with school and community health, human, social, psychological, and special education resources. In doing so, a triage system is used to account for need and availability of resources, decisions are made about special placements and IEPs, and a case management system is used to ensure communication and follow-up.

3. **Crisis/Emergency Assistance and Prevention**—requires a mechanism for responding to school-wide crises and minimizing the impact of crises.

> Besides emergency response, there are the related prevention tasks necessary for reducing the number of school-wide and personal crises (e.g., school safety/violence reduction, suicide prevention, child abuse prevention).

4. **Home Involvement in Schooling**—requires a mechanism for planning, developing, and maintaining comprehensive home involvement.

> This mechanism focuses on ways to directly involve the home in improving student functioning (e.g., through parent education and instruction in helping with schoolwork), meet specific parent needs (e.g., through ESL classes and mutual support groups), and so forth.

(cont.)

Table 11.1 (cont.)

5. *Volunteers and Community Outreach*—requires a mechanism to ensure planning, development, and maintenance of a volunteer program and comprehensive forms of community involvement.

> With respect to volunteers, this mechanism can focus on delineating the many ways a school can use volunteers (e.g., to assist staff, to assist targeted students) and establishing systems to find and effectively use a variety of volunteers (e.g., parents, college students, senior citizens, peer and cross-age tutors and counselors, professionals-in-training).

> With respect to community outreach, the emphasis can encompass (a) linking community-based health and human services directly to the school (e.g., recruiting local services to work at the school site, making formal linkages with other local services and resources), (b) involving local businesses in a variety of ways (e.g., adopt-a-school, providing resources, mentors, awards, jobs), (c) making contact with hard-to-involve homes/families, and (d) representing local services and resources on the School-Based Coordinating Committee.

6. *Transitions*—requires a mechanism for planning, developing, and maintaining a comprehensive focus on transition concerns.

> Examples of focus include concerns about (a) welcoming and providing social support for new arrivals, (b) before and after school activity, (c) articulation in moving to the next level of schooling, (d) vocational and college counseling, (e) transition into or out of special education, and (f) transition to post school living.

*Besides a Classroom Program Enabling mechanism, the school's curriculum planners need to include a specific focus on curricular approaches for fostering socio-emotional and physical development. Such a focus is a necessary element of efforts to prevent learning, behavior, emotional, and health problems.

Note: Not addressed here are the general tasks of governance and coordination related to all this activity.

resources; by attracting more volunteers, professionals-in-training, and community resources to work at the school site). By proceeding in this manner, a district can empirically determine what additional resources and mechanisms are necessary at the level of school complexes and clusters as well as systemwide to support the primary enabling activity taking place at each school.

At this time, there is no indication in the literature that any school district treats enabling activity as a primary component of efforts to accomplish its educational mission. Restructuring of schools that serve large numbers of students who are bumping into major barriers to learning will not lead to significant improvements in student learning and performance unless the reorganization includes a substantive focus on enabling activity. The concept of the enabling component suggests that nothing less than elevating such activity to equal parity with instruction will do.

As with other examples we offer throughout this monograph, the point is not to argue for the specific ideas presented. The concept of the enabling component is meant to illustrate that one way to move beyond the status quo related to psychological and educational interventions is to reformulate underlying rationales. Many of the intractable problems confronting psychologists and educators probably require not just refinements in existing rationales but also radical transformations in our thinking.

NOTES

1. D.W. Allen (1993). *Schools for a new century: A conservative approach to radical school reform.* New York: Praeger, p. 167.

2. The literature supporting the need for a range of programmatic activity to enable and enhance a school's teaching efforts is extensive. For a review of recent reports focused on this problem (selected from the twenty-five published between 1989 and 1991), see A.T. Lavin, G.R. Shapiro, & K.S. Weill (1992). *Creating an agenda for school-based health promotion: A review of selected reports.* Cambridge, MA: Harvard School of Public Health. For a historical perspective, see D.B. Tyack (1979). The high school as a social service agency: Historical perspectives on current policy issues. *Education Evaluation and Policy Analysis, 1,* 45–57 and D.B. Tyack (1992). Health and social services in public schools: Historical perspectives. *The Future of Children, 2,* 19–31. Also of both historical and continuing interest is the policy formulation of N.M. Lambert, E.M. Bower, G. Caplan, et al. (1964). *The protection and promotion of mental health in the schools.* Washington, DC: U.S. Government Printing Office. For a contemporary perspective, see H.S. Adelman & L. Taylor (1993). *Learning problems and learning disabilities: Moving forward.* Pacific Grove, CA: Brooks/Cole. L.A. Bond & B.E. Compas (Eds.) (1989). *Primary prevention and promotion in the schools.* Newbury Park, CA: Sage. Carnegie Council on Adolescent Development (1988). *Review of school-based health services.* New York:

Carnegie Foundation. G.M. Christopher, P.D. Kurtz, & P.T. Howing (1989). Status of mental health services for youth in school and community. *Children and Youth Services Review, 11*, 159–174. J.G. Dryfoos (1990). *Adolescents at risk: Prevalence and prevention.* New York: Oxford University Press. M.W. Kirst & M. McLaughlin (1990). Rethinking children's policy: Implications for educational administration. In B. Mitchell & L.L. Cunningham (Eds.), *Educational leadership and changing context of families, communities, and schools: Eighty-ninth yearbook of the National Society for the Study of Education* (Part 2, pp. 69–90). Chicago: University of Chicago Press. A. Mitchell, M. Seligson, & F. Marx (1989). *Early childhood programs and the public schools: Promise and practice.* Dover, MA: Auburn House. National Commission on the Role of the School and Community in Improving Adolescent Health (1990). *Code blue: Uniting for healthier youth.* Washington, DC: American Medical Association and National Association of State Boards of Education. M. Orr (1987). *Keeping students in school: A guide to effective dropout prevention programs and services.* San Francisco: Jossey-Bass. R.H. Price, M. Cioci, W. Penner, & B. Trautlein (1993). Webs of influences: School and community programs that enhance adolescent health and education. *Teachers College Record, 94*, 487–521. L.B. Schorr (1988). *Within our reach: Breaking the cycle of disadvantage.* New York: Doubleday. R. Slavin, B.J. Karweit, & N. Madden (Eds.) (1989). *Effective programs for students at risk.* Boston: Allyn & Bacon. U.S. Congress, Office of Technology Assessment (1991). *Adolescent health—Vol. 1: Summary and policy options*, OTA-H-468. Washington, DC: U.S. Government Printing Office. USOE/NIMH (1972). *Mental health and learning.* Washington, DC: U.S. Government Printing Office. E.F. Zigler & M. Lang (1991). *Child care choices.* New York: Macmillan.

3. For a sample of the literature discussing restructuring, see R.S. Barth (1990). *Improving schools from within: Teachers, parents, and principals can make a difference.* San Francisco: Jossey-Bass. R.F. Elmore & Associates (1990). *Restructuring schools: The next generation of educational reform.* San Francisco: Jossey-Bass. A.C. Lewis (1989). *Restructuring America's schools.* Arlington, VA: American Association of School Administrators. A. Lieberman & L. Miller (1990). Restructuring schools: What matters and what works. *Phi Delta Kappan, 71*, 759–764. J. Murphy (1991). *Restructuring schools: Capturing and assessing the phenomena.* New York: Teachers College Press. F.M. Newmann (1993). Beyond common sense in educational restructuring: The issues of content and linkage. *Educational Reviewer, 22*, 4–13, 22. S.B. Sarason (1990). *The predictable failure of educational reform: Can we change course before it's too late?* San Francisco: Jossey-Bass. P.C. Schlechty (1990). *Schools for the twenty-first century: Leadership imperatives for educational reform.* San Francisco: Jossey-Bass. Task Force

on Education of Young Adolescents (1989). *Turning points: Preparing American Youth for the 21st century*. Washington, DC: Carnegie Council on Adolescent Development. G. Wehlage, G. Smith, & P. Lipman (1992). Restructuring urban schools: The New Futures experience. *American Educational Research Journal, 29*, 51–93.

4. Policy makers all across the United States have recognized the critical importance of moving toward improved coordination and eventual integration of health, social, and human service programs. A variety of demonstration projects have adopted the concept of "one-stop shopping" whereby a center (e.g., a Family Service Center) is established at or near a schoolsite to house as many health, mental health, and social services as feasible. For examples of basic discussions, see Center for the Future of Children Staff (1992) in *The Future of Children, 2*, 6–18. H.L. Hodgkinson (1989). *The same client: The demographics of education and service delivery systems*. Washington, DC: Institute for Educational Leadership, Inc./Center for Demographic Policy. J.G. Dryfoos (1993). Schools as places for health, mental health, and social services. *Teachers College Record, 94*, 540–567. W.H. Holtzman (1992) (Ed.). Community renewal, family preservation, and child development through the School of the Future. In W.H. Holtzman (Ed.), *School of the Future*. Austin, TX: American Psychological Association and Hogg Foundation for Mental Health. S.L. Kagan (1990). *Excellence in early childhood education: Defining characteristics and next-decade strategies*. Washington, DC: Office of Educational Research and Improvement, U.S. Department of Education. S.L. Kagan, A.M. Rivera, & F.L. Parker (1990). *Collaborations in action: Reshaping services for young children and their families*. New Haven, CT: Yale University, Bush Center on Child Development and Social Policy. M.W. Kirst (1991). Improving children's services: Overcoming barriers, creating new opportunities. *Phi Delta Kappan, 72*, 615–18. A. Melaville & M. Blank (1991). *What it takes: Structuring inter-agency partnerships to connect children and families with comprehensive services*. Washington, DC: Education and Human Services Consortium.

5. See H.S. Adelman (1993). Restructuring education support services: Toward the concept of an enabling component (manuscript).

6. Despite statements continuing to support the goal of universal education in the United States, the lack of detail in the restructuring literature regarding how schools should reorganize and integrate education support programs and services is ample reason to question whether current reform agendas are addressing this goal in a realistic way. See F.M. Hechinger (1993). Schools for teenagers: A historic dilemma. *Teachers College Record, 94*, 522–39, and H.L. Hodgkinson (1991). Reform vs. reality. *Phi Delta Kappan, 73*, 9–16.

7. Webster defines *enabling* as "providing with the means or opportunity;

making possible, practical, or easy; giving power, capacity, or sanction to."

8. A visit to any poverty area school underscores this point vividly and poignantly. For a discussion of the dimensions of the problem, see Committee for Economic Development (1987). *Children in need: Investment strategies for the educationally disadvantaged.* New York: Author. Dryfoos (1990). *Adolescents at risk.* E.O. Nightingale & L. Wolverton (1993). Adolescent rolelessness in modern society. *Teachers College Record, 94,* 472–86. J. O'Neil (1991). A generation adrift? *Educational Leadership, 49,* 4–10.

9. Funding for health and social services almost always is less than is needed, and there are always a significant number in society who could benefit from such services who are hard to reach. In the 1990s, policy makers are attempting to increase cost effectiveness by developing models designed to enhance service coordination, collaboration, and eventual integration. To improve contact with hard to reach and underserved populations, the emphasis is on linking services to school sites and in some cases placing the services on campuses. For an annotated bibliography on the topics of service integration and school linkages, see A. Chaudry, K.E. Maurer, C.J. Oshinsky, & J. Mackie (1993). *Service integration: An annotated bibliography.* New York: National Center for Service Integration, as well as other previously cited references.

A Few Concluding Comments about the Underlying Rationale Problem

I find the great thing in this world is not so much where we stand, as in what direction we are moving.

Oliver Wendell Holmes

Throughout Part II, we have highlighted issues and problems related to understanding the bases and biases associated with intervention, with a special emphasis on interventions in psychology and education. We have not tried to be exhaustive, nor have we given equal emphasis to the various concerns covered. Rather, our intent has been to provide a broad look at the underlying rationale problem in a way that underscores its nature and scope and highlights some of its most interesting facets. Additional concerns related to the rationale problem will become evident in Parts III and IV.

Interveners make profound decisions in adopting or formulating an intervention rationale, albeit not always with full awareness of these decisions or their implications. Given the life-shaping nature of interventions in psychology and education (as well as in medicine, social work, etc.), a high level of awareness obviously is desirable. As professionals continue to grapple with the above concerns and many more, the result should be greater clarity about and articulation of underlying intervention rationales.

Clarity and articulation of rationales should facilitate creation of good client-intervention matches and provide a sound basis for establishing valid contracts. This should be associated with significant benefits to clients and to society at large. And, paraphrasing Lewin, one hopes that work on the underlying rationale problem will result in increased appreciation that *there is nothing as practical as a good rationale.*

PART III

THE PLANNING AND IMPLEMENTATION PROBLEM

The core of purposeful and creative action is design, the active building of relations between [people] and [their] world.

Jantsch[1]

We turn now to considerations related to translating a rationale into a specific plan of action and carrying the plan out. Analyses of planning and implementation activity provide a fundamental appreciation of what is involved in operationalizing intervention practices.

In this brief introduction to problems associated with planning and implementation, four topics are explored: (1) planning as a tool, (2) components of planning, (3) the role of assessment, and (4) key concepts and concerns associated with facilitating implementation. Before proceeding, however, a few words are warranted regarding society's role in supporting intervention planning and implementation.

In talking about improving education and dealing with psychosocial and learning problems, it has become fashionable to say "You can't solve problems by *throwing* money at them." It is a truism that money alone cannot solve such problems; it is not likely, however, that society can do so without a substantial financial outlay.

The real policy and resource issues are: What must be done? How much can we afford? How can we ensure that the money is used appropriately? How can we determine efficacy? All four of these complex questions deserve top priority in society's discussion of paths to an improved future. Instead of exploring these issues, educational and psychological interveners seem mired down in politically motivated accountability practices and business or managerial models for motivating improved performance.

No one can predict the future. The best bet, however, is that, even in the most developed countries, a relatively small amount of public taxes will be devoted to education and interventions to ameliorate psychological and social problems. At the same time, through their elected representatives, the general public and special interest groups will continue to demand greater cost efficiency and better outcomes. So, calls for improved intervention collaboration, consolidation, accessibility, and accountability are likely to remain central policy thrusts. But because of limited resources, such policies mostly mean shifting funds from one priority to another. This leads to serious dilemmas and political battles. For example, effective prevention programs arguably may yield long-range savings. If policy makers fully adopt the concept of prevention, large-scale programs increasingly will be favored. Unfortunately, at least in the short run, augmented support for prevention usually means reduced support for efforts to address current problems.

Intervention planning and implementation are dependent on existing policies as reflected in resource support. Thus, any discussion of intervention planning and implementation must encompass ideas about the impact of limited resources and the influence of policy makers.

NOTE

1. E. Jantsch (1981). *The evolutionary vision.* Boulder, CO: Westview Press.

12

Planning as a Tool

The ethics of planning lies within the individuals who use the tools of planning and not in the tools or the planning process itself.

Sybouts[1]

Some worry that too much planning can be stultifying and constricting. Without planning, however, intervention is a reactive process. This risks an overemphasis on the press of immediate events, at the expense of long-range aims implicitly or explicitly stated in an intervention's underlying rationale.

Planning, as formally defined by Hartley, is the unilateral or participatory task of "relating means to ends, formulating rationally feasible courses of action through systematic considerations of alternatives."[2] As with all tools, planning is undertaken for good or for bad, used mundanely or creatively, and done well or perfunctorily. It leads to interventions that are static or dynamic, reactive or proactive. Unfortunately, planning often is not done well because to do so methodically expends valuable time and effort and because planning is not a major focus of training for many practitioners.

De Neufville captures the dilemma of planners well. She notes that, on the one hand, we are confronted by an acute awareness that rational, comprehensive planning may well be futile, and on the other by a conviction that we should do it anyway.[3] Relatedly, Goodlad states with respect to education planning: "Carried to an extreme, the order implied in a rational system fails to square with what we know about human beings and human resources. Both are marked by irrationality, a substantial measure of which may be desirable. But there is little danger of the decision-making process in education becoming overly rational. When it does, I shall be delighted to argue the case for irrationality."[4] Emphasizing the importance of planning for psychological intervention, Urban and Ford state: "Ideally, . . . procedures for affecting behavioral change will be formulated in orderly, systematic, and explicit fashion; the more this is done, the more successfully some other person (therapist or researcher) can replicate them and the more successfully the effects of the specific procedures can be studied."[5] In *Future Shock*, Toffler notes, "Arguing that planning imposes values on the future, the anti-planners overlook the fact that non-planning does so, too—often with far worse consequences."[6]

Systems and management theorists are among the most active in discussing intervention planning. From these perspectives, a plan of action includes decision making to

- formulate general goals and objectives
- organize relevant data
- determine personnel, space, and material requirements
- examine alternative procedures and establish priorities
- provide for system communication and information retrieval
- analyze financial resources
- evaluate how well objectives are met
- anticipate future needs
- continuously review the system to reformulate objectives and prevent it from becoming static and rigid

Sybouts differentiates approaches to planning along a continuum from simple or intuitive planning to highly complex or strategic planning/management. He also stresses that complexity increases with the number of individuals and groups involved, when the stakes are higher related to the enterprise being planned, and when the focus is on persons and social and political concerns and not just on the physical environment.[7]

Although some practitioners function at an intuitive level, major intentional interventions require some form of "strategic planning" or "system design." Strategic planning, as described by Sybouts, is used to make forecasts with the intent of meeting the future proactively. The process begins by clarifying the organization's goal definition—the direction in which intervention is to take a system given the system's mission and needs. Defining goals is done with specific understanding of the setting (environment, climate) in which the system functions. Then, intervention options are identified and decisions made; that is, strategic goals are operationalized into working plans. As plans are implemented, performance is evaluated so plans can be revised.[8]

Systems design, as discussed by Banathy, also stresses that one's desired image of the future state for the system plays a key role in guiding creation of a plan for the future. Such planning is described as involving formulation of purposes—including the core definition of the system, specification of desired system characteristics, selection and systematic arrangement of functions for attaining stated purposes, design of a system model to guide the carrying out of functions, and design of appropriate organizational processes to accomplish the functions.[9]

Planning for development of prototypes and demonstration programs is almost always well supported. Recent examples in psychology and education are seen in the initiatives to encourage greater integration of social service and health programs and to develop new models for schooling. In both cases, significant funds are earmarked for planning stages. In the day-by-day practice of psychology and education, however, underwriting for planning often is sparse, and sufficient time is not scheduled. When inadequate resources are devoted to planning, both efficiency and effectiveness are jeopardized, and practitioners may even lose sight of the guiding vision for their work.

NOTES

1. W. Sybouts (1992). *Planning in school administration: A handbook.* Westport, CT: Greenwood Press, p. 8.

2. H.J. Hartley (1968). *Educational planning-programming-budgeting.* Englewood Cliffs, NJ: Prentice-Hall, pp. 2–3.

3. J.I. de Neufville (1986). Usable planning theory: An agenda for research and education. In B. Checkoway (Ed.), *Strategic perspectives on planning practice.* Lexington, MA: D.C. Heath.

4. J.I. Goodlad (1966). *School, curriculum, and individual.* Waltham, MA: Blaisdell Publishing Co., p. 8.

5. H.B. Urban & D.H. Ford (1971). Some historical and conceptual perspectives on psychotherapy and behavior change. In A.E. Bergin & S.L. Garfield (Eds.), *Handbook of psychotherapy and behavior change.* New York: Wiley & Sons, p. 16.

6. A. Toffler (1970). *Future shock*. New York: Random House.

7. Sybouts, *Planning in school administration*.

8. Ibid. In response to critics, the term *strategic management* has been proposed in place of *strategic planning*. Strategic management is seen as broadening the process, with special emphasis on plans for moving toward implementation and using feedback to enhance strategic control. To integrate various planning concepts, Sybouts has proposed a five-step progression from strategic planning through operational planning: (1) clarifying vision and commitment, (2) strategic planning (mission and goals statements), (3) strategic management (extends the strategic plan by formulating alternatives for implementation and strategic control), (4) operational planning (design of specific tasks for reaching goals), and (5) monitoring and evaluating.

9. B.H. Banathy (1991). *Systems design of education: A journey to create the future*. Englewood Cliffs, NJ: Educational Technology Publications, pp. 27–8. Banathy specifically distinguishes between planning and design. He juxtaposes the two as follows (p. 150):

PLANNING	DESIGN
works out from the existing system	works back from an ideal image
prescribes goals/objectives	explores values, aspirations, and expectations
sets forth specific steps to take within a time scheme	devises and describes the SYSTEM that has the potential to realize the aspirations
proceeds in a linear fashion	works in a spiral and recursive fashion
establishes an overall time frame (3–5 years) at the end of which another planning cycle starts	is continuous and becomes the approach to organizational change and renewal

Many thinkers have wrestled with the concept of design, trying to place it in the context of scientific activity. Herbert Simon, for example, distinguishes between approaches used in the natural and behavioral sciences and the use of the science of design in applied fields. He sees the former as describing what exists and how it works; design is seen as using and synthesizing existing knowledge to create and shape what should be (e.g., constructing and reconstructing systems). See H. Simon (1989). *The sciences of the artificial*. Cambridge, MA: MIT Press.

Planning as we use the term encompasses design as outlined by Banathy and Simon. Clearly, the concept (planning encompassing design) has implications for both advancing knowledge about intervention and applying that knowledge in everyday practice.

13

Components of Planning

Planners must understand the environment in which they work and acknowledge the chaos that is present.

Sybouts[1]

In discussing translation of an underlying rationale into a plan of action, we elaborate first on the four planning phases introduced in Part II; then, we explore planning as related to the five major intervention tasks (also introduced in Part II). Finally, we underscore the need for mechanisms that ensure ongoing attention to planning.

FOUR PHASES OF PLANNING

Intentional intervention logically includes a number of planning phases, even though many interveners probably don't think in terms of such phases. As illustrated in Part II (Figure 8.3), the phases involve (1) planning normatively, (2) translating the normative plan into specific practices, (3) accounting for administrative concerns, and (4) preparing to evaluate. A few brief comments are offered below to clarify the general nature of each phase and some related concerns. We stress at the outset that the phases are not strictly sequential, although normative planning logically comes first.

Normative planning is conceived as the process of translating comprehensive and highly abstract theories, beliefs, and values about ends and means into less abstract but still broadly stated intervention goals and procedures. The nature and scope of such planning are shaped by the nature and scope of the underlying intervention rationale. In particular, normative planning is guided by the rationale's image of the desired future state of the system(s) addressed. The process uses one or more general design models to clarify content, functions, and how intervention can be organized. This type of planning is seen in the work of (1) authors of texts on system change, counseling, psychotherapy, behavior change, and teaching, (2) curriculum developers, (3) academics who design programs for practitioners, and (4) individual interveners when they formulate general strategies.

Normative designs cannot account for many considerations found in a particular context. That is, each intervention requires detailing of specific ends and means for a targeted client given current circumstances and available resources. Thus, normative designs must be translated into a *specific* intervention plan. Such planning is based on informed analyses of client(s) and the intervention context. The intent is to design processes and specify objectives (products and outputs) to account for current intervention inputs or antecedent conditions, such as client characteristics and available administrative resources. The process includes, first, delineating immediate outcome options, and, second, selecting and arranging them systematically with reference to content, functions, and how intervention will be organized and scheduled (addressing collaboration with other interveners as appropriate). Specific planning is the *sine qua non* of all efforts to plan individualized or personalized intervention.

As already suggested, *administrative* planning plays a potent shaping role in moving from a normative to a specific intervention plan. Appropriate administrative planning involves decisions about deploying resources (finances, personnel, space, materials, equipment). While the hope is to translate an ideal rationale into ideal practice, resources are almost always limited, forcing planned compromises. Furthermore, when programs are carried out for profit or must divert limited resources to meet underwriters' accountability demands, administrative planning may conflict with efforts to approximate the ideal.

Logically, *evaluation* planning immediately follows each planning phase. It has two purposes. The first is to ensure that data are gathered on the appropriateness and adequacy of each intervention phase. To this end, processes are planned for determining the congruence between each phase and the intervention rationale and the logical consistency of each with the other. Second, such planning is used to prepare an evaluation is designed to describe and judge intervention antecedents, transactions, and outcomes (immediate and long-term). In both cases, evaluation should be, first and foremost, in the service of maximizing pursuit of ideas formulated in the underlying intervention rationale. However, as indicated above, administrative requirements, especially pressures for profits and accountability, may take immediate precedence and, over the long run, may reshape the underlying rationale. We reemphasize this concern because the underlying intervention rationale is the proper referent for all planning, including evaluation planning. A well-formulated rationale can be distorted and undermined when administrative and evaluative considerations become the primary referents.

Although the phases of planning are not strictly sequential, the logical steps for accomplishing each phase involves (1) identification, (2) analysis, (3) decision making, and (4) reformulation of plans as appropriate. These steps are taken with respect to antecedent conditions (intervention inputs), intended outcomes, intended transactions, other anticipated transactions and outcomes, and additional transactions to minimize anticipated negative outcomes.

PLANNING AS RELATED TO INTERVENTION TASKS

As also indicated in Part II, the activity planned during each of the above phases is associated with five intervention tasks: assessment, decision making, transition-in facilitation, facilitation toward outcomes, and transition-out facilitation (see Figure 8.4). These tasks are organized into specific programs and services designed to accomplish intervention aims. To illustrate, Figure 13.1 outlines a range of programs and services that may emerge in addressing emotional, behavioral, and learning problems. Intervention tasks encompass such complex sets of activity and concerns that space here precludes offering more than a brief sketch of the nature of planning for each.

Figure 13.1
Intervention Activity Associated with Emotional, Behavioral, and
Learning Problems

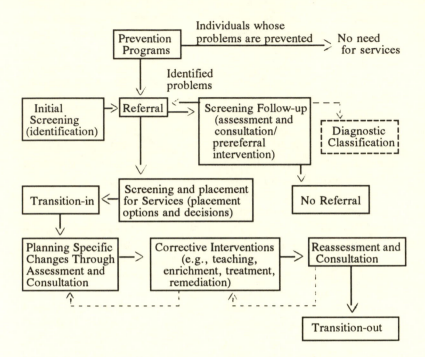

Note: All major intervention tasks and services are based on a rationale
         and require planning for implementation and evaluation.

Source: H.S. Adelman and L. Taylor (1993). *Learning problems and
         learning disabilities: Moving forward.* Pacific Grove, CA:
         Brooks/Cole. Reprinted with permission.

Assessment for Planning

Data gathering plays a key role in all facets of planning, implementation, and evaluation. That is why we discuss the role of assessment in detail in a subsequent section. Our emphasis here is on assessment for planning.

Assessment activity is directed by guidelines established as part of the underlying rationale. Resulting data provide essential information upon which interventions are designed. The earliest planning steps, therefore, involve delineating what information is necessary for planning and how to gather it.

For instance, administrative and specific planning require data about available resources, on the contexts in which intervention takes place, and on the preintervention status of the systems/subsystems toward which interventions are directed.[2] Data on preintervention status are gathered during initial assessments. Because planning is shaped by the way in which phenomena are classified, such data are used for purposes of informal and sometimes formal labelling.[3]

Initial assessments also are planned to gather data, during first contacts or subsequently, as a basis for decisions about specific intervention objectives and processes. For example, after a corrective program is initiated, processes for ongoing assessment and decision making must be planned to guide each encounter with respect to intended outcomes.

Finally, as intervention proceeds, plans must be made for evaluative reassessments. Reassessments include (1) ongoing *formative* evaluations to validate initial decisions, determine progress toward short-range objectives, and detect negative side effects, and (2) *summative* evaluation to document benefits and costs resulting from pursuit of intervention aims. That is, over time, the validity of each intervention decision must be reexamined and progress and problems must be monitored. (If a diagnosis was made, is it valid? Was the initial decision to intervene in a given way a good one? How satisfactory is progress? Is anything interfering with progress? What are the negative side effects? Has the program accomplished its objectives? Has it done all it should?)

Decision Making

Planning takes on new meaning as decisions are made. The first decisions are: Who is to make the decisions related to planning? and How will such decisions be made? Then, as each task is planned, a major focus is on clarifying: What decisions must be made? Who is to make them? and What processes should be used in arriving at the decisions?

For example, based on analysis of assessment data, decisions emerge about whether to design interventions to prevent or treat problems.[4] In either case, decisions arise about what intervention activity to use in addressing the concern (e.g., assessment, referral, selection/placement, teaching, remediation, treatment, enrichment). As part of planning, decisions must be made about program admission criteria and procedures. As an intervention proceeds, decisions must be made about whether to continue. And always there is the nagging question: Who decides?

Transitions

Each decision to intervene raises concerns about transitions. Planned transitions involve designing activity first to prepare organizations and persons for a transition and then for providing support and working collaboratively until the transition is successfully accomplished. For instance, interveners know that referrals are no guarantee that intervention will be pursued. And even when pursued, many barriers can make the initial experiences counterproductive.

Research on barriers has suggested a variety of familial, cultural, job, social class, communication, and intervener attitude factors that interfere with successful transitions to intervention settings. Barriers can be categorized as institutional, personal, or impersonal, with each type encompassing negative attitudes and emotions, lack of mechanisms and skills, or practical deterrents. Considerable attention is paid to personal barriers such as fear, anxiety, antipathy, or lack of social support and social skills, and impersonal barriers such as lack of finances and scheduling problems. Less systematic attention is paid to *institutional* barriers. These barriers encompass such concerns as inadequate resources (insufficient budgets, space, time), lack of interest or hostile attitudes on the part of staff, administration, and community, and failure to establish and maintain formal mechanisms and related skills. For instance, a major problem in many large urban schools is the flood of students and their families who come and go over the period of a school year. In many schools, there is no policy commitment to facilitating enrollment, adjustment, and involvement at the school (for students and their families) through enhanced strategies for creating a sense of community and welcoming students and families; there are no formal mechanisms for planning and implementing appropriate activity or for upgrading the skills of staff, students, and parents to carry out desired activity.

In general, *transition-in* interventions are designed to help ensure successful contact with appropriate interventions; interventions are introduced in ways that prevent and overcome initial transition and adjustment difficulties. Examples of activity for overcoming transition-in barriers include providing basic welcoming information, structuring initial contacts so that they are personalized, and offering supportive transition resources.

Barriers also may arise during *transition-out*. Thus, interventions are planned to help overcome anxieties at the time a program ends and to develop specific "survival skills" and provide support services during the period of transition.

Transition concerns arise in relation to all systems involved in intentional interventions. A vivid example of growing recognition for the importance of planning transitions is seen in legislation for individuals with disabilities. U.S. Public Law 101-476 makes it mandatory for the multidisciplinary teams that prepare written individualized education programs (IEPs) to specify transition services for persons with disabilities as they move from school to postschool status. What such services should entail is specified in some detail and is cited here to illustrate the nature of the transition tasks.

> Transition services include "a coordinated set of activities for a student, designated within an outcome-oriented process, which promotes movement from school to postschool activities including postsecondary education, vocational training, integrated employment (including supported employ-

ment), continuing and adult education, adult services, independent living or community participation. The coordinated set of activities shall be based upon the individual student's needs, taking into account the student's preferences and interests, and shall include instruction, community experiences, the development of employment and other postschool adult living objectives, and, when appropriate, acquisition of daily living skills and functional vocational evaluation."

The transition plan is to specify "interagency responsibilities or linkages (or both) before the student leaves the school setting" and is to be made annually beginning no later than age 16 and earlier when appropriate.[5]

Facilitation Toward Outcomes

Initial and ongoing planning to facilitate outcomes begins with the question: What should be done to accomplish intended outcomes and minimize undesired ones? At this point, a brief answer is, The process adopts a normative design, factors in administrative considerations, and develops a specific facilitation plan. That plan details a content focus, processes (including collaboration), and how formative evaluation data will be used. The specific plan undergoes continuous modification during implementation based on ongoing formal and/or informal assessment data and decision making. The extent of this activity is elaborated by our subsequent discussion of the role of assessment and concepts and concerns associated with facilitating implementation.

The preceding discussion underscores the value of systematic planning as a basis for rational and methodical intervention. An appreciation that planning is valuable, however, is no guarantee that interveners will pursue systematic planning. For this to happen, appropriate mechanisms must be established and maintained.

MECHANISMS FOR PLANNING

As emphasized above, planning manifests itself in the form of specific programs and services. Thus, critical indications of the need to improve planning are found through evaluating programs. Such data, however, say little about the quality of planning mechanisms. Therefore, efforts to improve planning must also include quantitative and qualitative analyses of planning mechanisms.

Planning mechanisms encompass processes by which plans are developed and approved for each phase of intervention and for intervention collaborations. For planning mechanisms to exist, their function and value must be recognized. Moreover, when organizations and agencies are responsible for the intervention, policy makers and governance bodies must support the establishment and maintenance of planning mechanisms. Such support encompasses (1) clarifying who is to participate and who is to approve plans, (2) allocating resources in the form of time, facilities, and competent and informed people, and (3) establishing policies that encourage and enable appropriate collaboration.

Planning by individual interveners usually involves only the practitioner's contemplations, with due recognition to the client. In effect, the planning mechanism is a committee of one. When many entities are involved, mechanisms generally incorporate groups of stakeholders and others included because of their special expertise.

The prevailing prototype mechanisms are collaborative planning committees and subcommittees, such as strategic planning and operational planning teams; their products are approved by governance bodies, such as boards and organization/agency administrators. Common examples of planning groups are organization executive committees, program steering committees, curriculum planning committees, and case management teams. Sometimes a special planning facilitator is employed, such as an outside process consultant. In addition, large-scale planning calls for the assistance of support resources, such as clerical staff and substantive experts. The processes used are data gathering, analysis, deliberation, and strategies for arriving at compromise and consensus. Because such processes require productive working relationships among participants, planners must understand group dynamics and facilitation.

A widely used example of a committee created to improve intervention planning and evaluation is seen in the field of special education. U.S. Public Law 94-142 includes guidelines requiring a multidisciplinary team to prepare a written individualized education program (IEP) for each student diagnosed as having a disability. At referral, the team can encourage prediagnostic interventions; team members do additional, multidisciplinary assessment; they write up a specific program plan and arrange for placement. The team also can provide a mechanism for case management, including monitoring of progress.

Systematic analyses of planning mechanisms for psychological and educational interventions are rare. Among the basics requiring clarification are (1) the nature of and relationship between planning tasks, (2) the best mechanisms for accomplishing specific tasks and ensuring appropriate linkages, and (3) the type of training and resources required to ensure that planning mechanisms function effectively and efficiently over time.

PLANNING: SHAPING THE FUTURE

Someone once noted that planning is the best substitute for good luck. Unfortunately, even the best planning is no guarantee that desired outcomes will be accomplished. After all, planning is a human endeavor and thus is subject to personal foibles and political and socioeconomic circumstances.

Still, if we are to have any control over intervention, if we are to improve practice, if we are to advance knowledge about intervention, we must choose to plan. And we must do so with commitment, system, sophistication, and imagination.

NOTES

1. W. Sybouts (1992). *Planning in school administration: A handbook.* Westport, CT: Greenwood Press.

2. Sometimes preintervention data are gathered as part of formal screening programs. When large-scale screening procedures are used, intervention planners must design appropriate follow-up screening and referral programs (including "prereferral" intervention). In the United States, for example, development of large-scale screening (child-find) programs is mandated by law. Intensive assessment and consultation are supposed to follow all such screening. How this should be done is controversial. Some screening follow-up consists of psychoeducational testing and results in diagnosis and referral for special help. Some experts argue that a more appropriate first step is to encourage family members, friends, teachers, physicians, and others to explore various corrective strategies. Those taking this position reason that, optimally, this "least intervention needed" approach can lead to

sufficient improvements so that an individual will not require testing and special interventions. At the very least, the process can provide additional data on specific needs.

A related form of consultation, support, and informal assessment is often called prereferral intervention. By improving the way problems are responded to prior to referral, this form of intervention is meant to reduce the amount of formal testing, diagnosis, and referral for special interventions. For example, prereferral consultation in the schools can result in a student staying in the regular classroom because the teacher has learned new ways to work with problems. Such activity also can add "authentic" assessment data, leading to increased validity of diagnoses and referrals.

3. When the focus is on persons, a formal diagnosis makes individuals eligible for services not necessarily available to those with undiagnosed problems. For example, among school-aged youngsters diagnosed as having serious emotional disturbance or learning disabilities, any of the following decisions may be made. (Although eligibility for many services requires assignment of a diagnostic label, the types of services described below generally are as appropriate, or inappropriate, for anyone with a problem.) Plans may be made with respect to (1) class placement—to keep an individual in regular classes or place her or him in a special classroom for all or part of the day; (2) extra help—those kept in regular classes may have a special teacher brought in at selected times to provide special instruction, or the individuals may be sent to a special class for part of the day; after-school tutoring also may be planned, instead of the other arrangements or in addition to them; (3) ancillary services—in addition to educational services, counseling/psychotherapy or speech therapy may be recommended; when physicians and other "medically related" specialists are involved in making decisions, then medication, special diets, vision correction, or various other services also may be recommended; and (4) private remedial school—those requiring a special class not available in a school district can receive public funds for tuition to attend a private remedial school. For adolescents and adults, plans also can include service programs designed to prepare individuals for a vocation or career. These plans may encompass career counseling, job training, and work-study programs that take into account an individual's special needs. Because few classroom programs are designed for adults with problems, planning for them often is limited to clinic tutorial programs or private tutoring.

4. In keeping with the principle of using the least intervention needed, prevention-oriented programs logically come first because, when they are completely effective, the necessity for further activity is eliminated. Prevention programs also provide a vehicle for screening problems early.

5. Public Law 101-476, enacted in 1990.

14

The Role of Assessment

Of course, there are limits to what different people are capable of achieving, but we should make no uninformed assumptions about what these limits are.

Stevenson & Stigler[1]

All intervention decisions involve use of assessment data. Thus, any discussion of systematic planning and implementation requires an informed appreciation of the nature of assessment.

People are continuously involved in assessment. Although such assessments usually are not as formal or systematic as those performed by professionals, the essential processes are the same: information is gathered and judgments formulated (and eventually decisions are made that draw on the data).

Among some practitioners, assessment is referred to as diagnosis, diagnostic testing, screening, and so forth. Following medical usage, these terms suggest application of procedures, such as tests, ratings, and interviews. From this perspective, the intent is to find, label, analyze, and prescribe treatment for an individual's problem. That is, the focus is person- and problem-centered, and the process is shaped primarily by the presumption that problems stem from and belong to targeted individuals.

In keeping with the "medical" model, a dominant perspective among interveners in psychology and education keeps assessment focused on physiological and psychological correlates of pathology, development, or both. This leads to an overemphasis on problems and views of cause and correction that stress person variables.

Until well into the twentieth century, attention centered on a highly delimited set of variables associated with behavior and learning. Over the last few decades, the focus broadened to encompass a range of correlates associated with social skills and temperament, as well as a variety of cognitive and metacognitive variables. For example, in education, criticism of "skill and drill" approaches to assessment and teaching eventually gave rise to renewed interest in practices for fostering higher order thinking. Continuing interest in a broader focus is reflected in calls for an expanded curriculum and greater use of "authentic" or performance assessment.[2]

Because of dissatisfaction with the prevailing person-oriented model, environmental research is attracting increasing attention. In psychology and education, procedures developed to assess home and school variables are enabling researchers to clarify the role such variables play in facilitating human functioning. The findings have major implications for addressing the causes and correction of problems.

Going a step further, transaction-oriented investigators hope to determine the degree of variance accounted for by the interplay of person and environment. Those who adopt transactional (interactional, reciprocal determinist) orientations tend to subsume, not reject, the other two models. Thus, research in this area has promise for understanding a full continuum of factors determining human functioning.[3]

Clearly, planning and implementation are shaped by views about what should be assessed. Therefore, understanding of the planning and implementation problem is facilitated through a broad-based appreciation of assessment. To this end, we offer a brief exploration of (1) a definition of assessment, (2) assessment purposes/functions, (3) single versus multistage assessment and decision making, (4) the concept of mediated assessment, and (5) preassessment interventions.

DEFINITION

The term *assessment* represents an attempt to avoid the conceptual limitations associated with medically related language. Since intervention is not restricted to persons, assessment is not limited to persons; that is, environments and person-environment transactions may also be assessed. And assessment is not restricted to problems; strengths and interests also are assessable.

Formally defined, assessment is the process by which attributes of phenomena are described and judged. Descriptions take the form of data gathered by formal and informal measures, such as tests and observations of behavior or settings. Judgments take the form of interpretive conclusions about the meaning of data, such as whether a phenomenon is good or bad, above or below standard, pathological or not.

In practice, the overall aim of assessment is to describe and make judgments as an aid to decision making. The judgments may represent a conclusion about the past (such as what led to the current state of affairs), a statement about the present (such as how severe a problem is), or a prediction about the future (such as how much change is expected).

FUNCTIONS

As seen in Figure 14.1, we divide assessment into four functions. Each represents the major areas of intervention decision making described below.

- Identification—Data are used to help find and label phenomena of interest. The focus may be on a person, environment, or both and may or may not be on problems.
- Selection—Data are used to help make decisions about the *general* nature and form of recommended intervention. For example: Should structural changes be made in an organization? Should a person pursue educational, psychological, or medically oriented services? Is placement in a certain type of setting indicated?
- Planning for specific practices—With reference to longer-range goals, data are used to decide about short-range objectives and procedures. Examples are specific plans or prescriptions for any given day's intervention encounters.
- Evaluation of intervention—Data are used to decide intervention effectiveness based on positive and negative outcomes. Decisions are made with respect to the impact on (a) particular persons or environments or both, (b) all experiencing a specific intervention, or (c) society as a whole.

Categorization may be done directly as part of identification. However, labelling of phenomena also may be a by-product of any

Figure 14.1
Assessment Processes and Purposes

Assessment defined: The processes by which attributes of phenomena are described and judged.

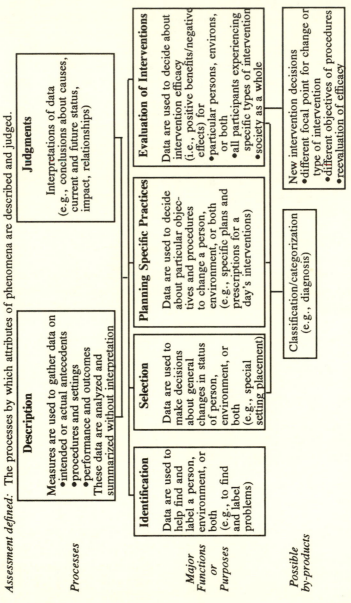

Source: H.S. Adelman and L. Taylor (1993). *Learning problems and learning disabilities: Moving forward.* Pacific
Grove, CA: Brooks/Cole. Reprinted with permission.

of the other three assessment functions.

An example may help clarify the above points. Achievement tests often are used to assess reading performance in a given school. The number of right and wrong answers provides a description of performance on a given set of items at a given time. Based on these data and available norms and prevailing standards, a variety of judgments are made.

Judgments differ regarding those with identical scores who differ in age. Different judgments may be made about groups living in economically advantaged and disadvantaged communities.

Decisions are made about whether to assign "diagnostic" labels to individuals and programs judged as performing poorly. That is, an individual might be formally diagnosed as having a learning disability; a school might be informally assigned a variety of negative labels for failing to do its job.

Decisions are made as to whether some individuals and schools require help; if so, specific plans may be formulated. At a later date, achievement tests provide data for evaluating subsequent performance.

As the example shows, the same form of data may be used to

- find and label programs and individuals (identification)
- decide whether a class, school, or district should consider different approaches to instruction and whether an individual requires special services (selection)
- decide what a given individual should be taught and what specific approach to instruction should be adopted (planning specifics)
- decide whether a school's reading program and whether an individual's progress are adequate (evaluation).

In planning assessment, intended judgments and decisions should guide choices about which data to gather and which to exclude. As the above example suggests, such planning facilitates use of the data as an aid in making a variety of practical and policy decisions.

In addition to having four functions, assessment activity occurs in steps and differs in focus and types of procedures (see Table 14.1). Planning what and how to assess requires understanding the sequence of steps and the range of options. The planner also must appreciate the reactive impact of assessors and their processes. For example, different stimulus-and-response conditions are produced

Table 14.1

Nature and Scope of Assessment Activity

I. *Functions of Assessment*

A. **Identification**
   1. Screening and referral
   2. Diagnostic labeling
   3. Nonpathological attributes

B. **Selection/Placement**
   1. Clarification of options
   2. Client decisions about general changes in status
   3. Professional and agency decisions to accept or reject applicants

C. **Planning specific practices**
   1. Detailed objectives
   2. Detailed procedures

D. **Evaluation of intervention**
   1. Individual efficacy
   2. Efficacy for all participants
   3. Impact on society

II. *Major Steps*

A. **Preparatory decisions about what is to be assessed** (implicit or explicit rationale for assessment)

B. **Description** ("measures" of specified variables and serendipitous data gathering, followed by analyses and descriptive summaries)

C. **Judgments** (interpretations)

D. **Communication and decision making with reference to assessment purposes**

III. *Focus of Assessment*

A. **Focal point**
   1. Person(s)—individuals or groups of individuals
   2. Environment(s)
   3. Person-environment transactions

B. **Nature of phenomena**
   1. Problematic-nonproblematic conditions
   2. Observable-inferred
   3. Proximal-distal
   4. Historic-current-future expectations

C. **Levels**
   1. Molecular-molar analyses of persons
   2. First, second, and third level contextual analyses
   3. Transaction of person-environment

D. **Areas or domains**
   1. Biological and psychological processes
   2. Motor and verbal functioning
   3. Physical environment
   4. Social environment
   5. Person-environment transactions

IV. *Types of Procedures/Instruments* (standardized, semi-standardized, or unstandardized)

A. **Interviews and personal reports** (oral or written questions, inventories, etc.)

B. **Observations**

C. **Verbal-performance measures** (objective instruments such as achievement tests; projective instruments such as thematic pictures; instruments developed by teachers, psychologists, and M.D.s that have not been formally and technically standardized)

D. **Biological tests** (electrorecording devices, chemical analyses)

E. **Available records and data** (analyses of current or cumulated records related to person, environment, transactions; analyses of natural performances and products, such as portfolio assessment) by altering the number of variables assessed, their complexity, and whether they are simulated or natural. Other variations arise with respect to (1) how ambiguous and subjective stimuli are, (2) how well standardized the administration procedures are, (3) how intrusive the procedures are, and (4) how much they cause unintended reactions. Also widely discussed are considerations about similarities and differences between the assessor and the assessed, especially with respect to race, cultural background, socioeconomic status, and gender. Concerns are rampant about how such variations influence assessment processes and outcomes; unfortunately, the data base is relatively weak.

SINGLE VERSUS MULTI-STAGE ASSESSMENT AND DECISION MAKING

For a variety of well-known technical and conceptual reasons, assessment data are limited and at times erroneous. Increasingly, sequential or multistage assessments are advocated as a way to enhance decision accuracy and improve many facets of intervention practice and research.

For example, in screening problems, the deficiencies of first-level screening data are generally acknowledged. At the same time, concerned professionals warn that diagnoses and placement decisions often are made solely on the basis of such data. Even when the best available assessment procedures are used, initial intervention decisions may be in error. In all cases, sound practice calls for taking additional steps to confirm or disconfirm the problem through further assessment prior to and after a program is implemented. Figure 14.2 illustrates a sequence for assessment and decision making related to screening, placement, and specific planning.

MEDIATED ASSESSMENT

Conventional psychometric approaches raise many validity concerns. A common example is that, under formal assessment conditions, poor performance among problem populations may be

Figure 14.2
Screening, Placement, and Specific Planning as a
Complex Sequence

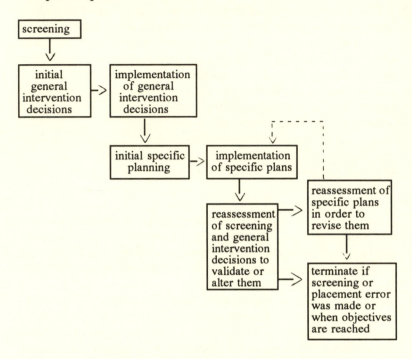

due to low or negative (avoidance) motivation resulting from high anxiety or negative attitudes. These factors and cultural differences can negatively affect the performance of persons from nondominant cultural backgrounds. Critics argue that it is impossible to know whether failure to demonstrate specific knowledge, abilities, or skills represents a real deficiency. That is, assessment results for such persons may be contaminated and cannot be taken at face value. Clearly, the implications are profound.

Within the psychometric tradition, several strategies are used to address validity concerns. These include (1) accounting for contaminants when interpreting findings, (2) improving task content and administration to reduce biasing conditions, including frequent reassessments, and (3) going beyond standardized administration to assess how much more the individual can do. In this last regard, procedures include lengthening time limits, prompting, and adding a brief teaching facet to the assessment process.

Going a step further, those in the dynamic assessment movement use a highly mediated approach to assess how much more individuals can do when comprehensively prompted and taught. That is, they actively monitor and modify the interaction with clients to induce successful functioning. Clients are "prodded, directed, and reinforced into a role of active seeker and organizer of information."[4]

Because the term *dynamic assessment* is used mainly in education and in a somewhat narrowly defined way, we contrast conventional practices with what we describe generically as mediated assessment. This term encompasses but goes beyond dynamic assessment to include all intervener activity designed to determine whether the system assessed can perform at a higher level. The intent of the assessor is not to replace but to supplement prevailing assessment procedures in order to seek data not available through prevailing approaches. In contrast to the nondynamic/static approach found in typical psychometric testing, such assessors assume a highly active "testing the limits" stance to facilitate increased levels of performance. The process often takes the form of an assess-teach-reassess approach, involving a reasonable interval of time for learning. Often data are gathered on a client's performance capability *in situ* and on intervention approaches that appear effective.

The main concern about mediated assessment is how improved assessment performance is interpreted. For instance, with respect to assumptions underlying dynamic assessment, critics stress that developmental deficiencies cannot be modified significantly over brief periods of time. Thus, in interpreting improved assessment performance, they see changes as primarily reflecting motivational rather than functional modifiability.

PREASSESSMENT INTERVENTIONS

Critics concerned about premature person-focused assessment argue that major efforts to improve programs should come first. In this context, we recall Hobbs' views on screening children's problems: "Ideally, special screening programs to identify health problems and developmental difficulties of children should not be necessary. All children regardless of economic status should be able to participate in a comprehensive health maintenance program."[5] And we would add that in kindergarten and the elementary grades, they should be provided comprehensive psychoeducationally oriented school programs.

Screening problems should be secondary to efforts to evolve programs to match clients' levels of motivation and development. Preventive and early-age intervention programs can reduce the numbers of those experiencing problems, provide improved *in situ* screening to identify those who continue to require special help, and thereby reduce the necessity for special assessment.

Considerable support exists for improving programs as the first step in a screening sequence for problems. In essence, the idea is that, prior to assessment, programs to ameliorate problems should (1) enhance general practices in the "mainstream" and (2) remedy problems that arise as soon as possible and with the least intervention needed. To accomplish these goals requires broadening general (mainstream) practices and increasing the availability of support mechanisms. Prominent among the advocated changes are (1) adding personnel, such as aides, trainees, volunteers, and peer support, (2) improvement of setting conditions, such as enhanced working relationships, and (3) upgrading the technical infrastructure through addition and sophisticated use of technological innovations (e.g., computers, interactive video, up-to-date science equipment). Proponents also stress providing mainstream interveners with training, consultation, peer support, and collaboration to increase use of corrective strategies prior to referral for specialized interventions.[6]

In the preceding discussion, we reviewed a range of basic complexities and controversies surrounding assessment for identification, selection, program planning, and evaluation. Some of the controversy stems from deficiencies and limitations of specific procedures. Additional concerns emerge from analyses of how assessment shapes research, practice, and related policy decisions. Rather than enumerate such concerns, we can simply reiterate implications of the overemphasis on assessing persons. As noted already, this overemphasis tends to exonerate environmental variables as causal factors and as the focus for corrective strategies. Ironically, it also appears to hinder development of procedures for assessing the role of the environment, thereby perpetuating the overly person-centered emphasis in research, practice, and policy. Appreciation of such concerns makes the need for improved practices and a broader focus evident.

Controversy related to assessment, and indeed any intervention activity, is inevitable. Even when relatively objective assessment data are used, subsequent decisions often are extremely subjective. This is not surprising given that most decisions involve consider-ations that go well beyond the availability of valid data. More often than not, complex socio-political-economic value questions are involved. In some cases, seemingly relevant data are ignored in order to arrive at a decision that the decision makers see as viable and beneficial. As Thorndike and Hagen have aptly observed, "The wisdom of the decider is crucial."[7]

Despite the deficiencies of prevailing assessment practices, each day planners are called upon to use assessment data in making decisions. Fortunately, as highlighted above, recent trends point to promising approaches that go beyond conventional procedures in gathering data. And the better the data are, the better the planning can be.

NOTES

1. H.W. Stevenson & J.W. Stigler (1992). *The learning gap: Why our schools are failing and what we can learn from Japanese and Chinese education*. New York: Summit Books.

2. The focus of authentic assessment is on performance-based evaluation using such procedures as essays, open-ended responses, responses to computer simulations, interview data, and analyses of an individual's journals and work that is accumulated over time in a portfolio. See D.A. Archibald & F.M. Newman (1988). *Beyond standardized testing: Assessing authentic academic achievement in secondary schools*. Washington, DC: National Association of School Principals. R.L. Linn, E.L. Baker, & S.B. Dunbar (1991). Complex, performance-based assessment: Expectations and validation criteria. *Educational Researcher, 20*, 15-21. G. Wiggins (1989). A true test:

Toward more authentic and equitable assessment. *Phi Delta Kappan, 70,* 703–713.

3. On environment and person-environment assessment, see the discussion in Part I.

4. C.S. Lidz (Ed.) (1987). *Dynamic assessment: An interactional approach to evaluating learning potential.* New York: Guilford Press, pp. 3–4. Also, on dynamic assessment, see A.S. Palincsar, A.L. Brown, & J.C. Campione (1991). Dynamic assessment. In H.L. Swanson (Ed.), *Handbook of assessment of learning disabilities: Theory, research, and practice.* Austin, TX: PRO-ED, pp. 75–94.

5. N. Hobbs (1975). *The future of children: Categories, labels, and their consequences.* San Francisco: Jossey-Bass.

6. Recent discussion about improving the response of mainstream interveners through consultation processes incorporate the concept of prereferral interventions in education. See D. Fuchs (1991). Mainstream assistance teams: A prereferral intervention system for difficult-to-teach students. In G. Stoner, M.R. Shinn, & H.M. Walker (Eds.), *Interventions for achievement and behavior problems.* Washington, DC: National Association of School Psychologists, pp. 241–67. J.L. Graden, A. Casey, & S.L. Christenson (1985). Implementing a prereferral intervention system: Part I. The model. *Exceptional Children, 51,* 377–84. L.J. Johnson & M.C. Pugach (1991). Peer collaboration: Accommodating students with mild learning and behavior problems. *Exceptional Children, 57,* 454–61.

7. R.L. Thorndike & E.P. Hagen (1977). *Measurement and evaluation* (2nd ed.). New York: Wiley, p. 20.

15

Facilitating Implementation: Concepts and Concerns

Changing the individual while leaving the world alone is a dubious proposition.

Neisser[1]

Not all that is planned is carried out; not everything done is planned. Appropriate implementation requires understanding what is intended and what isn't and how to accomplish the former and avoid the latter.

No intervener has control over all important elements involved in accomplishing intended intervention outcomes. Indeed, interveners can affect only a relatively small segment of the physical and social context surrounding a client. With specific respect to facilitation, however, interveners differ in the degree to which they dominate what occurs. As portrayed in Figure 15.1, at times highly motivated clients are able to self-select outcomes and pursue them on their own, even outside the intervention setting. This certainly constitutes the least intervention needed and is in marked contrast to times when the intervener selects outcomes and uses direct control techniques to accomplish them.

Clients with different interests and problems vary in how much intervention they require. And interveners differ significantly in their attempts to apply the principle of least intervention needed. Therefore, interventions vary considerably in the amount and source of intervener control. In the majority of educational and psychological settings, interveners probably select most outcomes, which then are pursued primarily through intervener facilitation.

Whether intervener-dominated or client-initiated, the problem of

Figure 15.1
Amount and Source of Intervention Control

Outcome Selection

Client-selected outcomes	Intervener facilitates outcome selection	Intervener-selected outcomes

< --- >

Least Intervention   **Most Intervention**

< --- >

Functioning on one's own	Intervener facilitates functioning	Intervener uses direct control techniques

Intervener Facilitation

attention. In what follows, we present our perspective on key concepts and concerns relevant to the problem.

Intervention often is described as an art. There may be considerable truth in this view. For most interveners, however, the art flows out of an intuitive or cultivated appreciation of what it takes to facilitate pursuit of outcomes.

Our interest here is in enhancing cultivated appreciation. We begin with a brief discussion of context considerations and then move on to the concept of structure, ideas about systematically addressing differences in motivation and capability, and the construct of personalized intervention. Finally, we address barriers to working relationships, organizational change, and mechanisms to facilitate intervention collaboration and consolidation.

INTERVENTION SETTING

Research on the effect of settings on behavior is helping clarify the impact of physical and social contextual variables.[2] Crowding, lack of privacy, and extremely ill-equipped or poorly arranged environments are widely discussed examples of factors that produce negative effects.

Key setting and context characteristics surface in the process of answering three questions: (1) What are the composition and organization of the social context? (2) What are the nature and facilitating implementation of planned intervention warrants special quality of the physical surroundings and resources (e.g., architecture, equipment, tools, materials, furnishings, design, color, lighting, temperature control)? and (3) How is the setting perceived (e.g., perceptions of physical, social, intellectual, political, and moral atmosphere)?

A few comments with specific regard to intervention are in order. In thinking about the social context, the central factor determining quality of facilitation may reasonably be viewed as the presence of interveners with at least minimal competence and an appropriate range of resources, especially enough time. How much competence and how many resources are necessary appear dependent on, first, the scope of the system (e.g., size of organization, number of clients) and, second, client needs and characteristics. In general, the larger the system and the greater its needs, the more crucial it probably is to have highly competent interveners and a full complement of resources.

In teaching, for example, the greater the number of students, the more critical is the ratio of students to personnel, such as teacher, aides, volunteers, and specialists. The ratio may be even more significant if a large percentage of the students have learning or behavior problems. A related consideration is group composition. For all students, one-to-one instruction is sometimes necessary. Conversely, some things are learned best in the context of a group, especially when the group is selected because its characteristics can facilitate what is to be learned. Furthermore, class composition shapes dynamics and thus can profoundly affect efforts to facilitate learning. For instance, working with others one likes or admires can change learning experiences from mediocre to exceptional. Comparable points can be made about programs designed to deal with psychosocial problems (such as substance abuse and delinquency) and about those that focus on organizational change.

Quality of physical surroundings and resources also is of concern. Think about the impact on interveners and clients of run-down buildings in urban ghettos as contrasted to the well-kept facilities found in most suburban areas. Think about settings equipped with the latest technology and software as contrasted to those that have little or no equipment and materials.

Of course, whether the environment appears good or bad to

others can be less significant than how it appears to the client and the intervener. Take the topic of intervener and client characteristics, for example. From the standpoint of a specific client and intervener, concern about the match between gender, race, ethnicity, age, and other intervener and client characteristics all may boil down to whether they perceive each other as acceptable.

STRUCTURE

The concept of structure provides another way to discuss setting variables and intervention facilitation. In talking about structure, some people seem to see it as all or nothing. That is, they see an intervention as structured or unstructured. Moreover, some equate structure only with limit setting and control. For instance, when someone misbehaves, observers often prescribe "more structure." Sometimes the phrase used is "clearer limits and consequences," but the idea is the same. The misbehaving individual is seen as out of control, and the observer perceives the solution as exerting greater control over the person.

Most interveners wish it were that easy. There comes a point when efforts to use external means to control behavior are incompatible with developing the type of working relationship that facilitates desired outcomes. Using the term *structure* as synonymous with external efforts to control the behavior of others ignores this consideration.[3]

Intervention structure involves communication, support, direction, and the type of limits or external controls that facilitate pursuit of long-range aims. The intent is to facilitate the ends specified in the underlying intervention rationale, not just to control behavior. Obviously, intended outcomes cannot be accomplished when clients are uncooperative or out of control. Equally obvious, however, is the fact that some procedures used to control behavior interfere with moving toward desired ends. In expending extensive time and resources on surveillance to control staff behavior, an organization is likely to negatively affect morale, and thereby inhibit pursuit of its goals. Clients on medication to control behavior may misbehave less but may be too sedated to pursue intervention aims and thus make no better progress than before drugs were prescribed. A teacher cannot teach a youngster who is suspended from school, and the youngster may be less receptive to the teacher when the suspension ends.

Structure does "control" behavior, but its primary purpose is to provide a client with the type of support and direction necessary for accomplishing intervention outcomes. Support and direction are used to clarify information; this includes providing information about limits or external controls, but as the last, not the first, consideration. Support and direction can be provided in little or great amounts. Furthermore, the amount offered can and usually should differ from task to task.

Ideally, the type and degree of support and direction used should vary with the clients' requirements. Some activities can and should be pursued without help; this avoids fostering dependency and undermining a client's intrinsic motivation. Other tasks require considerable help.

Persons designated as primary interveners are the single most important source of support and direction. However, peers, aides, volunteers, and various resources such as materials and equipment can be used to approximate the ideal of varying structure to meet client requirements.

Figuring out the best way to provide structure is central in building a working relationship with a client. The problem is to find the right balance so that the relationship is neither too controlling and dependency-producing nor too permissive. Few instances warrant creation of an authoritarian atmosphere, and no intervener wants a client to take liberties. In this regard, topics such as caring, mutual respect, and empathy often are discussed. Although a working relationship may be facilitative even if it is not positive and warm, the literature tends to support the value of these qualities. As a result, interveners often are taught that a positive working relationship requires mutual respect, and a warm working relationship requires mutual caring and understanding.

The concept of structure also has relevance in discussing intervention activities and the use of techniques. Some degree of structure is inherent in all activities and can be increased through the use of techniques. That is, appropriate activities support and direct functioning, and techniques are ways to enhance that structure. As we conceive techniques, they enhance structure by increasing an activity's attractiveness and accessibility and by decreasing avoidance and distraction. The following brief discourse is offered to elaborate on the facilitative role of activities and techniques.

Activities

Their prominence should make activities one of the most investigated facets of intervention. But the fact is that the study and conceptualization of intervention activities constitutes a much neglected area.

A staggering number of packaged and published intervention materials and "programs" are marketed. Some activities are useful in implementing a variety of content and techniques. Others, programmed materials for example, prescribe content and outcomes, incorporate a particular set of techniques, and reflect specific theories and ideas about the nature of intervention. Some activities are designed primarily for practice to solidify and consolidate capabilities. Practice activities present a special concern because they frequently involve the type of drill people find dull and prefer to avoid. "Homework" assignments are often cited as the prototype for this concern.

The diversity of activities makes it desirable to group or categorize them. One useful way to distinguish among activities is with reference to their purpose. Although this approach is straightforward and simple, it does not convey the complexities involved in making decisions about which to use.

Minimally, activities should be differentiated in terms of

- purpose (e.g., used to facilitate learning, performance, production, practice, problem solving, communication, exploration, recreation, creative expression, entertainment with respect to one or more areas of system function)
- form (e.g., printed materials; writing and performing; role playing; group and one-to-one discussions; computers, video, and other machines, tools, instruments, and equipment; games)
- source (e.g., commercially or intervener-made; noncommercial resources accessible in the community)
- provider (e.g., underwriters for costs).

Discussing learning and teaching, Brophy and Alleman define activities as "anything that students are expected to do, beyond getting input through reading or listening, in order to learn, practice, apply, evaluate, or in any other way respond to curricular content." They see activities as in the service of the content goals of the intervention; that is, activities are means to ends, not ends in themselves. For students, a good activity is one that engages them in actively processing content, "developing personal ownership, and appreciation of it, and applying it to their lives outside of school." The success of an activity is seen as dependent not only on the activity itself but on the nature of the intervention structure before, during, and after the activity.[4] In our terms, the activity's success is dependent on support, direction, and communication.

Brophy and Alleman formulate a rich set of principles and a framework to aid in the design, selection, and evaluation of activities. For example, as necessary criteria for an activity, they stress goal relevance, appropriate level of difficulty, feasibility, and cost effectiveness. Desired but not essential features include activities that meet multiple goals, have motivational value and topic currency, provide opportunities to complete whole tasks rather than practicing part-skills, foster higher order thinking, and are adaptable to accommodate individual differences in interests or abilities. For pursuing sets of activities, Brophy and Alleman place particular emphasis on variety, progressive levels of difficulty or complexity, and life and natural applications.

Practical decisions about what activities to use are shaped by their source; of particular concern is the cost of some manufactured materials. Costs aside, many decisions about the form and purpose of activities are related fundamentally to philosophical, psychological, and political views of the intervention process. For example, if one believes that the best learning takes place through carefully controlled and sequenced instruction, one is unlikely to choose discovery-oriented learning activities.

Whatever one's orientation, however, the job of matching client and intervention is made easier when multiple sources and forms of activities are drawn upon. Interveners often begin with as much ready-made material as can be accessed. Inevitably, however, some activities must be adapted to fit specific circumstances, especially when clients with major problems are involved. Techniques are used to make the necessary adaptations.

Techniques

In their discussion of activities, Brophy and Alleman stress the importance of introducing the activity, providing a scaffold that supports and directs, encouraging independent work, and concluding with reflection and assessment as a form of debriefing about what has been accomplished. Each point represents a technique by which an intervener can enhance the potency of any activity.

Techniques alter an activity's structure. We see their function as making activities more attractive and accessible and/or minimizing interfering factors, such as circumstances that lead to avoidance and distraction. Viewed in this way, techniques are fundamental processes used to address the reality that clients differ in the degree of support and direction they require on any given task and at any given time. The same activity can be varied to match a client's need for more or less structure by changing, for example, the amount of cueing and prompting. Some variations are "built in" at the time an activity is developed, such as special formatting in published materials; others are added as an activity is implemented.

In sum, we define techniques as *planned variations in the characteristics of a tool or the way it is applied, the immediate intent of which is to increase attraction and accessibility and decrease avoidance and distraction.* From a psychological perspective, techniques are used to enhance (1) motivation (positive attitudes, commitment, approach tendencies, follow-through), (2) sensory intake (perceptual search and detection), (3) processing and decision making (evaluation and selection), and (4) output (practice, application, demonstration). Techniques are categorized with reference to each of these aspects of human functioning in Table 15.1.

ADDRESSING MOTIVATION

Facilitating intervention involves arranging that relatively small

Table 15.1

Categorizing Techniques

I. For enhancing motivation

A. *Nurturance* (including positive regard, acceptance and validation of feelings, appropriate reassurance, praise, and satisfaction)
Specific examples:
- eliciting and listening to problems, goals, and progress
- statements to reassure students/clients that change is possible
- increasing nonauthoritarian/nonsupervisory interpersonal interactions
- increasing positive feedback and positive public recognition
- reducing criticism, especially related to performance
- avoiding confrontations

B. *Permission* for exploration and change (including encouragement and opportunity)
Specific examples:
- increasing availability of valued opportunities
- establishing and clarifying appropriate expectations and "set"
- modeling expression of affect (self-disclosing) when relevant
- encouraging pursuit of choices and preferences
- reducing demand characteristics such as expanding behavioral and time limits, reducing the amount to be done

C. *Protection* for exploration and change (including principles and guidelines—rights and rules—to establish "safe" conditions)
Specific examples:
- reducing exposures to negative appraisals
- providing privacy and support for "risk taking"
- making statements to reassure clients if risk taking is not successful
- reducing exposure to negative interactions with significant others through eliminating inappropriate competition and providing privacy
- establishing nondistracting and safe work areas
- establishing guidelines, consistency, and fairness in rule application
- advocating rights through statements and physical action

D. *Facilitating effectiveness* (see techniques for enhancing sensory intake, processing, decision making, and output)

II. For sensory intake, processing, decision making, and output

A. *Meaning* (including personal valuing and association with previous experiences)
Specific examples:
- using stimuli of current interest and meaning
- introducing stimuli through association with meaningful materials, such as analogies and pictorial representation of verbal concepts, stressing emotional connections
- presenting novel stimuli
- participating in decision making

B. *Scaffolding* (including amount, form, sequencing and pacing, as well as source of support and guidance)
Specific examples:
- presenting small, discrete units of material and/or information
- increasing vividness and distinctiveness of stimuli through physical and temporal figure-ground contrasts (patterning and sequencing), such as varying context, texture, shading, outlining, use of color

(cont.)

Table 15.1 (cont.)

- varying levels of abstraction and complexity
- using multisensory presentation
- providing models to emulate, such as demonstrations, role models
- encouraging self-selection of stimuli
- using prompts and cues, such as color coding, directional arrows, step-by-step directions
- using verbally mediated "self"- direction ("stop, look, and listen")
- grouping material
- using formal coding and decoding strategies such as mnemonic devices, word analysis and synthesis
- rote use of specified study skill and decision-making sequences
- allowing responses to be idiosyncratic with regard to rate, style, amount, and quality
- reducing criteria for success
- using mechanical devices for display, processing, and production, such as projectors, tape recorders, and other audiovisual media, typewriters, calculators, computers
- using person resources to aid in displaying, processing, and producing

C. *Active contact and use* (including amount, form, and sequencing and pacing of interaction with relevant stimuli)
  Specific examples:
  - using immediate and frequent review
  - allowing for self-pacing
  - overlearning
  - small increments in level of difficulty, such as in "errorless training"
  - using personally valued opportunities for practice
  - role playing and role taking
  - using formal reference aids, such as dictionaries and charts
  - use of mechanical devices and person resources to aid in interactions

D. *Feedback* (including amount, form, sequencing and pacing, and source of information/rewards)
  Specific examples:
  - providing feedback in the form of information/rewards
  - providing immediate feedback for all processes and/or outcomes or provided on a contingency basis (reinforcement schedules or need)
  - peer and/or self-evaluation
  - using mechanical monitoring and scoring

III. **"Technical methods."** Sometimes groups of techniques are combined into comprehensive and complex sets of tools (activities/experiences/ materials and techniques). Despite the fact that they are complex methods, they usually are referred to simply as techniques as they are communicated from intervener to intervener.
  Specific examples:
  - kinesthetic techniques
  - desensitization and relaxation techniques
  - problem-solving strategies
  - reciprocal teaching

Note: While we have attempted to conceptualize discrete categories, all the examples are not mutually exclusive.

but critical facet of the setting that can be affected. As discussed above, one aspect of this is providing appropriate structure for client efforts to pursue intervention outcomes. More comprehensively, the intent is to create an "environment" (objectives, processes, content) that mobilizes and then maintains client mobilization until the intervention is successful. The view of motivation incorporated into an underlying intervention rationale profoundly shapes how these concerns are understood and addressed. For our purposes here, we draw on cognitive-affective theory and research and highlight intrinsic motivation as a primary concept for understanding facilitation.[5]

Ready examples of why motivation must be addressed in a systematic manner are seen every day by those who work with individuals in clinical and classroom settings and in every effort to accomplish institutional changes. Two contemporary institutional examples include reforms designed to restructure schools and the movement to integrate a wide range of health and social services and link them to school sites. In both these cases, one of the first concerns is how to mobilize and direct the energy of those involved. Negative attitudes must be overcome. New attitudes must be engendered. New working relationships must be established. New skills must be learned.

Once all this is addressed, the problems of maintaining energy and direction arise. The novelty and excitement of newness wear off. The demands of change sap energy. New skills are mastered only through practice.

The substance of comprehensive change usually is achieved only when fairly high levels of positive energy among those involved can be mobilized over extended periods of time, and the sustained energy is appropriately directed. For interveners, this means systematically planning and implementing motivationally oriented processes.

Mobilizing the Client

Interveners rarely have enough control to force clients to pursue major intervention outcomes. Consequently, motivation-oriented strategies are a primary facilitation concern. An appreciation of strategies that mobilize client initiative requires understanding what is likely to affect a client's positive and negative motivation with respect to intervention processes, content, and outcomes. Particular attention to the following ideas seems warranted:

- Optimal functioning requires motivational readiness. Readiness is not viewed in the old sense of waiting until a client is interested. Rather, it is understood in the contemporary sense of designing interventions to maximize the likelihood that processes, content, and outcomes are perceived as vivid, valued, and attainable.
- Interveners must not only try to increase motivation, especially intrinsic motivation, but must also avoid practices that decrease motivation. For example, they must be careful not to overrely on extrinsics to entice and reward because to do so may decrease intrinsic motivation.
- Motivation is a process and an outcome concern. For example, with respect to outcomes, interventions should be designed to maintain, enhance, and expand intrinsic motivation for pursuing relevant activity beyond immediate intervention efforts.
- Increasing intrinsic motivation involves affecting a client's thoughts, feelings, and decisions. In general, the intent is to use procedures that can reduce negative feelings, thoughts, and coping strategies and increase positive ones with respect to intervention outcomes, processes, and content. For problematic conditions, this means especially identifying and minimizing experiences that maintain or may increase avoidance motivation.

Factors that appear basic in efforts to mobilize clients encompass (1) availability of options, (2) client participation in decision making, and (3) client awareness of accomplishments. Each of these overlapping notions is discussed below.[6]

Options. If the only choice clients have is between doing something they hate and doing something they loathe, the options are unlikely to please them, and their motivation to make a choice will be low. Even if they do choose one over the other, desired motivational effects are unlikely to occur. Furthermore, one client may not like participating in any intervention in any way. Another may want to participate but may dislike the planned approach. A third has her own ideas about what outcomes should be pursued. A fourth will try anything if someone will direct him through each step. Such differences underscore the necessity of options for processes (including content and structure) and outcomes.

Every practitioner knows the value of variety. Variety helps address the reality of differences among clients in current interests and capabilities. This reality is of particular concern in dealing with that significant proportion who are not interested and perhaps have avoidance tendencies toward common intervention approaches. Such clients probably will be unreceptive to approaches that look like "the same old thing." When few of the currently available options are appealing, exceptional efforts seem necessary if clients are to perceive intervention outcomes and activity as personally valuable and obtainable and the intervener as supportive. This may involve (1) further expansion of the range of options, including, if necessary, replacing established processes; (2) accommodating a wider range of their behavior than usually is tolerated, such as widening limits with respect to the amount of deviance permitted; and (3) choice processes that encourage personal and active decision making.

Decision making. Given valued and feasible options, ultimately, the facilitative impact of the options is dependent on how clients are involved in making decisions about which to pursue. Decision-making processes can lead to perceptions of coercion and control or to perceptions of real choice and self-determination. Such differences in perception can affect whether a client is mobilized to pursue or avoid planned activities and outcomes.

People who have the opportunity to make decisions among valued and feasible options tend to commit to following through. In contrast, people not involved in decisions often have little commitment to what is decided. And if individuals disagree with a decision that affects them, failure to follow through may be paired with hostile reactions.

Thus, decision-making processes that affect perceptions of choice, value, and probable outcome are primary considerations in mobilizing clients. Optimally, the intent is to maximize perceptions of real choices from among valued and attainable process, content, and outcome options. At the very least, it seems basic to minimize perceptions suggesting that there is no choice, that there is little value in available options, or that failure is probable.

Three special points about decision making are worth underscoring. First, we note that the most fundamental decision for some clients is whether they want to participate. In such cases, the decision to do so in a proactive way often depends on whether the client perceives intervention options as positively and significantly different from previous ones that didn't work out. For this reason, it may be necessary temporarily to put aside established options and standards, especially when clients with serious problems are involved.

Second, decisions reflect participants' current perceptions. As perceptions shift, decisions must be reevaluated and modified in ways that maintain client mobilization.

Third, effective and efficient decision making is a basic skill that is poorly developed in some clients. Involving these clients in decision making provides an opportunity not only to enhance their motivation but to improve this basic skill.

Client awareness of accomplishments. Research warns that too much intervener surveillance and use of rewards and punishment can produce serious negative consequences. Sparing use of external monitoring and extrinsic appraisals is indicated since such approaches may be perceived by clients as efforts to control. Moreover, close monitoring may be viewed as a sign of intervener doubt about client competence to perform without assistance. Both perceptions can undermine a client's sense of well-being and may even lead to psychological reactance. Procedures for providing clients with information on accomplishments must be designed with all this in mind.

Self-monitoring techniques, personal record keeping, and client-intervener dialogues are examples of recommended procedures. They can provide information to clarify progress and effectiveness without seriously threatening feelings of competence and self-determination. Many clients are ready and able to self-evaluate—to say what's working well and what isn't from their perspective. In such cases, dialogues are the easiest and most direct way to learn about how they perceive the match between themselves and the intervention.

Some clients, of course, have yet to develop the abilities for self-evaluating at the desired level. Others are motivated to make excuses, to overstate how well they are doing, or to avoid discussing the matter at all. Some do this because they do not perceive the personal value in self-evaluating, or they may not feel it's safe to say what is on their minds. Here, too, participating in self-evaluation and engaging in dialogues with sufficient support and direction can be opportunities for individuals to develop appropriate skills and attitudes.

To maintain mobilization, feedback also can stress effectiveness in making decisions and can relate outcomes to the client's intrinsic reasons for participating in the intervention. Handled well, such information should contribute to clients' feelings of competence, self-determination, and relatedness and should clarify directions for the future. Of course, as discussed next, maintaining mobilization encompasses more than attending to the form and content of feedback.

Maintaining Mobilization

Because there is no proven set of procedures and principles for maintaining mobilization, interveners continue to synthesize current ideas. Our efforts along these lines are reflected throughout this discussion. (Also see Part II regarding matching the client's current levels of motivation and development, and review the techniques outlined in Table 15.1).

In general, maintaining mobilization requires processes that, over time, can instigate and enhance client perceptions of valued opportunities (e.g., options), control (e.g., feelings of self-determination), and accomplishment (e.g., feelings of competence). For motivated clients, ongoing facilitation stresses ways to maintain and possibly enhance intrinsic motivation, and to enable the client to pursue outcomes effectively, efficiently, and with a minimum of negative side effects. At times, all that may be necessary is to help clear the way of external hurdles and to structure the situation so that clients can proceed on their own. At other times, maintaining mobilization requires leading, guiding, stimulating, clarifying, and supporting. And, as we have stressed, mobilization probably is best facilitated when procedures are perceived by clients as good ways to reach desired outcomes.

Efforts to maintain mobilization build on processes used initially to mobilize the client. The procedures are conceived in terms of nine comprehensive facilitation or enabling objectives. These emphasize that the focus in designing interactions with the clients is to

- establish and maintain an appropriate working relationship (e.g., through creating a sense of trust, open communication, providing support and direction as required)
- clarify the purpose of activities and procedures, especially those designed to help correct specific problems
- clarify why procedures should be effective
- clarify the nature and purpose of evaluative measures
- build on previous capabilities and interests
- present outcomes, processes, and content in ways that structure attending to the most relevant features (e.g., modeling, cueing)
- guide motivated practice (e.g., suggesting and providing opportunities for meaningful applications and clarifying ways to organize practice)
- provide continuous information to ensure awareness of accomplishments
- provide opportunities for continued application and generalization (e.g., concluding the process by addressing ways in which the client can pursue additional, self-directed accomplishments in the area and/or can arrange for additional support and direction).

The focus for maintaining mobilization is not on one procedure at a time. Interveners' rationales usually provide an overall theory, model, or concept that guides them to certain procedures and away from others. In general, procedures and content are tightly interwoven, with procedures clearly seen as means to an end.

Motivated Practice

Facilitating motivated practice appears to require a variety of task options that are perceived as challenging but not too hard. And, as we have stressed, the processes by which tasks are chosen must lead to client perceptions that activities or outcomes (preferably both) are worthwhile—especially as sources of personal satisfaction. Within limits, the stronger the sense of potential outcome satisfaction, the more likely practice will be pursued even when practice activities are rather dull. When expectations of potential outcome satisfaction are low, interveners and clients must design practice activities that are positively motivating in and of themselves.

A primary intervention emphasis on intrinsic motivation is not without its critics.

> In the real world, people need to work and solve problems even when they aren't "motivated" to do so. Also, if a person wants to be good at something, they need to practice it day in and day out, and that's not fun! Too much emphasis on intrinsic motivation spoils people so that they don't want to do anything unless it's personally relevant and interesting.

We recognize that people must do many things in their lives that they do not experience positively. How we all learn to put up with such circumstances is an interesting question, but one for which psychologists have yet to find a satisfactory answer. (We doubt that interveners must manufacture experiences involving long periods of drudgery in order for people to learn to tolerate what is boring.)

Motivational theory suggests that even if intervention activities are not enjoyable, they can be viewed as worthwhile and experienced as satisfying. Task persistence, for example, seems facilitated by the expectation that one will feel smart or competent while performing the task or at least will feel that way afterwards. Therefore, even if a task isn't fun, expectation of feeling some sense of satisfaction related to the process or outcome still can be a powerful intrinsic factor motivating client behavior.

ADDRESSING CAPABILITIES

Matching motivation is seen as a first-order consideration in facilitating intervention. To do so, however, is difficult without simultaneously matching the client's capabilities. Consequently, addressing variability in development as reflected in functioning must be given simultaneous consideration.

Because the literature on individualized intervention has covered this topic rather extensively, we only underscore two points here. First, psychologists and educators interested in differences in capability find it useful to stress four key performance dimensions: (1) *rate*—the pace at which the system performs, (2) *style*— preferences with regard to ways of proceeding, (3) *amount*—quantity of work the system produces, and (4) *quality*—care, mastery, and aesthetic features demonstrated in performance.

Although each dimension is recognized as representing significant developmental differences, many efforts to facilitate intervention do not systematically address all four. Available evidence suggests that some accommodation for differences in rate and amount occurs with regularity. But there is less agreement and consistency about addressing variations in style and quality.

Our second point is a reminder that indices of performance rate, style, amount, and quality not only reflect development but also are influenced by levels of motivation to perform. Low or negative motivation can confound efforts to assess a system's capacities in any area of development. This is especially likely when previous experiences reduce motivation to perform. The implications for the use of such data in planning and implementation are obvious.

PERSONALIZING INTERVENTIONS

The construct of personalization offers a concept around which to organize thinking about facilitating intervention. As we use the term, personalization is a best general practice approach designed to address the problem of the match. The focus is a broad one in that it emphasizes matching client differences with respect to both motivation and developmental levels.[7]

Equally as important, the client's perception is used to assess how good the match is. That is, the construct of the match is operationalized by accepting the client's perspective. This approach to defining "goodness of fit" also is an aid in assessing how well an intervention balances between using the   least intervention and providing what is needed—in terms of both programs and structure.

More specifically, personalized interventions are built on the following assumptions:

- Client functioning is determined by the ongoing transactions between the client and the intervention.
- Optimal functioning results from an optimal match between the client's accumulated capacities and attitudes and current state of being and the intervention's processes and context.
- Matching a client's motivation must be a primary process objective.
- Matching the client's pattern of acquired capacities must also be a primary process objective.

- The client's perception is the critical criterion for deciding whether a good intervention-client match exists.
- Procedures for facilitating client choice from among a relatively wide range of desirable process, content, and outcome options are essential.

In keeping with the above assumptions, the major elements of personalized interventions are (1) regular use of dialogues to explore client perceptions of how well the intervention matches current levels of motivation and capability, (2) a broad range of outcome, content, and process options from which the client can make choices, (3) procedures to facilitate active decision making on the part of the client, (4) formulation of specific intervention plans, (5) establishment of mutual agreements about the plan and the ongoing relationship between the client and intervener(s) and the client and other clients, and (6) regular reassessments of decisions, reformulation of plans, and renegotiation of agreements based on mutual evaluations of progress, problems, and current client perceptions of the client-intervention match.

Besides improved functioning and problem solving, the above strategies are intended to enhance intrinsic valuing of intended outcomes and a sense of personal responsibility for pursuing them. And the fundamental emphasis on individual differences may have the positive side effect of increasing acceptance and even appreciation of such differences.

BARRIERS TO WORKING RELATIONSHIPS

As we have mentioned throughout, facilitating intervention requires establishing and maintaining productive working relationships. In this regard, each concept and concern discussed above comes into play. Other factors, of course, can get in the way. These, too, must be studied to clarify their implications and how to counter them.

Dynamics and Differences as Barriers

Working relationships, like other interpersonal transactions, often reflect patterns of poor communication, avoidance, and conflict. Many individuals (clients, interveners, colleagues) who have been treated unfairly, discriminated against, or deprived of opportunity and status at school, on the job, and in society use whatever means they can to seek redress and sometimes to strike back. Such individuals may promote conflict in hopes of correcting power imbalances or to call attention to other problems. And even when this is not the case and there are no other serious barriers at initial contact, common dynamics arise over time as people work together. These can be anticipated and steps taken to deal with them in ways that facilitate cooperative task-oriented behavior.

A common manifestation of working relationship problems is captured by the phrase *You don't understand!* In most situations, accusations that another does not understand are valid. Indeed, they are givens. After all, one cannot fully understand complex situations or what others experience and feel. Also given is the fact that such accusations make recipients (an intervener, a client, a family member, an employee, a colleague) uncomfortable and put them on the defensive.

The phrase *You don't understand* provides a prototypical illustration of confrontations engendering negative attitudes that interfere with effective working relationships. In encounters with clients and colleagues, a variety of human, community, and institutional *differences* usually can be expected. Moreover, intervention settings foster an extensive range of interpersonal *dynamics*.

With respect to differences, unproductive working relationships are associated with variations in sociocultural and economic background, current lifestyle, primary language spoken, skin color, gender, power, status, intervention orientation, and on and on. Examples of interfering dynamics include excessive dependency and approval seeking, competition, stereotypical thinking and judgmental bias, transference and countertransference, rescue-persecution cycles, resistance, reluctance, and psychological withdrawal. Differences and dynamics become barriers to effective working relationships with colleagues and clients when they generate negative attitudes that are allowed to prevail.

It is self-defeating when barriers arise between clients and interveners or hinder staff from working together effectively. Barriers undoubtedly interfere with the help-seeking behavior of large numbers of individuals who need intervention. Among staff, conflicts contribute to collaborative failure and burn out.[8]

Overcoming Barriers

As suggested above, an understanding of barriers requires an appreciation of the role played by previous experiences and the ongoing impact of the politics and psychology that characterize intervention situations. Interventions to overcome barriers are built on such an understanding.

When poor working relationships are due to lack of awareness and poor skills, the problem may be relatively easy to resolve. Most motivated individuals can be directly taught ways to improve understanding and communication and to avoid or resolve conflicts that interfere with working relationships.

Often the task of overcoming barriers to a working relationship involves countering negative attitudes. There are no easy solutions to overcoming deeply embedded negative attitudes. (We are reminded of H.L. Mencken's quip: "There's always an easy solution to every human problem—neat, plausible and wrong.")

Discussions that directly focus on overcoming barriers to working relationships are found in the psychotherapy, counseling, group process, and management literatures. As outlined in Table 15.2, building working relationships involves actions that minimize barriers and facilitate task-focus and accomplishment. In part, this requires avoiding ego-oriented behavior and building rapport and connection. Helpful in this regard is Sue and Zane's analysis, which suggests that proactive steps toward building positive connections entail establishing one's credibility and demonstrating that something of value can be gained from working together.[9] Toward these ends, much of what we have already discussed regarding facilitating implementation applies. For instance, as with any relationship, working together can benefit from the efforts of participants to convey genuine empathy, warmth, regard, and respect. Other specific recommendations for creating an atmosphere where defensiveness is minimized stress ensuring confidentiality, risking self-criticism and self-disclosure, and expressing appreciation for efforts in the right direction.

Table 15.2

Building Working Relationships

To be effective in working with others requires building a positive relationship around the *tasks* at hand. Necessary ingredients in building a working relationship seem to include:

- minimizing negative prejudgments about those with whom one works

- taking time to make connections

- identifying what will be gained from the collaboration in terms of mutually desired outcomes—to clarify the value of working together

- enhancing expectations that working relationships will be productive— important here is establishing credibility with each other

- establishing a structure that provides support and guidance to aid task focus

- periodic reminders of the positive outcomes that have resulted from working together

With specific respect to *building relationships* and *effective communication*, three factors that seem relevant are:

- conveying empathy and warmth (e.g., the ability to understand and appreciate what others are thinking and feeling and to transmit a sense of liking)

- conveying genuine regard and respect (e.g., the ability to transmit real interest and to interact in a way that enables others to maintain a feeling of integrity and personal control)

- talking with, not at, others—active listening and dialogue (e.g., being a good listener, not being judgmental, not prying, sharing one's experiences as appropriate and needed)

Before leaving this topic, we reemphasize that matching *individual differences* is the most fundamental determinant of whether a good relationship is established. That is, facilitating a working relationship requires a personalized approach that accounts for the client's perceptions. This point was poignantly illustrated by an event experienced by a psychologist we know.

A Korean student who had been in the United States for several years and spoke comprehensible English came to the school's psychologist seeking help for a personal problem. Trying to be sensitive to cultural differences, the psychologist referred the student to an Asian counselor. The student met with the counselor, but did not bring up his personal problem and did not return for a second scheduled session.

In a follow-up interview conducted by a non-Asian staff member, the student explained that the idea of telling his personal problems to another Asian was too embarrassing.

Then, why had he come in the first place?

Well, he did not understand that he would be sent to an Asian; indeed, he had expected to work with the "blue-eyed counselor" a friend had told him about.

Anyone potentially can work together with others; on first impression, many do not want to do so. Building and maintaining working relationships are among the most basic concerns for those who plan and implement intervention.

ORGANIZATIONAL CHANGE

Organizational change raises additional considerations for interveners.[10] Examples are seen in efforts to restructure schools and the movements to integrate community health and social services. Such major organizational changes call for comprehensive planning and implementation to introduce and institutionalize desired changes in a chosen organizational setting, and to address the problem of diffusion into other settings.

In formulating plans for organizational change, it is important to recognize some basics:

- The process must begin with solid *policy* commitments.
- Then, *mechanisms* must be established and adequate *resources* provided to operationalize the policy.
- The problems involved in making major institutional changes (especially given limited financial resources) require implementing change *in phases*.
- During the early stages, evaluation must be oriented primarily toward facilitating program development and organization change (i.e., *formative evaluation*).
- Major attention must be directed at (a) *mobilizing and maintaining proactive effort* that consistently moves in the direction of desired outcomes, and (b) *overcoming barriers to working relationships*.

Creating a Climate for Change

As is well known, institutions tend to resist change, and even when demonstration programs are implemented they generally aren't maintained over the longrun. Thus, the question arises as to how to overcome resistance and maintain new programs. One somewhat naive approach involves simply mandating program restructuring and implementing related accountability measures. Advocating change, of course, is relatively easy to do. Producing desired changes is quite a bit harder.

The administrative/organizational literature says a great deal about institutional change. For example, creation of an appropriate climate for change is seen as requiring at least the following conditions: (1) appropriate incentives for change, such as intrinsically valued outcomes, expectations of success, recognitions, and rewards; (2) procedural options so that those expected to implement change can select one they see as workable; (3) establishment of mechanisms that facilitate the efforts of those responsible for installing change, such as participatory decision making, special training, resources, rewards, and procedures for improving organizational health; (4) agents of change who are perceived as pragmatic rather than as idealistic; (5) not trying to accomplish too much too fast, including facilitating readiness and phasing in changes using planned transitions; (6) appropriate feedback regarding progress of change activity; and (7) ongoing support mechanisms to maintain changes as long as they remain appropriate.

As discussed in a preceding section, there must be a primary and constant focus on intrinsic motivation to ensure positive attitudes whenever the intent is to create an "environment" that mobilizes and then maintains participant mobilization. For interveners, this means systematically planning and implementing motivationally oriented processes. It also means including a mechanism that has primary responsibility for the change process. Such a mechanism is an agent of change.

Change Agents

With respect to new programs and approaches, change agents are catalysts and facilitators in establishing structures, implementing processes, solving problems, and linking resources. The role they play involves understanding the general model to be introduced into the organization and facilitating and phasing in desired changes.

As a guide for change agents, it helps to think about the process and problem of introducing organizational change in terms of stages and related tasks. The stages are (1) *readiness,* (2) *initial implementation,* (3) *institutionalization of the model,* and (4) *evolution of the model.* As amplified in Table 15.3, the major tasks in facilitating and phasing in desired changes include:

- generating the necessary readiness and commitment
- overcoming barriers to change
- anticipating and addressing negative reactions and dynamics related to change
- establishing and maintaining the necessary infrastructure (i.e., organizational and operational mechanisms)
- developing effective working relationships
- enhancing intrinsic motivation for maintaining and evolving newly acquired ideas and processes

MECHANISMS FOR COLLABORATION AND CONSOLIDATION

Widespread agreement exists among policy makers regarding the desirability of intervention collaboration and consolidation.[11] Relatedly, there is interest in ensuring that collaboration and integration produce a comprehensive package of accessible programs with proven or highly promising utility.

Despite all the interest and agreement, insufficient attention is paid to how to get there from here. In particular, as discussed above, considerable work is required on the problem of addressing barriers to working relationships and organizational change. More work also is required to delineate the formal processes that can facilitate proactive movement toward intervention collaboration and consolidation.

Little agreement exists about matters such as what the scope of coordination and integration and governance should be, where integrated programs should be located, how to create a climate where

Table 15.3

Some Factors Relevant to Organizational Change Tasks

Generating Readiness and Commitment
Understanding the nature of the organization and its stakeholders
Involving stakeholders in making substantive decisions
Clarifying benefits and their personal relevance
Eliciting public statements of commitment

Overcoming Barriers to Change
Arranging for new policies or exceptions to existing policies
Guaranteeing necessary financial and material resources are available
Intervening to enhance positive attitudes and capabilities of those
implementing changes

Anticipating and Addressing Negative Reactions/Dynamics
Ameliorating
  • reactance—emotions and behaviors
      (this includes emotions such as anger, fear, suspicion, and anxiety,
      and behaviors ranging from passivity to direct hostile reactions and
      efforts to undermine proposed changes; much of the negative
      reaction is motivated by threats to competence, self-determination,
      and interpersonal relationships)
  • apathy and low valuing
  • apprehension
  • information/communication breakdowns
      (this includes problems of understanding, information overload,
      miscommunications, rumor-mills)
  • unrealistic expectations

Establishing and Maintaining Infrastructure
  (i.e., organizational and operational mechanisms for model development
  and for program planning, implementation, and evaluation)
Model Design Team
Model Implementation Facilitator
On-site Implementation Steering Committee
Program Teams
Coordinating Teams

Developing Effective Working Relationships
Overcoming barriers to working together
  (e.g., negative attitudes stemming from differences and from threats to
  competence, self-determination, and interpersonal relations)
Building rapport and connection
Developing knowledge and skills
Resolving conflict and providing ongoing relationship support

**Enhancing Intrinsic Motivation for Maintaining and
Evolving New Ideas/Processes**
Ownership (empowerment)
Ongoing support for maintaining infrastructure and expanding
  knowledge and skills

interveners are committed to working together, and so forth. And little attention is paid to developing the mechanisms required for moving away from current, piecemeal practices.

The implications of all this will be familiar to anyone who has tried to accomplish major institutional change. To be direct: in the absence of policies that create and maintain facilitation mechanisms, it seems inevitable that the desire for comprehensive, integrated programs will go unfulfilled.

Even though work on the problems of large-scale intervention collaboration and consolidation is in its infancy, it is evident that getting from here to there requires major institutional change. As we have stressed, institutions tend to resist change.

Based on a general understanding of necessary conditions for organizational change, we currently conceptualize the processes leading to coordinated and integrated programs in terms of three arenas of activity and the mechanisms necessary for carrying the activity out effectively. Minimally, we see a need for formally sanctioned mechanisms designed to ensure (1) governance and planning, (2) initiation of desired changes, and (3) maintenance and enhancement of productive changes (see Figure 15.2). Because the literature says little on this topic, we offer a somewhat extended discussion of our analysis as a stimulus for further work on these problems.

Mechanisms for Governance and Planning

Given that the goal is to have a set of comprehensive, integrated programs, some group must accept responsibility for assuring that there is ongoing oversight and planning of activity for achieving this end. In some instances, one body can assume both the oversight and planning functions. Factors such as large catchment areas and the need to involve policy makers usually result in the need for separate governance (e.g., policy/steering committees) and planning groups.

The functions of governance, of course, have to do with policy, political, and economic concerns. These include ensuring that there are appropriate incentives for change and mechanisms and resources for carrying out plans. For instance, decisions must be

Figure 15.2
Key Tasks and Mechanisms in Moving Toward Integrated Services

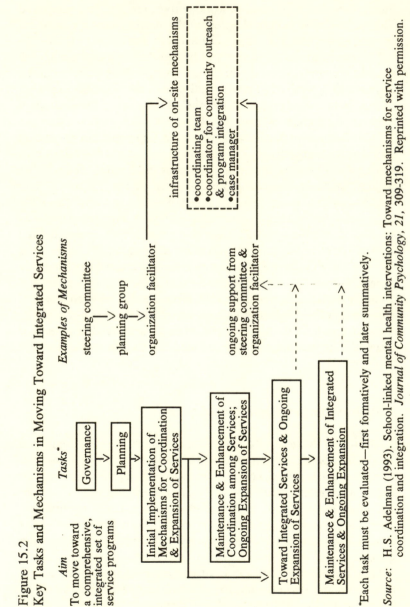

*Each task must be evaluated—first formatively and later summatively.

Source: H.S. Adelman (1993). School-linked mental health interventions: Toward mechanisms for service coordination and integration. *Journal of Community Psychology, 21,* 309-319. Reprinted with permission.

made about who to include in decision making about proposed changes and related budget considerations; what types of personnel, training, and other resources will be required; and whether to experiment with demonstration sites before attempting widespread change.

The planning group's function is to design the *general* framework for evolving an integrated and comprehensive set of programs and to work out *specific* details. Guided by the literature on organizational change, such planning includes an emphasis on pacing change, designing optional procedures that likely will be seen as workable by those expected to implement change, identifying appropriate agents of change, and so forth.

The planning group logically consists of persons who represent programs to be linked, those charged with administering the changes, and someone with basic understanding of the process of institutional change. One of the first activities for such a group is to formulate general ideas for initiating and maintaining mechanisms that can (1) improve coordination among existing programs and (2) eventually lead to a comprehensive, integrated set of programs. Then, because such groups generally are too large for hammering out a detailed plan of action, a small subcommittee of the planning group can work out specifics and bring them to the larger group for final ratification.

Mechanisms to Initiate Desired Changes

Once a set of detailed plans is generated, formal implementation mechanisms must be established. As a first mechanism, we conceive of designating and training someone formally as an *organization facilitator*. This person's functions are to go on-site to introduce ideas for programmatic change and to facilitate establishment of an infrastructure of on-site mechanisms for implementing (and maintaining) the desired changes. At a minimum, such a change agent must understand organizational change, how to establish collaborative working relationships toward accomplishing desired changes, and the specific activities and mechanisms required for establishing and maintaining comprehensive, integrated interventions. Also, given that interventions are based in a particular community and site, an understanding of the culture of the community and site is essential. Models for training such personnel range from workshops to comprehensive apprenticeships and include provision for on-the-job training and consultation.

The infrastructure of on-site mechanisms can be viewed as formal processes for interprogram communication and problem solving related to coordinating and integrating interventions. For instance, for community-based programs, the infrastructure seems to require a *team of program representatives* from interfacing programs, a *coordinator for interprogram coordination*, and a *case manager*. A segment of those who served on the planning group may constitute the core of the on-site team. Such a team meets regularly (e.g., weekly) to share information, discuss coordination of activities, space, and other resources, and explore solutions for problems. An on-site coordinator provides a means for following through on ideas and plans generated by the team; in addition, such a coordinator can observe how programs work together and help improve the process. Finally, at the case level, the concept of a case manager represents not only a mechanism for improving coordination of service delivery for individual clients, but an additional way to improve interprogram communication and problem solving.

With the on-site infrastructure in place, initial efforts are directed at developing effective and efficient *coordination* among participating programs. Coordination first must be accomplished among relevant existing programs (e.g., school programs and community services designed to address psychosocial, mental health, medical, and health education concerns).

After programs are functioning in a coordinated manner, the feasibility of true *integration* can be explored. The difficulty of accomplishing genuine integration stems from the fact that such a move requires that programs do more than cooperate with each other; it requires that they cede much of their autonomy and pool resources. Most programs probably need to work together for some time before they are convinced that the benefits of true integration are worth the costs. Alternatively, policy makers can mandate rapid program integration; in doing so, it is hoped that they will provide appropriately for the problems such mandates produce.

Mechanisms to Maintain and Enhance Productive Changes

After implementation mechanisms are created, they must be monitored and supported to ensure that their functional integrity is maintained and that they evolve appropriately. Maintaining and enhancing changes can be at least as difficult as making them in the first place.

Maintenance and enhancement require ongoing steering activity by the governance body (with emphasis on program advocacy, ongoing policy concerns, maintaining and enhancing financial support, long-range planning). In addition, efforts to counter forces that break down coordination are facilitated by use of an external support mechanism to detect problems and provide staff training for ongoing problem solving. For instance, it is inevitable that mental health professionals working together in a school-linked consortium will need someone who has the time, energy, and expertise to anticipate continuing problems related to communication and sharing of resources and who can bring the involved parties together for problem solving. An organization facilitator may be a logical resource in this connection; such a professional can meet periodically with program representatives to support their efforts to maintain and evolve program coordination and integration.

Parallel to the above activity, a mechanism is required for evaluating program efficacy in an appropriate manner. That is, some individual or group must have the time, energy, and relevant expertise to establish and maintain an evaluation system. And that system must do more than gather data on outcomes. As discussed in Part IV, evaluation must also provide essential information on processes, such as mechanisms for collaboration and consultation.

NOTES

1. U. Neisser (1976). *Cognition and reality: Principles and implications of cognitive psychology*. San Francisco: W.H. Freeman, p. 183.

2. See Part I.

3. Limits may be defined as the degrees of freedom or range of choices allowed an individual in any given situation. Stated differently, limits are the

restraints placed on an individual's freedom of choice and action. The concept of limits provides a basis for understanding the difference between permissiveness and license. The term *license* is used when someone goes well beyond or is encouraged to go well beyond commonly accepted boundaries for behaving. *Permissiveness* is used to describe efforts to expand commonly accepted limits short of encouraging license. In practice, if one agrees with efforts to expand limits, one sees them as a move toward establishing greater freedom and liberty; if one doesn't like the direction, the efforts probably are seen as a step toward license and anarchy. The diagram below graphically suggests that varying criteria may be used in establishing limits.

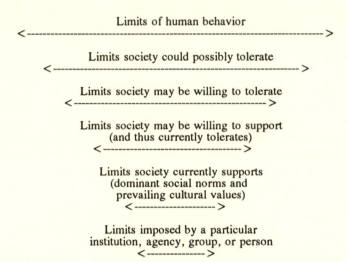

Limits of human behavior

Limits society could possibly tolerate

Limits society may be willing to tolerate

Limits society may be willing to support
(and thus currently tolerates)

Limits society currently supports
(dominant social norms and
prevailing cultural values)

Limits imposed by a particular
institution, agency, group, or person

Every day we experience differences in the limits within which we are expected to stay. As we go from one setting to another, we observe that different criteria are used to measure acceptable behavior. What is appropriate at home is not appropriate at work or school. What friends expect is not usually the same as what family members expect. For individuals with problems, intervention settings often are the places where they experience the greatest sense of external control and loss of freedom. Often the narrow limits imposed are much more restrictive than those the individuals are likely to encounter anywhere else currently or later in life. This excessive control probably adds to clients' dislike of interventions and interveners. Many writers, for example, suggest that the overreliance on power and tight limits in many classrooms probably is short-sighted and counterproductive. Such tactics may have an immediate impact on some negative behaviors, but they also may interfere with learning and even with the intended long-term socialization. What seems surprising is not that many rebel and misbehave under such circumstances but that so many accept as much control as they do. This raises the problem of how practitioners and parents can avoid an *overemphasis* on using power and tight limits to establish control and, relatedly, learn to use procedures that can lead to cooperation and appropriate social functioning.

4. J. Brophy & J. Alleman (1992). Activities as instructional tools: A framework for analysis and evaluation. *Educational Researcher, 20*, 93–23.

5. For a review of the literature on cognitive-affective theories of motivation and their application to intervention, see E.L. Deci & R.M. Ryan (1985). *Intrinsic motivation and self-determination in human behavior*. New York: Plenum Press.

6. We discuss these topics in detail in H.S. Adelman & L. Taylor (1993). *Learning problems and learning disabilities: Moving forward*. Pacific Grove, CA: Brooks/Cole.

7. We prefer the term *personalization* over *individualization*. Individualization connotes intervention designed to match differences related to developmental capabilities (with the primary emphasis often only on differences in rate and amount). Personalization, as we define it, encompasses individualization. That is, the term stresses the importance of designing intervention to match current developmental capabilities but assigns equal and primary significance to matching levels of motivation and especially attending to intrinsic motivation. Furthermore, we treat personalization as a psychological construct by operationalizing it in terms of client perceptions.

8. For a discussion of burnout among human service workers, see B.E. Gilliland & R.K. James (1993). *Crisis intervention strategies* (2nd ed.). Pacific Grove, CA: Brooks/Cole.

9. S. Sue & N. Zane (1987). The role of culture and cultural techniques: A critique and reformulation. *American Psychologist, 42*, 37–45.

10. See P.E. Connor & L.K. Lake (1988). *Managing organization change*. New York: Praeger. S.B. Sarason (1982). *The culture of school and the problem of change* (2nd ed.). Boston: Allyn & Bacon. C. Argyris (1993). *Knowledge for action: A guide to overcoming barriers to organizational change*. San Francisco: Jossey-Bass. G. Braiger & S. Holloway (1978). *Changing human services organizations: Politics and practice*. New York: Free Press. W.B. Brookover (Ed.) (1981). Changing school social systems. *The Generator, 11*, 1–59. L. Cuban (1990). Reforming again, again, and again. *Educational Researcher, 19*, 313. Y. Hasenfeld (1983). *Human service organizations*. Englewood Cliffs, NJ: Prentice-Hall. K. Heller (1990). Social and community intervention. *Annual Review of Psychology, 41*, 141–168. C.R. Hickman & S.A. Michael (1984). *Creating*

excellence: Managing corporate culture, strategy, and change in the new age. New York: New American Library. S.B. Sarason (1990). *The predictable failure of educational reform: Can we change course before it's too late?* San Francisco: Jossey-Bass. R.H. Waterman (1987). *The renewal factor.* New York: Bantam Books.
    11. See Part II.

A Few Concluding Comments about the Planning and Implementation Problem

All parties interested in facilitating implementation of planned interventions should strive to understand the nature and scope of what is involved. In doing so, they will soon appreciate the immense amount of work remaining to be done on the planning and implementation problem. Such appreciation is a prerequisite to creating conditions conducive to designing and developing better practices.

Requisite conditions for improving practices include realistic time frames, adequate financial resources, and use of initial evaluation primarily for formative purposes and evaluative research. Those concerned with better intervention theory and practice must help develop and shape attitudes in ways that lead to policies that support such tactics. To do less is to ensure continuance of a very unsatisfactory status quo.

PART IV

THE EVALUATION PROBLEM

Evaluation practiced at the highest level of the state-of-the-art is one means of speeding up the processes that contribute to human and social progress.

Rossi, Freeman, & Wright[1]

Increased concern about evaluation in psychology and education has advanced the way evaluation is conceived.[2] Despite the breadth of this scholarly activity, widespread demands for accountability continue to narrow the way professionals, clients, policy makers, underwriters, and the general public think about evaluation. Social and political forces literally have shaped the whole enterprise of program evaluation.[3]

The prevailing cry is for specific evidence of efficacy—usually in terms of readily measured immediate benefits—and for cost containment. Although understandable in light of the unfulfilled promise of so many programs and the insatiable demands on limited public finances, such naive accountability demands ignore the complexities of intervention. The problem is well exemplified by the narrow focus found in reviews, analyses, and reanalyses of data on psychotherapy, behavior change, and early education programs.[4]

Besides responding to accountability pressures, two unfounded presumptions are at the core of most current evaluations in psychology and education. One premise is that an intervention in widespread use must be at a relatively evolved stage of development and thus warrants the cost of summative evaluation. The other supposition is that major conceptual and methodological problems associated with evaluating intervention efficacy are resolved. The truth, of course, is that interventions are frequently introduced prior to adequate development with a view to evolving them based on what is learned each day. Moreover, many well-institutionalized approaches remain relatively underfunded and underdeveloped. As to the process of evaluation, every review of the literature outlines comprehensive, unresolved concerns. Given this state of affairs, accountability demands are often unreasonable and chronically reflect a naive view of research and theory.

Overemphasis on immediate evaluation of the efficacy of underdeveloped interventions draws resources and attention away from the type of intensive research programs necessary for advancing intervention knowledge and practice. Cost-effective outcomes cannot be achieved in the absence of cost-effective development of interventions and related intervention research. *Premature* efforts to carry out comprehensive summative evaluations clearly are not cost-effective. Consequently, policies mandating naive accountability run the risk of generating evaluative practices that are neither cost-effective nor wise.[5]

The evaluation problem, then, involves more than determining the efficacy of current interventions and more than finding better ways to evaluate efficacy. Broadly stated, it encompasses concerns about how to expand the focus of evaluation not only to contribute to improving practice, but also to aid in evolving theory and basic knowledge about intervention.

In the following sections, our intent is to briefly highlight (1) the concept of evaluation, (2) how the evaluation problem relates to the other three fundamental intervention problems, and (3) the key role of evaluative research in improving practice and advancing basic knowledge about intervention.

NOTES

1. P.H. Rossi, H.E. Freeman, & S. Wright (1979). *Evaluation: A systematic approach* (3rd ed.). Beverly Hills, CA: Sage.

2. For a comparison of evaluation models, see D.L. Stufflebeam & W.J. Webster (1983). An analysis of alternative approaches to evaluation. In G.F. Madaus, M.S. Scriven, & D.L. Stufflebeam (Eds.), *Evaluation models*. Boston: Kluwer-Nijhoff; also see P.H. Rossi & H.E. Freeman (1989). *Evaluation: A systematic approach* (4th ed.). Newbury Park, CA: Sage. E.J. Posavac & R.G. Carey (1989). *Program evaluation: Methods and case*

studies (3rd ed.). Englewood Cliffs, NJ: Prentice-Hall. For recent reviews of the topic, see W.R. Shadish, Jr., T.D. Cook, & L.C. Leviton (1991). *Foundations of program evaluation: Theories of practice*. Newbury Park, CA: Sage. L. Sechrest & A.J. Figueredo (1993). Program evaluation. *Annual Review of Psychology, 44*, 645–674. M. Scriven (1993). *Hard-won lessons in program evaluation*. San Francisco: Jossey-Bass.

3. Recent reviews stress that the evolution of program evaluation in general and evaluation theory specifically has been shaped to a significant degree by evaluation researchers who were unprepared for their confrontations with complex social and political realities—including those associated with the shift from an industrial to a postindustrial (cybernetic) era. The demand for greater external validity has forced program evaluators to move beyond the prevailing paradigms and methods guiding the social sciences. For the most part, this demand reflects the socio-political-economic nature of intervention and evaluation. That is, interventions compete for limited societal resources and evaluation feeds into political decision making about which interventions are funded and levels of support.

4. See L. Bond & B.E. Compas (Eds.) (1989). *Primary prevention and promotion in the schools*. Newbury Park: Sage, pp.106–45). A. Kazdin (1990). Psychotherapy for children and adolescents. *Annual Review of Psychology, 41*, 21–54. M.J. Lambert, D.A. Shapiro, & A.E. Bergin (1986). The effectiveness of psychotherapy. In S.L. Garfield & A.E. Bergin (Eds.), *Handbook of psychotherapy and behavior change* (3rd ed.). New York: Wiley. A. Mitchell, M. Seligson, & F. Marx (1989). *Early childhood programs and the public schools: Promise and practice*. Dover, MA: Auburn House. R.E. Slavin, N.L. Karweit, & N.A. Madden (1989). *Effective programs for students at risk*. Boston: Allyn & Bacon. J.R. Weisz, B. Weiss, & G.R. Donnenberg (1992). The lab versus the clinic: Effects of child and adolescent psychotherapy. *American Psychologist, 47*, 1578–1585.

5. Accountability pressures can lead to an overemphasis on immediate behavioral outcomes. Usually, decisions as to what and how to evaluate are made by those administering or funding an intervention. For example, with respect to specifying outcomes for evaluation, the primary focus in preparing IEPs for special education is on remedial outcomes. Furthermore, the prevailing emphasis is on specifying outcomes in terms of behavioral and criterion-referenced objectives. Similar trends are seen in psychology for interventions underwritten by third party payers. These trends no doubt are a major aid in efforts to evaluate whether outcomes are accomplished. However, the limited focus ignores the broader responsibility many interveners have for facilitating ongoing development and providing enrichment opportunities. A narrow focus on correcting problems also can be counterproductive to overcoming problems if the intervention involves

little more than a set of laborious and deadening experiences. Moreover, many important facets of a program are not easily measured and thus may be given short shrift (e.g., self-concept, attitudes toward system improvement and problem solving). In general, the danger is that valuable intervention aims and goals are lost when *all* ends are specified in terms of highly concrete and easily measurable objectives. Not all complex long-range aims that an intervention should pursue can be stated as short-term or behavioral objectives. Indeed, only a relatively limited set of skills can be specified in highly concrete, behavioral terms—and even in these instances, it may not be desirable to do so for intervention purposes. In education, beside the fact that specifying everything in this way would result in far too many objectives to teach, the trend stresses *teaching* at the expense of *learning*. Moreover, attitudes, motivation, and creative functioning in the arts and sciences, for example, do not lend themselves to formulation in simple behavioral terms.

The dilemmas raised by accountability pressures are well illustrated in an article on mental health services for children: see J.D. Burchard & M. Schaefer (1992). Improving accountability in a service delivery system in children's mental health. *Clinical Psychology Review, 12*, 867–882.

16

The Essence of Evaluation

When the cook tastes the soup it is formative evaluation and when the guests taste the soup it is summative.

Stake[1]

Evaluation involves determining the worth or value of something.[2] In formal terms, we define comprehensive evaluation as a systematic process designed to describe and judge an intervention's antecedents, transactions, and overall impact and value for purposes of making decisions and advancing knowledge.[3]

Everyone evaluates interventions with which they come in contact. Whenever anyone decides that an intervention is or isn't a good one, an evaluation is made.[4] Interveners judge whether their own and others' programs are going well. Clients are quick to formulate likes or dislikes of interveners and their programs. Administrators know which programs they think are working and which aren't.

Some evaluative judgments simply reflect an individual's or group's informal observations. Other judgments are based on careful data gathering and analyses and use of appropriate sets of standards. Some evaluations only offer conclusions about the degree to which a program is effective. Most, however, also incorporate the conclusions of those judging the program in terms of whether they agree with what it is trying to do. Since what a program intends to do stems from its rationale, program evaluations inevitably influence views about the appropriateness of its underlying rationale.

Systematic evaluation planning requires decisions about (1) the focus of evaluation (e.g., person or environment, immediate objectives vs. long-range aims), (2) whose perspective (e.g., client, intervener, program underwriter) is to determine the evaluation focus, methods, and standards used, and (3) the best way to proceed in gathering, analyzing, and interpreting information (e.g., specific measures, design). In making such decisions, concerns arise because what can be evaluated currently is far less than what a program may intend to accomplish. Furthermore, inappropriate bias and vested interests shape evaluation planning and implementation, thereby influencing whether a program is seen as good or bad. And all aspects of evaluation have the potential to produce negative effects; for instance, evaluation can lead to invasion of privacy and an undermining of the ability of clients and interveners to self-evaluate, and over time, what is evaluated can reduce and reshape a program's intended aims.

PURPOSES

Intervention evaluation can aid efforts to (1) *make decisions* about whether to undertake, continue, modify, or stop an intervention for one or more clients and (2) *advance knowledge* about interventions in ways that can advance understanding of and improve practices (including utility), training, and theory. Evaluation is useful in relation to a great variety of interventions as an aid in assessing efficiency, effectiveness, and impact. As Rossi and Freeman state:

> The mass communication and advertising industries use fundamentally the same approaches in developing media programs and marketing products; commercial and industrial corporations evaluate the procedures they use in selecting and promoting employees and organizing their work forces; political candidates develop their campaigns by evaluating the voter appeal of different strategies; . . . administrators in both the public and private sectors are continually assessing clerical, fiscal, and interpersonal practices of their organizations. The distinction between these uses of evaluation lies primarily in the intent of the effort to be evaluated . . . to benefit the human condition . . . [or] for other purposes, such as increasing profits or amassing influence and power.[5]

Providing a broad categorical view of the areas in which evaluation is applied, Scriven outlines the "Big Six" plus others. The Big Six are listed as product, performance, personnel, program, proposal, and policy evaluations. To these, he adds two other applied fields. "The first is the evaluation of evaluations (meta-evaluation). . . . The second is a field comprising a set of fields: It might be called 'intradisciplinary evaluation,' the evaluation of the data, sources, explanations, definitions, classifications, theories, designs, predictions, contributors, journals, and so on within a discipline." Scriven concludes: "In toto, intradisciplinary evaluation is by far the largest part of evaluation, and having practitioners do it with reasonable skills is the price of admission to the company of disciplines. Other applied fields besides the Big Six range from literary criticism and real estate appraisal to quality control in industry."[6]

Stake's evaluation matrix is reproduced in Figure 16.1 as an example of a framework designed to outline the general nature of information for meeting many evaluation purposes.[7] As the framework suggests, evaluation encompasses the acts of *describing* and *judging* an intervention's (1) rationale, including assumptions and intentions, (2) standards for making judgments, (3) actual activity, including intended and unintended procedures and outcomes, and (4) costs—financial, negative effects, and so forth. To achieve the above ends in a comprehensive manner, both immediate and long-term information on an intervention must be gathered.[8]

TASKS FOR PLANNING

Awareness of tasks involved in planning an evaluation provides another perspective on the process. Such tasks reflect the necessity in evaluation planning of making decisions about the focus of the evaluation, its specific objectives, and appropriate methodology and measures.

Our formulation identifies the following seven key planning tasks:

- *Clarifying the intended use of information.* Most important here is awareness of who wants the information and why they need it. Ultimately this translates into the question: What types of decisions are to be made? Also important is the matter of anticipating the use and political and motivational impact of evaluation processes and findings. This includes a significant appreciation of the often conflicting interests among the variety

Figure 16.1

Layout of Statements and Data to Be Collected During Evaluation

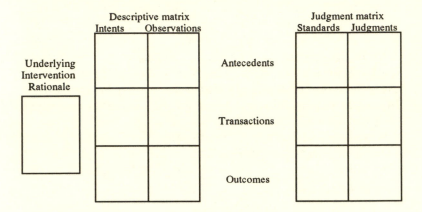

Source: R. Stake (1967). The countenance of educational evaluation. *Teachers College Record, 68*, 523-40. Reprinted with permission.

of interested parties (i.e., stakeholders).

- *Understanding the intervention's rationale.*   In cases where evaluation includes judging the intervention rationale, pursuit of the above task (clarifying the intended use of evaluation information) will result in gathering information about the rationale. However, when the evaluation is designed with reference to a standardized set of objectives, clarification of the rationale becomes a separate task. In either case, an understanding of the intervention rationale can provide a separate basis for deciding about other intervention facets to evaluate.
- *Formulating evaluation questions.* Evaluative concerns are translated into a set of questions. For example: Were intended antecedent conditions present during the intervention? Which procedures were effective for which clients? Were there undesirable transactions? Were specific objectives achieved? Were long-range aims achieved? Did expected negative outcomes occur? Were there unexpected negative outcomes?
- *Specifying information to be gathered.* Relevant descriptive information that can answer each major question is specified. The more things one is interested in evaluating, the more one has to settle for samples of information. Some of the information likely will be of a quantitative nature; some may be qualitative.[9]

- *Specifying procedures.* Decisions about information gathering are shaped first by what one wants to know and then are tempered by practical considerations. Problems related to gathering desired information become evident as one attempts to specify procedures. Limitations related to time, money, sample availability, valid measures, multivariate statistics, and personnel usually lead to major compromises in evaluation planning. For example, sometimes a good measuring instrument exists; sometimes only weak procedures are available; sometimes gathering desired information is not currently feasible. A special set of problems stems from the socio-political-economic concerns (e.g., threats to current status) and psychological reactance (e.g., fear-based resistance) that are common phenomena when evaluation is introduced.[10]
- *Specifying a design.* An evaluation design is used so that information can be gathered and interpreted appropriately. When someone asks how good an intervention is, judgments are based on the available information and are relative to some standard of comparison. A sound design ensures that appropriate bits of information (e.g., data) are gathered, including information for use as standards for judgments. A sound evaluation design also includes provision for the gathering and use of information for revising interventions as the process proceeds.[11]
- *Designating time and place for collecting information.* Further practical considerations arise when evaluations are scheduled. The design sets the general parameters; the particulars are determined by practical factors such as resource availability.

One major evaluation concern not reflected above involves decisions about the role of various interested parties. For example, as suggested throughout, rationales may differ with respect to what should be evaluated. If so, whose rationale should prevail? Every facet of an evaluation is influenced by the answer to this question.

Another matter not specifically addressed above involves ethical concerns associated with evaluation. Naturally, these are similar to those discussed in relation to assessment in general. For instance, evaluators must be concerned with how to minimize possible bias and conflicts of interest, as well as negative consequences that can arise from evaluation itself.

IMPACT ON PROGRAM BREADTH

As the discussion to this point underscores, a common use of evaluation is to determine if one agrees with what the intervention is trying to accomplish and how well the intervention is accomplishing the full range of outcomes desired. The less a program is trying to achieve, the easier it is to determine these matters. It is hard to evaluate large-scale social programs, community agencies, and most school programs, for example, because they are trying to accomplish so many different goals.[12]

Ironically, the longer a program is subjected to external, formal evaluation, the less it may try to accomplish. At least this seems to be one negative effect of the big push toward behavioral and criterion-referenced outcomes as ways to improve accountability. That is, such approaches can cause a shift away from a program's long-range aims toward a limited set of immediately measurable objectives. This is a negative form of "teaching to the test" because, in the process, many important things are ignored simply because they will not be directly evaluated.[13] If one is not careful, the desire for information on effectiveness can redesign a program's underlying rationale in ways that inappropriately reduce its breadth of focus.

Comprehensive evaluation should stress the full scope of desired intervention aims. That is, even when certain processes and outcomes are not easily measured, they still must be evaluated as well as is possible and kept in the forefront of discussions about a program's worth. For example: from a motivational perspective, a basic concern is whether a program enhances clients' interest, desire, and participation in improving their functioning. Because none of these outcomes is readily measured, the danger is that they will not be afforded the attention they warrant.

In sum, evaluations of whether an intervention is any good must first address the question: Is what it is trying to accomplish appropriate? The frame of reference for such evaluations may be the intervention rationale or what others think the program should be doing or both. After judging the appropriateness of what is wanted or expected, a program's intended breadth of focus should guide efforts to evaluate effectiveness. Because not everything is measurable in a technically sophisticated way, some things will be poorly measured or simply reviewed informally. Obviously, this is less than satisfactory. Still, from a rational perspective, continued emphasis on the entire gamut of what is intended is better than limiting evaluation to approaches that inappropriately narrow the breadth of focus for intervention.[14]

In this context, we are reminded of Yankelovich's commentary on measurement:

> The first step is to measure whatever can be easily measured. This is okay as far as it goes. The second step is to disregard that which can't be measured or give it an arbitrary quantitative value. This is artificial and misleading. The third step is to presume that what can't be measured easily isn't very important. This is blindness. The fourth step is to say what can't be measured really doesn't exist. This is suicide.[15]

NOTES

1. R.E. Stake (1976). *Evaluating educational programs: The need and the response.* Paris: Organization for Economic Cooperation and Development, p. 19.

2. We recognize the deficiencies of this simple definition. Still, it conveys the essence of the process. Reviewing the matter, Scriven states: "Evaluation is a process of determining certain evaluable properties of things, but there is more than one kind of such properties. Perhaps the most fundamental and important distinction among them is between merit or quality and worth or value." Using the example of a high school French teacher, he notes that the teacher may be the best in a school, but if enrollment patterns shift away from French, that teacher's worth or value to the school diminishes. The teacher's merit (i.e., quality in terms of professional standards) has not declined, but his or her benefit (vis à vis meeting the school's needs) has. M. Scriven (1993). *Hard-won lessons in program evaluation.* San Francisco: Jossey-Bass, p. 67.

3. Rossi and Freeman use the terms *evaluation* and *evaluation research* interchangeably. Their definition states: "Evaluation research is the systematic application of social research procedures for assessing the conceptualization, design, implementation, and utility of social intervention programs." See P.H. Rossi & H.E. Freeman (1989). *Evaluation: A systematic approach* (4th ed.). Newbury Park, CA: Sage, p. 18.

4. Conclusions of good or bad clearly are value judgments. Shadish and colleagues note that "Early evaluators mostly ignored the role of values in evaluation—whether in terms of justice, equality, liberty, human rights, or anything else. . . . such evaluators believed their activities could and should be value-free. But it proved to be impossible in the political world of social programming to evaluate without values becoming salient. Social programs

are themselves not value-free." W.R. Shadish, Jr., T.D. Cook, & L.C. Leviton (1991). *Foundations of program evaluation: Theories of practice.* Newbury Park, CA: Sage, pp. 46–47.

5. Rossi & Freeman, *Evaluation,* p. 19.

6. Scriven, *Hard-won lessons in program evaluation,* p. 44.

7. R.E. Stake (1967). The countenance of educational evaluation. *Teachers College Record, 68,* 523–40. Among program evaluators, Robert Stake is one of the early and long-term contributors. See Shadish, Cook, & Leviton, *Foundations of program evaluation,* for a comprehensive overview of his ideas and contribution, as well as those of other influential leaders such as Michael Scriven, Donald Campbell, Carol Weiss, Joseph Wholey, Lee Cronbach, and Peter Rossi.

8. A relatively new form of evaluation practice is a process called "prospective evaluation," which has been developed by the Program Evaluation and Methodology Division (PEMD) of the U.S. General Accounting Office (GAO). The purpose of the process is to predict or forecast the impact of a proposed program or policy change (e.g., as an aid to legislators). The potential value of such forecasts is obvious; so are the problems associated with efforts to make accurate predictions. See General Accounting Office (1989). *Prospective evaluation methods: The prospective evaluation synthesis.* GAO/PEMD-89-10. Washington, DC: Author.

9. Among academics, there is a running argument about the relative merits of quantitative and qualitative evaluations. In response to the many who argue primarily for quantitative evaluation, Guba and Lincoln have argued strongly for qualitative evaluation. See E.G. Guba & Y.S. Lincoln (1989). *Fourth generation evaluation.* Newbury Park, CA: Sage.

Sechrest and Figueredo suggest that a compromise may be possible "in light of the realization that although rigorous theory testing is admittedly sterile and nonproductive without adequate theory development, creative theory construction is ultimately pointless without scientific verification." L. Sechrest & A.J. Figueredo (1993). Program evaluation. *Annual Review of Psychology, 44,* 645–74, p. 654.

10. Posavac and Carey enumerate and discuss how political and psychological factors can undermine evaluation efforts, and suggest ways to plan for dealing with them. See E.J. Posavac & R.G. Carey (1989). *Program evaluation: Methods and case studies* (3rd ed.). Englewood Cliffs, NJ: Prentice-Hall.

11. Tharp and Gallimore describe a fine example of program development based on a progressive series of formative and summative evaluations. Over a period of ten years, they made a succession of process and outcome evaluations using the quantitative data and qualitative information gathered on variables affecting the outcomes to improve the program. That is, data

gathered at each stage of program development were used as feedback for revising the intervention. See R.G. Tharp & R. Gallimore (1979). The ecology of program research and evaluation: A model for evaluation succession. In L. Sechrest, S.G. West, M.A. Phillips, R. Redner, & W. Yeaton (Eds.), *Evaluation Studies Review Annual* (Vol. 4, pp. 39–60). Beverly Hills, CA: Sage.

12. Besides being difficult to carry out, evaluations of large-scale social and educational programs are costly, and the history of efforts to evaluate such programs is characterized by weak and often poorly conceived methodology as well as findings that are subject to varying interpretations. At the same time, it is evident that such evaluations must be pursued, and we must learn to do them better. In this regard, each new national and state evaluation provides a unique opportunity to improve the process of evaluation.

13. Charles Silberman cogently noted in his 1970 book, *Crisis in the classroom* (Vintage Books): "Elementary school students almost invariably regard mathematics as the most important subject in the curriculum—not because of its elegance, but because math has the most homework, because the homework is corrected the most promptly, and because tests are given more frequently than in any other subject. The youngsters regard spelling as the next most important subject, because of the frequency of spelling tests" (p. 147).

We would add that, with increasing demands for accountability, teachers quickly learn what is evaluated and what is not, and slowly but surely greater attention is given to teaching what will be on the tests. Over time, what is on the tests becomes viewed as what is most important. Because only so much time is available to the teacher, other things not only are deemphasized, they also are dropped from the curriculum. If allowed to do so, accountability procedures have the power to reshape the entire curriculum.

What's wrong with that? Nothing—if what is evaluated reflects everything we want students to learn in school. Unfortunately, this is not the case.

Current accountability pressures reflect values and biases that lead to evaluating a small range of basic skills and doing so in a narrow way. For students diagnosed with problems, this is seen in the fact that their school programs increasingly have been restricted to improving skills they lack. As a result, they are cut off from participating in learning activities that might increase their interest in overcoming their problems and that might open up opportunities and enrich their future lives.

14. The issues related to the impact of a narrow focus on evaluation also arise in the context of discussions about evaluating intervener competence. That is, narrowly focused competency evaluations may constrict rather than expand intervener growth with respect to the broad range of knowledge,

skills, and attitudes needed to properly plan, implement, and evaluate interventions.

15. Cited in A. Smith. *Supermoney*. New York: Random House, p. 286.

17

Evaluation and the Other Basic Intervention Problems

In the last analysis, we see only what we are ready to see. We eliminate and ignore everything that is not part of our prejudices.

Charcot

The complexity of evaluation is best appreciated when viewed in the context of the other three fundamental intervention problems (see Figure I.1 in the Introduction). That is, each problem has implications for evaluation. Reciprocally, research of an evaluative nature is essential in advancing knowledge about these intertwined problems; each must be reasonably well addressed before interventions can be optimized. For instance, appropriate decisions about processes and outcomes cannot be made logically in the absence of valid differentiation among systems with regard to intervention needs. If appropriate process and outcome decisions cannot be made, appropriate planning and implementation are jeopardized. Thus, even when valid evaluation practices are available and feasible, the logical prerequisites for a sound summative evaluation of efficacy may be absent. The following discussion highlights a few basic implications for evaluation of the classification, underlying rationale, and planning and implementation problems.

CLASSIFICATION

Because the most used classification schemes in psychology and education focus on person problems, it is particularly instructive to look at evaluation in that context. As discussed in Part I, common approaches to classifying psychological and educational maladies categorize them in terms of current dysfunctioning, causal factors, prescriptive implications, or some combination of all these. The variables and criteria used in defining a category usually are chosen because they have immediate relevance for research, intervention, administrative, or policy matters.

When the emphasis is on current dysfunctioning, both severity and pervasiveness of dysfunction are relevant concerns. That is, a narrow or broad range of areas of human functioning may be affected, such as one or more developmental areas or facets of school, family, or job performance. Additionally, severity of dysfunction may range from mild to profound, depending on normative expectations related to factors such as levels of development and competence and socioeconomic and subcultural status. As graphically suggested in Figure 2.1 (see Part I), the combination of pervasiveness and severity yields nine classification groups when treated as discrete categories rather than continuous variables. When the paradigmatic cause of the dysfunction is added as a third dimension, the schema jumps to twenty-seven groups. Adding duration results in an another exponential increase in categories.

One clear implication of the relatively simple nine-group classification (see Figure 17.1) is that outcomes are likely to be easier to achieve with the Z''' category than for those in the X' group. With regard to efficacy, then, groups *minimally* should be separated for evaluation based on degrees of pervasiveness and severity of dysfunctioning at the onset of intervention.

Classification in terms of cause demonstrates other complexities. At times, causal factors and their effects logically are key indicators for intervention decisions and are potential predictors of outcome. In these cases, classification based on causal factors and their current manifestations are of great significance in evaluating intervention. Such categorization can be done using primary instigators, secondary contributing factors, or both. (The situation becomes extremely complex once secondary factors begin interacting with primary instigators.) The type of primary instigator and the degree of dysfunction produced by it determines the degree to which secondary factors exacerbate problems. In Part I, we pointed to the example of physiological "insult" causing a major CNS disorder, the effect of which is so severe and pervasive that result-

Figure 17.1
Evaluation with Reference to Classification of the Severity and
Pervasiveness of Dysfunctioning

		Broad	Moderate	Narrow
	Mild	X'''	Y'''	Z'''
Severity	Moderate	X''	Y''	Z''
	Profound	X'	Y'	Z'
		Broad	**Moderate**	**Narrow**
			Pervasiveness	

ant dysfunctioning cannot be significantly worsened. We contrasted
this with cases of minor CNS disorders where a great many secondary variables can aggravate existing dysfunctions and create other
problems. Outcomes differ for such contrasting groups and for
groups that vary in the degree to which the pathological impact of
causal factors can be compensated for or reversed. Therefore, such
group variations should be accounted for in evaluating interventions.

Failure to identify appropriate subgroups is a key factor in controversies over intervention efficacy. Examples are plentiful: the
Head Start program evaluations, psychotherapy outcome studies,
the evaluation of alcoholism treatments, investigations of learning
disability interventions. In most cases, inadequate efforts are made
to discriminate between important subgroups in analyzing findings,
and as a result, premature conclusions are reached about efficacy
or lack thereof.

Researchers who focus on the intervention-client match have
stressed that the question is not: Does an intervention work? The
proper question is, To what degree does a specific intervention
work for a given subgroup? In evaluating efficacy, classifications
are used to specify relevant subgroups that can help clarify sources
of variance in process and outcome data. Analyses of evaluation

findings are shaped in basic ways, then, by work done on the classification problem.

UNDERLYING RATIONALE

Concerns about the quality of underlying rationales and factors that bias the formulation of such rationales highlight the importance of initiating evaluation processes *prior* to the onset of intervention. For instance, evaluations can end up reifying biased rationales and undermining alternative points of view. The common example in psychology and education arises when a rationale inappropriately designates individuals as the problem, thereby blaming the victim. Under such circumstances, efforts to correct the problem and measure outcomes primarily focus on individuals. Ignored are alternative views of cause and correction, such as the possibility that the environment is the source of the problem and the proper focus for intervention.

When alternatives are not considered, prevailing biases tend to go unchallenged. Such consequences are minimized through preimplementation evaluations of intervention rationales and plans. These allow one to judge a priori the appropriateness of decisions about who or what will be the focus of intervention and about the nature and scope of outcome objectives. Furthermore, given the importance of the rational relationship between means and ends, a priori judgments can be made about the compatibility between procedures and projected outcomes. (This is the type of predictive process the U.S. General Accounting Office calls prospective evaluation and uses to forecast the impact of a proposed program or policy change as an aid to legislators.) Also, well before the time comes for analyzing outcomes, decisions can be made about whose objectives will be weighted most heavily in case of conflicting interests.

In general, evaluative investigations of the utility and validity of intervention rationales can have an immediate impact on practice, for example by minimizing the perpetuation of systematic biases and the implementation of interventions that are likely to produce more harm than good. And such research also should have a cumulative impact on basic knowledge and theory.

PLANNING AND IMPLEMENTATION

Implications of the planning and implementation problem for evaluating efficacy are so straightforward as to seem simpleminded. Sound planning calls for a logical consistency among intended antecedents, processes, and outcomes. Desired outcomes are unlikely when antecedent conditions necessary for intervention success are significantly lacking or when planned processes are not a logical match with antecedents. As suggested above, one basic evaluation implication is that intervention plans should be judged prior to implementation. Such judgments decide (1) whether there is a logical consistency among intended antecedents, processes, and outcomes, (2) likely costs and benefits, (3) the degree to which intended antecedents are present, and (4) whether observed antecedents are congruent with planned processes.

With respect to implementation, processes should be monitored from the moment they are initiated to determine if intended transactions occur and to detect unintended interfering transactions. Such information enables comparisons of optimal, average, and unsatisfactory implementations. For instance, when intended antecedents and transactions are not well approximated, desired outcomes are unlikely. An extreme but commonplace example is seen when a client terminates an intervention prematurely because of factors such as poor motivation or financial difficulty. By definition, an intervention is not optimally implemented in such cases. Consequently, outcome information on these clients obviously should be differentiated from findings on those for whom the intended antecedents and processes were logically consistent and carried out as planned.

A comparable example arises when clients stay but are not motivated to cooperate with interveners. Sound planning, implementation, and efficacy evaluation calls for addressing motivational differences among clients. This highlights another focus for classification. That is, clients should be differentiated in terms of degree of motivation (high, moderate, low) and its valence (positive, negative). This example, once again, underscores the interrelationship among intervention problems.

18

Studying Intervention—Not Just Evaluating Efficacy

Do not follow where the path may lead. Go instead where there is no path and leave a trail.

Anonymous

As the preceding presentation stresses, discussions of the evaluation problem generally deal with how to maximize the quality of information on intended outcomes. To a lesser degree, the literature also highlights the significance of gathering information on unintended outcomes, especially negative side effects, in evaluating costs versus benefits.[1]

Because the primary focus is on evaluating efficacy, the critical importance of evaluating other facets of intervention is less appreciated. Analyses of the evaluation problem can be instrumental in altering this situation, especially when bolstered by implications derived from work on the other three fundamental intervention problems. Such analyses underscore that, not only should other facets be evaluated, but at times these facets should be the primary and even the only focus of intervention evaluation.[2] Indeed, this must happen in order to improve the evaluation of programs *and* advance basic knowledge about intervention as a general phenomenon.[3]

IMPROVING INTERVENTION EVALUATION

Obviously, practitioners should improve their interventions and be accountable. Equally evident is the need to upgrade the methodological and technological infrastructure for evaluation.

We have stressed that evaluations can as easily reshape interventions in negative as in positive directions.[4] As an example, we have described how some accountability practices can inappropriately narrow a program's focus. This is seen in programs that limit evaluation to specific treatment and remedial objectives and overemphasize processes for pursuing these outcomes at the expense of those that foster ongoing client development in unaffected areas.

Finding out if an intervention is any good is a necessity. But in doing so, evaluation is not simply a technical process. The processes involve decisions about what and how to measure, and these decisions are based in great part on values and beliefs. As a result, limited knowledge, bias, vested interests, and ethical issues constantly influence the descriptive and judgmental processes and shape the decisions made at the end of the evaluation. Ultimately, the decisions made affect not only individuals but the entire society.

For new and evolving major interventions, evaluation must be extremely broad and used for formative purposes. Expending limited resources on comprehensive summative evaluations in the early stages of an intervention's development usually is premature. Resources are better devoted to formative evaluations. For instance, the activity might encompass the type of programmatic research and development required to test and improve unvalidated, large-scale treatments. Even for an established intervention, more than outcome information is necessary for describing and judging an approach's ongoing impact and value.

As we have also emphasized, preimplementation evaluations are essential for making judgments about whether a plan is worth carrying out. To fill out our preceding discussion just a bit: Evaluation can answer many questions before an intervention is implemented. One such question is whether the underlying intervention rationale is coherent, logical, and well grounded theoretically and empirically. If it is not, there may be little justification for proceeding. Similarly, prior to implementation, determination should be made of how well key variations in antecedent conditions are addressed. For example, do the intended processes account for existing individual and subgroup differences? That is, do they address differences in the severity and pervasiveness of problems, differences in motivation for overcoming problems, and so forth? When such variations cannot be validly classified, subsequent efforts to judge the impact of specific interventions often are futile.

Given the presence of relevant antecedent conditions, key evaluative concerns include whether intended processes actually occur and whether potent unintended processes transpire. Findings related to such matters are basic in deciding whether to evaluate efficacy and how to interpret assessed outcomes. Also basic to such deliberations are conclusions about whether projected outcomes and available measures are proper indicators of efficacy. When they are not, outcome evaluation probably won't be productive, and the resources would be better used to refine the intervention or validate evaluation measures.

ADVANCING INTERVENTION KNOWLEDGE

Beyond expanding awareness about the nature and scope of intervention evaluation, understanding the evaluation problem underscores the role of evaluative research in advancing basic knowledge about interventions. Such activity is essential if intervention practices are to meet society's needs and expectations. As Campbell has suggested, evaluative research can be part of an experimental approach to social reform "in which we try out new programs designed to cure specific social problems, in which we learn whether or not those programs are effective, and in which we retain, initiate, modify, or discard them on the basis of apparent effectiveness on the multiple imperfect criteria available."[5] Obviously, knowledge-driven research and decision-driven research are not necessarily incompatible. The danger in both cases arises when the fuel supply (financial support) is scarce and its distribution is tied to naive or biased accountability practices.

On a theoretical level, evaluation research is advancing knowledge about classes of intervention (e.g., community, organizational, educational, mental health) and about intervention as a pervasive phenomenon. Increasingly, such research is guided by and contributes to model building about the general nature of intervention. Initial efforts to evolve a comprehensive model of intervention use frameworks and concepts as aids to investigating significant commonalities and differences among interventions. This work also shows promise for stimulating more comprehensive and systematic research and theory designed to improve cross-intervention understanding of what works and what does not, and why.

Examples of the types of questions for which answers are beginning to emerge are: What is the essence of intervention? Are there specific philosophical and theoretical concepts that underlie all intervention activity? What are the major elements found in all interventions? These and other questions raised throughout this monograph represent researchable topics that can contribute to fundamental knowledge and theoretical thought regarding the phenomenon of intervention.

NOTES

1. For a prototypical illustration of the importance of gathering data on unintended outcomes, see G.L. Barkdoll (1992). Strong medicine and unintended consequences. *Evaluation Practice, 13*, 53–57

2. Shadish and colleagues point out that intervention evaluation contributes to understanding related to (1) social programming (e.g., how programs and policies develop), (2) knowledge construction (e.g., how we learn about social action), (3) valuing (e.g., how interventions are judged), (4) knowledge use (e.g., how available knowledge is used as rationales for intervention), and (5) evaluation practice (e.g., how evaluations are conducted and improved). See W.R. Shadish, Jr., T.D. Cook, & L.C. Leviton (1991). *Foundations of program evaluation: Theories of practice*. Newbury Park, CA: Sage.

On evaluative research, also see H. Chen & P. Rossi (Eds.) (1992). *Theory-driven evaluations in analyzing policies and programs*. Westport, CT: Greenwood Press. R.T. Gottfredson (1984). A theory-ridden approach to program evaluation: A method for stimulating researcher-implementer collaboration. *American Psychologist, 39*, 1101-12. J.C. Masters (1984). Psychology, research, and social policy. *American Psychologist, 39*, 851–62. R.G. Tharp & R. Gallimore (1979). The ecology of program research and evaluation: A model of evaluation succession. In L. Sechrest et al. (Eds.), *Evaluation Studies Review Annual* (Vol. 4). Beverly Hills, CA: Sage.

Note also that professionals concerned about advancing the state of the art related to evaluation are organized in the United States as the American Evaluation Association and in Canada as the Canadian Evaluation Association. The two groups plan to hold the First International Congress on Evaluation in 1995.

3. As Sechrest and Figueredo note, extending evaluation into new areas will help differentiate generic from specific concerns. See L. Sechrest & A.J. Figueredo (1993). Program evaluation. *Annual Review of Psychology, 44*, 645–74.

4. A much neglected area for research is the *psychology of evaluation*. From observation and personal experience, most of us know that anticipating and experiencing evaluation produces major reactive effects. Systematic studies are needed of the prospective, in-process, and antecedent psychological impact of evaluation on (1) systems that are evaluated, (2) evaluators, and (3) those who use evaluation findings.

5. D.J. Campbell (1969). Reforms as experiments. *American Psychologist, 24*, 409–29, p. 409.

A Few Concluding Comments about the Evaluation Problem

No longer is it assumed that well-meaning individuals or groups
. . . [responsible for] health, education, training, rehabilitation, or
other service actually help.

Posavac & Carey[1]

Intervention evaluation is difficult, and a task many would prefer to
avoid.[2] This is part of the evaluation problem.

Everyone agrees that practitioners should be accountable, but
there are major disagreements about what that means. Obviously,
practitioners must show that their work is effective. But effective
in what way? To what degree? At what cost? These questions
underscore another aspect of the evaluation problem.

In choosing what we look at, how we observe, what we perceive,
and what we report, interveners are strongly influenced by society's
values, policies, priorities, and rewards. These influences, of course,
usually are mediated by the predilections of those who employ us
and by our personal and professional codes of ethics and values,
favored models, and so forth. When one doesn't agree with an
intervention's rationale, one will not likely approve of the intervention, even if evaluation findings indicate that it is effective. These
also are facets of the evaluation problem.

Methodologically, evaluation must be carried out with exceedingly
limited tools. So technical limitations add significantly to the
problem.

And almost everyone has experienced negative consequences from
evaluation. Those evaluated often are harmed, and consumers of
evaluation reports frequently are misled. Evaluations create

tensions and dilemmas and can be misused to create undesirable degrees of uniformity and conformity. Ultimately, we should be as concerned with the consequences of evaluation as we are with improving our technical capability to conduct better evaluations.

All this said, perhaps the biggest problem related to intervention evaluations is that they rarely are designed in ways that truly improve programs and advance knowledge.

Evaluation is the door to the future. Ironically, prevailing evaluations of intervention seem to be closing rather than opening that door.

NOTES

1. E.J. Posavac & R.G. Carey (1989). *Program evaluation: Methods and case studies* (3rd ed.). Englewood Cliffs, NJ: Prentice-Hall, p. 3.

2. On the topic of what types of difficulties to anticipate, see M.S. Scriven (1993). *Hard-won lessons in program evaluation*. San Francisco: Jossey-Bass.

Next Steps

You see things; and you say, "Why?" But I dream things that never were; and I say, "Why not?"

George Bernard Shaw

Our exploration of fundamental intervention problems leads us to conclude that less is known about the basic nature of intervention than should be the case given the prevalence and consequences of such activity. And, as we have stressed throughout, we mean consequences not only for individuals, but for society.

At the same time, it is evident that a good foundation exists upon which to build and that work on basic intervention problems continues. Unfortunately, a relatively small group of professionals appears to be involved. This seems particularly ironic given the profound limitations these problems impose on efforts to advance knowledge and its application to practice in fields such as psychology and education. Few major breakthroughs are likely as long as systematic efforts to address the classification problem are narrowly focused, articulation of underlying intervention rationales is given so little attention, analyses of planning and implementation are approached primarily as managerial concerns, and evaluation is reduced to accountability.

To advance understanding of intervention as a generic phenomenon will require multiple methodologies, not the least of which are conceptual, qualitative, and transformational approaches. In looking at what is, we must develop heuristic frameworks to guide investigation and analyses of what is found. In particular, we must do more to capture not only the actions, but the thinking and affect of interveners and their clients, especially what they think and feel about each other and about intervention processes. Such data are critical to delineating (1) the cognitive and motivational underpinnings for current rationales, planning, implementation, and evaluation, and (2) the relationships between intervention antecedents, transactions, and outcomes.

In pursuing transformation from what is to what can be, we must develop visions of what is desired and desirable and create opportunities to pursue innovation. We must do more in the way of building ideal prototypes, particularly comprehensive, integrated approaches. Such prototypes are essential to clarifying future aims, why they should be valued, and optimal means for reaching them. Concomitantly, creation of prototypes should accelerate fundamental and generic understanding of intervention.

Many professionals caught up in the day-by-day pressure of intervening feel that efforts to address fundamental intervention problems are just additional unnecessary chores that take time away from the work at hand. Ironically and poignantly, programs often get into trouble because everyone is so busy "doing" that there is no time to find a better way. Certainly, the fields of psychology and education suffer from excessive pressure to "do." One is reminded of Winnie-the-Pooh: "Here is Edward Bear, coming downstairs now, bump, bump, bump, on the back of his head behind Christopher Robin. It is, as far as he knows, the only way of coming downstairs, but sometimes he feels that there really is another way, if only he could stop bumping for a moment and think of it."[1]

Obviously, our brief discussion has barely tapped the surface of the problems we have sketched. The intent has been simply to stop bumping long enough to think about them.

Based on the ideas explored throughout this monograph, we have prepared the following Guide to Analyzing Interventions. We hope this guide, intended as an aid to researchers and practitioners, provides a useful coda to this monograph.

NOTE

1. A.A. Milne (1926). *Winnie-the-Pooh*. New York: E.P. Dutton.

Guide to Analyzing Interventions

As an aid to research on intervention practice, the
following questions are intended to guide (a) construction
of semi-structured interviews, (b) analyses of written
descriptive material, and (c) observations. Practitioners
and supervisors may also find the guide a useful stimulus
in reviewing their work.

I. CLASSIFICATION

A. Was a *formal label* used in describing the phenomena?   Y N

If yes, specify the label.

Which of the following indicators support the
validity of the label?

1. label is part of a well-validated classification scheme   Y N
2. well-validated measures were used   Y N
3. well-validated criteria were used to judge findings   Y N
4. no reason to think the label is valid   Y N
5. no information available to answer this question   Y N

If no formal label, indicate the *informal labelling* that was used.

B. Label conveys

1. *cause(s)* of the phenomena   Y N
2. *current functioning* (e.g., strengths, weaknesses, limitations) Y N
3. general nature of *intervention needs*   Y N
4. none of the above   Y N

C. If the label focuses attention on an individual, were
   contributing roles of the environment or system
   appropriately accounted for?   Y N

D. If the label is meant to denote a problem, were any
   steps taken to *minimize negative consequences of labelling*? Y N

E. Briefly describe the processes used.

(cont.)

II. UNDERLYING RATIONALE FOR THE INTERVENTION

Based on the explicitly articulated rationale or the implicit rationale deduced from analyses of interviews with intervener(s) and/or observation of intervention planning, implementation, and evaluation:

A. *Philosophical* (including *ethical*) commitments (specify major ones)

B. *Theoretical* positions (specify major ones)

C. *Empirical* (including pragmatic) factors (specify major ones)

D. *Legal* considerations (specify major ones)

Of particular interest are such matters as positions about

- determinants of behavior
- purposes and focus of intervention
- general orientation to intervention
- how to plan an intervention
- the role of assessment (including evaluation)
- how to formulate outcomes
- processes for facilitating outcomes—including such concepts as structure, activities, techniques, working relationships, personalizing intervention, addressing transitions
- the role of the client in decision making
- how to deal with negative consequences
- what constitutes fairness in offering and carrying out interventions
- how to advance knowledge about intervention

E. Was the intervention's underlying rationale explicitly *articulated*? Y N

If yes, briefly describe how this was accomplished.

If no, why not?

(cont.)

III. PLANNING AND IMPLEMENTATION

	Rationale	Reflected in Planning	Implementation

A. *Model of Determinants of Human Behavior*

	Rationale	Planning	Implementation
1. person oriented only	Y N	Y N	Y N
2. environment oriented only	Y N	Y N	Y N
3. oriented to both person and environment	Y N	Y N	Y N
4. oriented to person-environment transactions	Y N	Y N	Y N
5. no model of determinants	Y N	Y N	Y N

B. *Purposes*

Focus is on:

	Rationale	Planning	Implementation
an individual	Y N	Y N	Y N
several individuals	Y N	Y N	Y N
an environment/system	Y N	Y N	Y N
both	Y N	Y N	Y N
maintenance	Y N	Y N	Y N
change	Y N	Y N	Y N
transformation	Y N	Y N	Y N
socialization	Y N	Y N	Y N
helping	Y N	Y N	Y N
both	Y N	Y N	Y N
capabilities	Y N	Y N	Y N
attitudes	Y N	Y N	Y N
both	Y N	Y N	Y N

C. *Intervention Orientation*

	Rationale	Planning	Implementation
a specific model	Y N	Y N	Y N
naive eclecticism	Y N	Y N	Y N
applied eclecticism	Y N	Y N	Y N
scholarly eclecticism	Y N	Y N	Y N

D. *Uses of Assessment*

	Rationale	Planning	Implementation
to determine validity of "referral" label	Y N	Y N	Y N
to reclassify phenomena	Y N	Y N	Y N
to select/place	Y N	Y N	Y N
to plan specific practices	Y N	Y N	Y N
to evaluate intervention	Y N	Y N	Y N
used as a single stage process	Y N	Y N	Y N
used as a multi-stage process	Y N	Y N	Y N
used in interventionist ways	Y N	Y N	Y N

(cont.)

	Rationale	Reflected in Planning	Implementation
E. *Preassessment Interventions*	Y N	Y N	Y N
F. Desired *outcomes* are addressed as:			
aims	Y N	Y N	Y N
goals	Y N	Y N	Y N
concrete objectives	Y N	Y N	Y N
G. If addressed as *concrete objectives*, to what degree do they seem to be an appropriate translation of intervention aims?	1 2 3 4*	1 2 3 4*	1 2 3 4*
H. To what degree are *unintended outcomes* addressed (e.g., negative consequences)?	1 2 3 4	1 2 3 4	1 2 3 4
I. To what degree is *communication with previous interveners* addressed?	1 2 3 4	1 2 3 4	1 2 3 4
J. To what degree is the problem of an appropriate *balance* between a *comprehensive* response and providing the *least intervention needed* addressed?	1 2 3 4	1 2 3 4	1 2 3 4
K. To what degree is the problem of *cooperation* or *coordination* with concurrent interventions addressed?	1 2 3 4	1 2 3 4	1 2 3 4
L. To what degree are *developmental differences* appropriately considered in addressing			
needs?	1 2 3 4	1 2 3 4	1 2 3 4
desired outcomes?	1 2 3 4	1 2 3 4	1 2 3 4
processes?	1 2 3 4	1 2 3 4	1 2 3 4
M. To what degree are *motivational differences* appropriately considered in addressing			
needs?	1 2 3 4	1 2 3 4	1 2 3 4
desired outcomes?	1 2 3 4	1 2 3 4	1 2 3 4
processes?	1 2 3 4	1 2 3 4	1 2 3 4

(cont.)

	Rationale	Reflected in Planning	Implementation
N. To what degree can the intervention model be considered a *sequential approach* (i.e., a step-wise approach with each subsequent step implemented only if necessary)?	1 2 3 4	1 2 3 4	1 2 3 4
O. To what degree can the intervention model be considered a *hierarchical approach* (i.e., to be used at more than one level if necessary)?	1 2 3 4	1 2 3 4	1 2 3 4
P. *Time Frames for Intervention*			
Short	Y N	Y N	Y N
Moderate	Y N	Y N	Y N
Long	Y N	Y N	Y N
Q. *Source of Consent*			
Client	Y N	Y N	Y N
Surrogate for client	Y N	Y N	Y N
Society	Y N	Y N	Y N
No consent			
If no consent, why not?			
Minor's assent NA	Y N	Y N	Y N
If no, why not?			
R. To what degree is client *participation involuntary?*	1 2 3 4	1 2 3 4	1 2 3 4
S. Explanation of *Costs vs. Benefits*			
during consent process	Y N	Y N	Y N
during assent process	Y N	Y N	Y N
T. To what degree are *client perceptions of the intervention* addressed?	1 2 3 4	1 2 3 4	1 2 3 4
U. To what degree does *client* participate in *decision making?*			
V. Is *fairness* addressed with respect to intervention			
availability?	Y N	Y N	Y N
intervention accessibility?	Y N	Y N	Y N
limit setting (rules)?	Y N	Y N	Y N
consequences for nonconformance?	Y N	Y N	Y N

(cont.)

	Rationale	Reflected in Planning	Implementation
W. *Fairness Principles* used:			

Approach deals with clients
(and potential clients)

	Rationale	Planning	Implementation
1. in the same way	Y N	Y N	Y N
2. giving due recognition to their specific needs (including making up for past discrimination)	Y N	Y N	Y N
3. in keeping with their worth to the society	Y N	Y N	Y N
4. according to what they deserve based on merit (e.g., earned privilege)	Y N	Y N	Y N
5. according to what they can pay for	Y N	Y N	Y N

X. To what degree are the
following addressed?

	Rationale	Planning	Implementation
1. *structure*	1 2 3 4	1 2 3 4	1 2 3 4
2. *activities*	1 2 3 4	1 2 3 4	1 2 3 4
3. *techniques*	1 2 3 4	1 2 3 4	1 2 3 4
4. *personalizing intervention*	1 2 3 4	1 2 3 4	1 2 3 4
5. *working relationships*	1 2 3 4	1 2 3 4	1 2 3 4
6. *change and transitions*	1 2 3 4	1 2 3 4	1 2 3 4

Y. To what degree is the
advancement of knowledge

	Rationale	Planning	Implementation
about intervention addressed?	1 2 3 4	1 2 3 4	1 2 3 4

Z. In general, is *planning* done *systematically*?

1. If not, is this because of
   a. lack of interest in planning? Y N
   b. pragmatic reasons (e.g., not enough
      time or other resources)? Y N
   c. lack of know-how? Y N
   d. lack of organization (e.g., no formal
      planning mechanisms)? Y N

2. Does planning
   a. reflect use of a guiding framework? Y N
   b. start from a normative plan for intervening? Y N
   c. deal with administrative considerations? Y N
   d. modify general approaches to fit the specific case? Y N

3. Briefly describe any other notable facets of planning.

(cont.)

AA. In general, is *implementation* done *systematically*?

1. If not, is this because of
  a. lack of interest?   Y N
  b. pragmatic reasons (e.g., not
       enough time or other resources)?   Y N
  c. lack of know-how?   Y N
  d. lack of organization (e.g., no
       formal support mechanisms)?   Y N

2. Does implementation reflect use of
  a. a guiding framework?   Y N
  b. continuous feedback?   Y N
  c. strategies to modify general approaches
       to fit the specific case?   Y N

3. Briefly describe any other notable facets related to implementation.

IV. EVALUATION

A. *Purpose of Evaluation*

1. To what degree is evaluation used
     to improve the intervention in use?   1 2 3 4

2. To what degree is evaluation used
     to advance knowledge about intervention?   1 2 3 4

In particular, is the evaluation used to improve knowledge
related to:
               classification   Y N
               underlying rationales for intervention   Y N
               planning and implementation   Y N
               evaluation of interventions   Y N

B. *Processes*

1. To what degree is evaluation
      focused on inappropriately
         formulated outcomes?   1 2 3 4
      using poorly standardized measures?   1 2 3 4
      using inappropriate criteria for
         making judgments?   1 2 3 4

2. To what degree does evaluation account for
      the relationship between antecedent
         conditions and outcomes?   1 2 3 4
      the relationship between intervention
         processes and outcomes?   1 2 3 4

(cont.)

C. In general, is *evaluation* done *systematically*?

1. If not, is this because of
   a. lack of interest in evaluation?   Y N
   b. pragmatic reasons (e.g., not
      enough time or other resources)?   Y N
   c. lack of know-how?   Y N
   d. lack of organization (e.g., no
      formal evaluation mechanisms)?   Y N

2. Does evaluation
   a. reflect use of an evaluation framework?   Y N
   b. start from a normative plan for evaluation?   Y N
   c. deal with administrative considerations?   Y N
   d. modify general approaches to fit the specific case?   Y N

3. Briefly describe the processes used.

- -

* 4 point scale for ratings:

                        1 = completely
                        2 = moderately well
                        3 = somewhat
                        4 = not at all

Name Index

Subject Index

About the Authors

HOWARD S. ADELMAN is a Professor of Psychology at UCLA and Co-director of the School Mental Health Project. He is actively involved in several projects designed to restructure intervention in psychology and education. His diverse publications include journal articles, book chapters, and three previous books.

LINDA TAYLOR is a Clinical Psychologist at the School Mental Health Center of the Los Angeles Unified School District and Co-director of the School Mental Health Project at UCLA. She is also Director of the federally funded Early Assistance for Students and Families Project. Her work has appeared in three books and in a wide range of psychology and education journals.

ISBN 0-275-94888-9

HARDCOVER BAR CODE